Praise for *[digital] Modeling*

"This book does a great job of covering the many aspects of digital modeling. William explains everything in detail with full-color references and pictures. What I found most useful was his explanations for why he performed specific modeling tasks. This is the first book that I have read on 3D modeling that isn't just a rehash of what I can find in a software manual. I'd highly recommend this book to not only modelers, but also anyone looking to improve their understanding of production pipelines."

—Brian Arndt, BioWare

"William's skill as a 3d modeler is legendary. His passion for teaching and abilities are just as well known. The combination of his knowledge of the art of modeling, and his clear and patient style of teaching make this book a "must have" for anyone, regardless of their current skill level."

—Jack "Deuce" Bennett II, owner, Creative Imagineering, Inc.

"William is an amazing teacher and one of the best designer/modelers I have ever met. His digital modeling book is just another in a long list of gifts from the master."

—Nicholas Boughen, owner, CG-Masters.com

"In his trademark natural writing style, William concisely explains not only how to model but also how to think and solve problems like a professional. This book is an absolute must-have for those who wish to get a solid understanding of the digital modeling process."

—Alan Chan, Digital Domain

"You'd be hard pressed to find a more talented or prolific artist in the industry today. William is one of a truly rare breed: someone who can both do the work and teach it to others. His methods have shaped my own practices in countless ways. I've learned a great deal from William, and so will you!"

—Jarrod Davis, Emmy Award–winning VFX artist

"Think of this book as THE BIBLE—not just for digital modeling but for applying a fun, professional attitude towards a career in the digital arts. I don't think you can get a clearer picture of what is expected of a digital artist in a production environment than what is shared in this glorious tome. But don't just take my word for it... really, you should stop reading my quote and get to page one already."

—David A. Maldonado, Deluxe Digital

"With his industry insights, thorough explanations and relevant examples, William's new book, *[digital] Modeling*, is required reading not only for those new to the industry but veterans who've come to rely on just a small subset of available tools and techniques as well."

—Chris O'Riley, V | 4 Digital

"William Vaughan is not teaching techniques as much as he is teaching the necessary mindset one must have for success as a digital modeler. Having been a student of William's, in my opinion this book is the best learning experience possible aside from sitting in on one of his classes. From the very first page it is clear that his experience and passion for his craft are the driving forces behind this amazing book."

—Kurt Smith, Pixomondo

"William Vaughan has the rare ability to share his in-depth knowledge of 3D modeling and the CG industry with others in an easy to digest way. He has trained hundreds of artists working in the industry and has influenced the way I approach modeling. This book is a must-read for anyone interested in creating digital models."

—Ron Thornton, award-winning VFX/CG Leader and recognized industry pioneer

"I've had the privilege of working with William for over a decade at many training events. His ability to explain difficult concepts in a simple, precise manner regarding the concepts of 3D modeling and animation is rare and exceptional. His insight and explanation of methodology to me over the years has been invaluable, and this modeling guide pulls it all into one amazing resource."

—Graham Toms, 3D educational specialist, NewTek

"Truly William Vaughan has a passion for teaching and shares that passion within the pages of this book. He is one of the best teachers I have had and I'm excited that he's able to share his modeling knowledge outside the boundaries of a single classroom."

—April Warren, Digital Domain

[d i g i t a l]
MODELING

New
Riders

HAN

[digital] Modeling
William Vaughan

New Riders
1249 Eighth Street
Berkeley, CA 94710
(510) 524-2178
Fax: (510) 524-2221

Find us on the Web at www.newriders.com
To report errors, please send a note to errata@peachpit.com
New Riders is an imprint of Peachpit, a division of Pearson Education

Senior Editor: Karyn Johnson
Developmental Editor: Corbin Collins
Copy Editor: Anne Marie Walker
Production Editor: Lisa Brazieal and Katerina Malone
Composition: WolfsonDesign
Proofreader: Roxanna Aliaga
Indexer: Emily Glossbrenner
Interior Design: Maureen Forys, Happenstance Type-O-Rama
Cover design: Aren Straiger
Cover Image: William Vaughan

ISBN-13: 978-0-321-70089-6
ISBN-10:   0-321-70089-9

9 8 7 6 5 4 3 2 1

Printed and bound in the United States of America

Image Credits

Many people have come in and out of my life over the years, and have helped to shape me into the artist I am today, but one stands out over the rest. Von Kwallek, one of my high school art instructors, instilled in me the importance of problem solving, which has carried me through my entire career. My teaching style can be directly attributed to Kwallek's passion for education and his unbelievable ability to share his knowledge.

Thank you, Thank you, Thank you.

Author Acknowledgments

I need to start by thanking my long-time, good friend, Deuce Bennett. Deuce recommended to Peachpit that I write this book and then graciously came on board to handle the technical editing. He also made himself available for countless conversations during the creation of the book, offering his vast knowledge of 3D. Deuce has always been quick to offer assistance in anything I've reached out to him for and has been a great friend for many years. I can't think of a better person to have had on board for the production of this book.

Along with Deuce's help, many other industry professionals and friends played a role in the development of this book, offering insights and sharing their expertise in the field. I'd like to thank all of them for their contributions. Some of the artists that played a role include:

Saham Ali, Nick Boughen, Alan Chan, Jarrod Davis, Joe DiDomenico, Aaron Juntunen, Jonny Gorden, Matt Gorner, Kory Heinzen, K. C. Ladnier, Lewis, David Maldonado, Ed McDonough, Elmar Moelzer, Angel Nieves, Chris O'Riley, Rob Powers, Jay Roth, Kurt Smith, Glen Southern, Lee Stringer, Aristomenis Tsirbas, Ben Vost, Farrah L. Welch, and James Willmott.

I'd like to thank Karyn Johnson and the entire team at New Riders for the opportunity to create this book and for their support in its creation. Special thanks to Corbin Collins for his attention to detail, guidance, and countless hours devoted to this project. I'm without a doubt a better writer thanks to Corbin's shared expertise.

Images play a major role in this book, and I'd like to thank the following for either contributing images they created or worked on, and/or images they allowed me to use that I produced for/with them:

Deuce Bennett, Eric Braddock, Bruce Branit, Alan Chan, Ed Chichik, Joe DiDomenico, The Foundation TV Productions Limited/Decode/Blue Entertainment, Fabian Nicieza, Steve Lerner, Dave Jacobs and the entire crew at FunGoPlay, Frima Studio, Ed Gabel, Erik Gamache, Kory Heinzen, John Karner, Kari Kim, Johan Lefkowitzz and the team at Inhance Digital, Dan Katzenberger, Lewis, Dave Maldonado, Sam Mendoza, Steve Mitchum, Elmar Moelzer, Jon Troy Nickel, Chris O'Riley, Alejandro Parrilla, Chris Patchell, Demi Patel, Jason Pichon, Rob Powers, Serena Martinez, Kevin Reher and the entire team at Pixar, Marv Riley, Sylvain Saintpère, Jay Schneider, Baj Singh, Kurt Smith, Kevin Snoad, Sound-o-Rama, Glen Southern, Lee Stringer and the team of Iron Sky, Rocco Tartamella, Graham Toms, Steve Varner, April Warren, Worldwide Biggies, and Joe Zeff.

Although they've been thanked already, I'd like to give David Maldonado special recognition for his pep talks, unwavering support, and advice during the creation of this book—and Glen Southern for his guidance and contributions to the digital sculpting sections of the book.

I'd also like to thank my business partners at Applehead Factory, Joe DiDomenico and Phil Nannay, for supporting this book and for their friendship over the years.

I'd like to thank my wife Addie and dog Jack for waiting patiently over the two months it took to write the book and for understanding my absence and allowing me to work.

And last but certainly not least, I'd like to thank you, the reader, for your interest in this book. I hope it aids you in the creation of countless digital models.

About the Author

Originally from Texas, now happily residing in Philadelphia with his wife Addie and dog Jack, William Vaughan's CG work can be seen in all forms of media over the past 20 years. He's worked on projects ranging from children's books to toys, video games, broadcast, and film, and for clients like *Rolling Stone* magazine, Hasbro Toys, and Pixar Animation Studios.

William has always had a passion for creating as well as teaching. For over six years, he played a major role in the evolution of the industry-leading software, LightWave 3D. While working for NewTek as its LightWave Evangelist, he helped write the manual and provided the training for CGI artists all over the world, authoring more than 300 tutorials and instructional videos. His online tutorials are required reading for anyone interested in learning 3D. William has been published by every major CGI magazine and has contributed to 17 books. However, his writing is not limited to tutorials and case studies. He has also written and directed several award-winning animated short films, such as *Batman: New Times*, *X-Men: Dark Tide*, and the Tofu the Vegan Zombie animated short, *Zombie Dearest*.

For several years, William was the Director of Industry Relations and Head of Curriculum at the Digital Animation and Visual Effects School at Universal Studios in Orlando, Florida. He has personally trained hundreds of students to become professional animators at major studios, such as Rhythm and Hues, Digital Domain, Weta Digital, Monolith, and EA Sports. Among his prized pupils are the art department at NASA's Johnson Space Center and actor Dick Van Dyke.

After spending two years in New York creating content for Nickelodeon, SyFy, Spike TV, and others, William recently moved to focus on his Philly-based toy company, Applehead Factory. As co-owner and Creative Director, he works with his business partners Joe DiDomenico and Phil Nannay on building brands and creating memorable characters.

About the Technical Reviewer

Jack "Deuce" Bennett II is a freelance CGI artist whose background is in physical special effects for motion pictures and television. Deuce has been working in the film industry his entire life and has such movies as *Robocop*, *Lonesome Dove*, and *Jimmy Neutron: Boy Genius* to his credit, as well as TV shows such as *Walker, Texas Ranger*. Deuce has been using computers since he was nine, and he started off writing his own graphic programs. He is a unique combination of physical knowledge and virtual know-how.

Table of Contents

Foreword

Several years ago, while I was trying to finish my first book, exhausted, demoralized, and with a deadline looming, my publisher told me I needed some sort of CG expert—some well-known public figure—to read a draft and write a foreword for my book. I told him I didn't know anyone who matched the description, because back in those days I was just a struggling artist and had met only a handful of others who pursued computer animation as a career. You have to remember, there just weren't that many of us in those days. "I have just the person," he said. "Proton."

"What's a Proton, other than a positively charged subatomic particle?" I asked.

"Exactly," he replied.

I was pretty puzzled at the time, but I soon came to learn exactly what he meant.

"Positively charged." That's the key. William Vaughan is one of those people who is able to discover the amazing in anything that possesses it and who has no compunction about sharing those discoveries with the world. If something is awesome, he lets everyone know about it. So when I received his feedback from the first draft, it was so positive and filled with such excitement that it gave me the energy I needed to finish the book and get it out there. That was very early in my career, and the success of that book is reflected in nearly everything I do professionally today.

Now here we are many years later, and I am faced with the privilege and problem of writing this foreword for William. My immediate urge is to write, without regard for the contents of the book, a glowing review so that I can repay William for his enthusiasm and advice over the years. But I don't need to do that because the book stands on its own, without my platitudes. William is an artist of immense integrity, which means that he puts the best of himself into everything he does.

Over the years, I have seen so many artists, hundreds certainly, perhaps thousands, benefit from the influence of this man's work, and I know this book is simply another expression of William's love for the art—just another way he can share his passion with the world, just another in a long list of gifts to us.

So why should you read this book? Because passion drives excellence and because William is one of the most passionate artists I have ever known, so I know with certainty that he brings all his excellence to it. Why on earth would anyone not want to read that?

Nicholas Boughen
VFX Supervisor
Owner CG-Masters.com

CHAPTER ONE

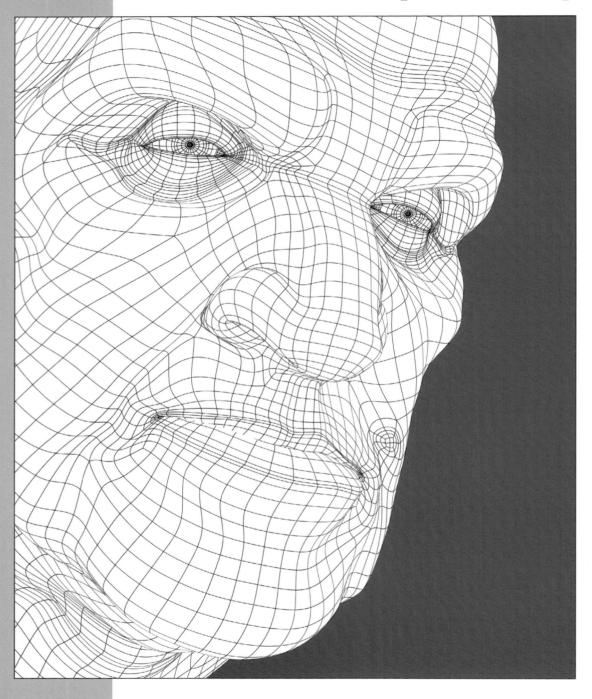

Introduction

Over the past 20 years, I've worked in various roles as an artist, from traditional designer and illustrator to jobs in all disciplines of 3D production. Only one area has been more rewarding to me than digital modeling, and that is teaching.

The information in this book is an accumulation of what I have learned during my career, and now I would like to share it with you. From understanding your role as a modeler in a production pipeline, to learning professional modeling methods and practices, to getting a job and much more, this book gives you the essential tools a digital modeler needs to work in the 3D industry.

I encourage you to read every page to fully benefit from this book's contents and hope it serves you well in your own career as an artist.

What Is Digital Modeling?

You've probably picked up this book with some understanding of what digital modeling means, but to make sure we're on the same page I thought I'd start off by defining it.

Digital modeling refers to the process of creating a mathematical representation of a three-dimensional shape of an object.

The result of this creation is what the industry calls a *3D model* or *3D mesh*. The 3D model of the character Tralfazz (from the indie comic series, *Patchkey Kidz*) went through the digital modeling process by starting as a 2D concept drawing, shown on the left in **Figure 1.1**. I created a 3D digital model of the character (center) and finished with a final 3D rendered image for print (right).

[Figure 1.1] Tralfazz 2D concept art created by Chris Patchell (left). A wireframe mesh is generated (center) and a final 3D render is made (right).

In the simplest of terms, digital modeling is 3D modeling.

You can create 3D models manually or automatically. The most common sources of digital models are those generated by an artist or technician using 3D software, as well as meshes that have been scanned into a computer from real-world physical objects using specialized hardware.

Digital modeling is an important component of any 3D production and is, hands down, my favorite aspect of a production pipeline. Throughout this book I explore various techniques and practices to generate a wide range of digital models.

Who Can Become a Professional Digital Modeler?

The fact that you are holding this book is a good sign that you can go on to be a successful digital modeler. You are already either taking steps to explore the world of modeling or to expand your current knowledge as a digital modeler.

Once limited to careers in the science and entertainment markets, digital modelers have more opportunities now than ever before. The demand for high-quality 3D graphics and animation is on the rise, and according to the Bureau of Labor Statistics (BLS) the job market for 3D artists is expected to grow at a rate of 12 percent through 2018 (www.bls.gov).

You see 3D graphics literally everywhere these days, and at their core are digital models. Digital modelers work in television and feature films, game design, medical illustration and animation, print graphics, product and architectural visualization, and many other markets that make up this growing field. I've had my fingers in a lot of these markets over the years, and it has been interesting to see that I can use the same core skills for all of them. The subject matter and delivery method may change, but the fundamental toolset remains the same. The 3D models used in **Figure 1.2** (on the following page) are just a few examples of how digital models are being used today.

To be successful in this field, you need to become a problem solver with good observation skills and a desire to create things. You never stop learning in this field. You face new challenges with every new project, many of which require innovative solutions that you must discover on your own. If you get to a point where you stop seeing these challenges as lessons that help build your ever-growing skill set, it's probably a sign that you've lost your passion for the medium and it may be time to explore other career options.

[Figure 1.2] Four examples of 3D models.

3D render of the Marc Jacobs Lola bottle used in print advertisements.

Frame from the Kanakas 3D animated pilot.

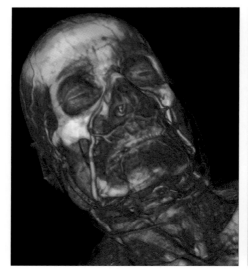

3D Medical Pre-vis used for an editorial illustration.

3D render of Worldwide Biggies' character, Bigby.

I've been teaching digital art almost as long as I have been creating it. When it comes to generating digital models, I've been asked just about every question there is. What kind of hardware to use, which specific techniques I apply to my model making, what to do about erratic sleeping habits, what kind of music I listen to, and just about anything else you can think of. But the most common question I've been asked by people interested in this industry is, "Can I become a digital artist?"

My response is always, without reservation, yes! I don't even need to know anything about the person asking, either. At the risk of sounding like Bob Ross or Mister Rogers, I always say that you can be anything you want to be as long as you have a passion for it and are willing to roll up your sleeves and put in the time to gain the skills needed to succeed.

I've trained students with a wide range of backgrounds and skill sets. Some started with more experience than their peers, which enabled them to work on major productions rather quickly. I've also instructed students with little to no experience in computer graphics (CG) who, despite their limitations, still managed to create a career in the industry by applying themselves. A few years ago I instructed a student who worked as a janitor at a Florida high school and had a passion for movies. That passion drove him to focus on building his skill set to allow him to pursue his lifelong dream of working on feature films. He's now happily working in California with several movie credits under his belt (I recently spotted his name in the credits of Marvel's *Thor* and *Captain America*).

Remember that talent is only one very small part of the equation and counts for nothing if it isn't backed up by perseverance, determination, resilience, and practice. If you want to be good at anything, learn as much as you can and work at it every day until you've mastered it.

So, in short, you *can* become a professional digital modeler.

Who Should Read This Book?

Those interested in expanding their knowledge in the creation of professional, production-ready, digital models—including but not limited to modelers, animators, texture artists, and technical directors—can benefit from the valuable information covered in this book.

"To follow, without halt, one aim: There's the secret of success."

—ANNA PAVLOVA

Use this guide if you are

- A professional 3D modeler wanting to enhance your problem-solving skills and explore alternate modeling techniques.

- A professional technical director, texture artist, or animator interested in other areas of the production pipeline and in using knowledge of digital modeling to enhance your current workflow.

- An instructor looking for new ways to teach aspects of digital modeling and its role in the industry.

- A student of CG looking to improve the artistic quality of your work and to learn about professional approaches to modeling before entering the industry.

- A hobbyist interested in real-world production techniques and strategies.

As with the entire series of [digital] books from New Riders, this book is written to be clear, not condescending, and to act as a reference and guide to contribute to the ongoing growth of your work.

What Can You Expect from This Book?

Although this book focuses on the art and science of digital modeling, it doesn't turn a blind eye to the other roles in an animation or visual effects production pipeline. It is my intention not only to share with you valuable production-proven modeling techniques and ideologies, but also to prepare you for a successful career as a digital artist.

This book is far from a rehash of information found in your 3D software's manuals and Help files. It's a compendium designed to complement your current skill set. You'll learn

- The modeler's role in a production pipeline

- How to prepare for a modeling session

- The fundamentals of digital modeling

- Multiple modeling techniques

- Professional practices

- How to land a job in the industry

- And much more

What You Should Know

For me to focus on the core attributes of what makes for efficient production-ready models and how to achieve them, I've made some assumptions on your skill level in a few areas. I'm assuming you have a fundamental understanding of Mac and/or Windows computers, including basic file structure protocol, working with peripherals, using Internet search engines, and using portable storage drives.

You should have a working knowledge of at least one 2D paint and one 3D graphics program of your choice, basic experience with 3D digital modeling, and a fundamental understanding of 3D space. It's important to remember that this book is not designed to replace your softwares' manuals and Help files. Whenever you need to use those, do so.

You don't have to have a working knowledge of every application used in this book. I cover the topics in a way that allows you to apply them to modeling in any 3D software.

I can't think of a single 3D modeling application that supports every feature or function covered in this guide; so the more comfortable you are with the software you are using, the easier it will be for you to translate any tool-specific process to the tools available in your application of choice.

Don't be discouraged if you feel that you don't currently have the knowledge required to continue. In this digital age you can easily get up to speed by doing some research on the Internet.

What You Will Need

Although I spend a great deal of time in this book focusing on the fundamentals of 3D modeling, some sections use a project-based approach to cover specific principles and techniques. The easiest way to absorb this material and commit it to muscle memory is to roll up your sleeves and actually do the projects as you read. So, you will definitely want to have a computer and the necessary software to get the most out of this book.

Most 3D modeling applications come in versions for both Mac and Windows, so whatever type of system you prefer, you should have no problem as a digital modeler. If you are buying a computer, make sure that its specifications are up to the requirements of the software you want to run. Don't feel like you have to run out and get the latest and greatest monster machine, as many may suggest. You might be surprised at how a modest system configuration can be all you need to work comfortably. That said, the more powerful the system, the more you can throw at it.

RAM

Random access memory (RAM) is where the data set you are currently working with resides in your computer. This data can be in the form of images or 3D point data, such as models. The more RAM you have, the more data you can simultaneously access without having to wait for the system to load it from the hard disk. Loading from the hard disk is slow.

CPU Speed and Number of Cores

With today's multi-core CPUs, computer processor speed is becoming less and less important. The more cores you have, the better off you are, so CPU speed is to be considered in relation to how many cores your computer has. Simply put, speed and number of cores are the main features that make rendering and data processing faster.

Graphics Card and GPU

A decent graphics card is an important factor for digital modelers, because it's responsible for displaying your data onscreen. Because most applications use OpenGL (Open Graphics Library)—the industry-standard Application Programming Interface (API) for writing applications that produce 2D and 3D computer graphics—a strong graphics card allows you to view your digital models as smoothly as possible.

The more geometry or hi-res (high-resolution) textures, the harder your graphics card has to work. Having a good graphics card definitely increases productivity as projects become more complex. NVIDIA is a graphics card industry leader and has the most stable platform for the CG industry.

Another factor to consider is Graphics Processing Unit (GPU) technology. The industry is starting to make a shift towards GPU-based rendering, essentially harnessing the power of the graphics card, which often is 50–100 times more powerful than a CPU for performing certain tasks. When choosing a graphics card, it's best to consider the amount of GPU cores it has; the more, the better.

If you're unsure of what type of system is best for you, visit one of the many online community forums—for example, CGSociety (www.cgsociety.org), 3DTotal (www.3dtotal.com), or Foundation 3D (www.foundation3d.com)—talk to artists who use these systems, research what's available, and most importantly, know your options.

Two Monitors

Something I have strong opinions about when discussing workstations is the need for a dual monitor setup. I believe dual monitors are a must for any digital artist and can't imagine accomplishing my work using just one monitor. That doesn't mean you have to invest in the largest, most expensive monitors available. For years I used two modestly priced 19-inch Viewsonic monitors that would satisfy even a tight budget.

Several extremely nice wide-screen monitors are available today that some might argue are just as good as using two monitors, but in my opinion, if you go that route, you might as well get two of them. Most studios I've visited have multiple monitors for their artists (**Figure 1.3**).

[Figure 1.3] Digital artists at BranitFX take advantage of multiple monitors while working on television shows like *Breaking Bad*, *Californication*, and *Fringe*.

A digital modeler working with just one monitor is like a draftsman working on an end table instead of a large drafting table. Having two monitors gives you more than just a comfortable workspace—it affords you the room needed to display multiple applications at the same time, as well as the ability to display your reference material on one screen while you work on the other.

About This Book's Approach to Software

Every working artist in CG has a preferred modeling application when generating meshes. I'm willing to bet that if you randomly asked professional artists throughout the industry which tools they use when they create, you would find a distinctive mix of software that each swears by. Usually, it's the software that they either started out using when they were learning about CG, or it's the software in which they have the most experience in. This makes perfect sense, but it has created something known as *software wars*.

Software wars are as old as the software applications, and as far as I'm concerned, arguing about them is a complete waste of time. Don't even bother getting into a debate with someone over which software is the best; you'll only exhaust yourself justifying why your software of choice is "better." No matter what is said during this argument, it is very likely that each of you will leave the conversation convinced that you are still using "the best" software.

Have you ever heard the phrase, "It's not the tool, it's the craftsman (or craftswoman)"?

Take a few minutes to explore any 3D software's online gallery, and you'll see breathtaking work being created. Whether the software is free, cheap, or super expensive, artists are creating amazing pieces of art with it. Don't get too caught up in software, because throughout your career as a digital artist you will most likely use various modeling and sculpting applications. Each comes with its own workflow, but the core fundamentals of modeling stay the same. That principle guides my approach to software in this book.

One of the main aspects of the [digital] series that attracted me to writing this book is that it doesn't focus on using any specific software. Hence, my book teaches you essential skills and concepts that you can apply to modeling in *any* 3D software.

Whatever software you own or decide to buy, be sure to read the manual. You need to become familiar with its tools and how that particular software works. You can use *[digital] Modeling* to help you generate professional meshes with those tools.

The bottom line is this: With some creative problem solving and an understanding of your toolset, you can accomplish anything you set out to create using any modeling application.

Software Requirements

Note that most applications have 30-day trial versions available on their Web sites. Also, several open source 3D applications, such as Blender (www.blender.org), are quite capable and absolutely free. A 2D paint and image manipulation application is also recommended.

3D Software

Although this book is software agnostic, I'll mention particular modeling packages throughout, because not every application supports the wide range of features and functions covered. However, most areas of this book describe several alternate techniques to achieve a given effect, so you can accomplish tasks no matter which program you use. Leading 3D software programs I mention include

- **3ds Max:** www.autodesk.com/3ds-Max

- **LightWave 3D:** www.lightwave3d.com

- **Maya:** www.autodesk.com/Maya

- **Modo:** www.luxology.com

- **Silo:** www.nevercenter.com

- **XSI:** www.autodesk.com/Softimage

- **ZBrush:** www.pixologic.com

2D software

A 2D paint and image manipulation application should be part of any digital modeler's toolkit to create and manipulate reference material and to generate texture maps. Adobe Photoshop (www.adobe.com) is the industry standard, but if you can't afford it, remember that there are a wide range of options available today, such as

- **Paint Shop Pro:** www.corel.com

- **GIMP:** www.gimp.org

- **Paint.net:** www.getpaint.net

Many other applications are available, too, that work perfectly fine.

What's on the Disc

Over six hours of training videos are included on the accompanying DVD and support the topics covered in this book. Although the examples in the videos use NewTek's LightWave 3D and Pixologic's ZBrush, the information covered can be easily translated to any 3D software. There are 18 videos that explore a wide range of modeling tools and techniques and 3 videos located in the ZBrush directory that show the entire sculpting process of the creature maquette in Chapter 12. I recommend viewing these videos once you have finished reading the book to fully benefit from the information covered. In addition to the training videos, I've included a video that shows 100 character models and their topology that can be used as inspiration and reference to study poly flow.

Some of the images printed in the book contain fine lines in the 3D program that may not show up clearly on the printed page. You'll find high-res versions of the images from the book on the disc, allowing you to see more detail.

Mentioned throughout the book is the Tofu the Vegan Zombie award-winning animated short, *Zombie Dearest*. This short can also be found on the disc so grab some popcorn and enjoy.

A Final Word: Change Your Thinking

Now that the formalities are out of the way, we're almost ready to get to the meat of this book. But first I want to cover a topic that is extremely important to your success.

When I start teaching someone about digital modeling, I usually find myself having the same conversations I've had a thousand times regardless of whether the artist I'm talking to has zero experience or is working in the industry. They all have the same desire to succeed, but in each of their paths to 3D mastery one thing stands in their way. Once they get past this roadblock, it's all smooth going.

What is this "one" thing that you have to get past (or *passed*, if you are a student of mine)? Could it be Booleans? Polygon flow? Radiosity? A corn-free diet?

The answer is none of those things, although the corn-free diet makes for a creative answer. Actually, the one thing you need to get past is simply *the way you think*.

It's my experience that most people have a can't-do attitude, especially when it comes to learning new things. When I say most people, I'm not limiting that to artists new to 3D. I witness this on just about every forum online and at the industry shows I attend. Most people assume that things are *not possible*, they are *too difficult*, or special software/hardware is needed to solve the *problem*. I always suggest a different approach.

It may sound cliché, but the power of positive thinking goes a long way when working in this industry. Every day you'll be asked to tackle the impossible, and if you go in with the attitude of *can do*, you'll be able to see the task to completion. If your attitude is *not possible*, you will most likely not complete the task. It's called a self-fulfilling prophecy. Robert K. Merton, the man who is credited with coming up with the expression, explains it this way:

"The self-fulfilling prophecy is, in the beginning, a false definition of the situation evoking a new behavior, which makes the original false conception come 'true.' This specious validity of the self-fulfilling prophecy perpetuates a reign of error. For the prophet will cite the actual course of events as proof that he was right from the very beginning."

Simply put, go into every new venture with a positive attitude, and you will be able to accomplish things you never knew you could. I get asked to do something I've never done all the time, so I always go in with the idea that I will be able to do it and will have that much more experience when it's done. Accept the fact that you haven't done that task, but don't dwell on it.

I always tell people, "I know everything I need to know to do the things I've already done."

Even I have to admit that it sounds silly but it's a great way to approach each new task. Really give thought to that statement. The next time you feel like giving up before you even begin, recite that phrase. Say it out loud if you have to. It's very similar to one of my favorite quotes from René Descartes, which states, "Each problem that I solved became a rule which served afterwards to solve other problems." In this industry, we are not *modelers*, *lighters*, *animators*, or *compositors*. The best title for what our job is on a daily basis is *problem solvers*. As production artists, we are thrown problem after problem, and we have to devise solutions to move on to the next phase in production. Then when you wonder if something is possible, say, "I bet it is; I just need to figure out how to do it." Do that and I believe you'll have far better results than giving up before you begin.

One of the biggest hurdles for new users to overcome when problem solving is actually trying to use the tools currently available instead of wishing for the tools of tomorrow. I once had a student who wasn't producing tell me that he couldn't complete his tasks because he was waiting for technology to catch up with his ideas. He left me speechless! To this day he is still waiting for those magical tools to catch up with his unrealized ideas, whereas others who have the right attitude are realizing even better ones. Maybe I'll check back with him in a few years to see if the tools he was waiting for were ever released and see if he has any of those incredible ideas left to realize.

I like to call this magical tool the Do My Job button. You know, the button that you click and it creates whatever you're currently tasked with in one simple step (**Figure 1.4**). Many people waste valuable time looking for the "easy" way out of their problem. Although this method sometimes leads to a breakthrough, usually the end result is lost time. The sooner you realize there isn't a Do My Job button and that you need to put a little elbow grease into each project, the sooner you will be on your way to producing amazing work.

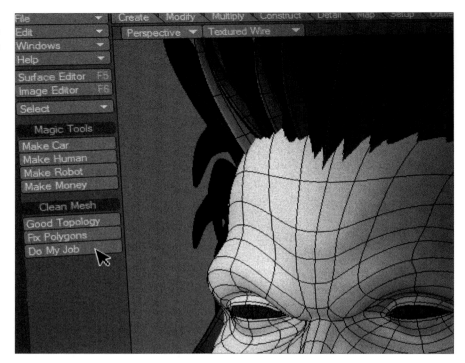

[Figure 1.4] Although many artists search for these buttons in their 3D software, they've yet to find them.

I tend to use the phrase "back in the day" all the time—which is surely a sign of getting older—yet I can't help but explain to new artists the stuff we used to have to do to solve what seem like minor hurdles with today's tools. Not having the tools didn't stop us. When we needed a flag blowing in the wind and there were no cloth dynamics to be found, we simply ran a procedural texture through a segmented plane and called it a day, and at the end of the day (to use another overused phrase) what it is really about is solving each task with the tools and techniques *that you currently have*. Sure, the tools will improve and so will your bag of tricks, but you already have the things you need to accomplish today—not tomorrow!

Don't get me wrong. I'm not saying don't push for new tools and improvements from the software developers. I push for new tools all the time. What I don't do is let the tools I currently have in hand stop me. This type of positive thinking and problem solving is what has helped most successful artists and studios flourish. Otherwise, studios with massive teams of programmers to write every tool needed for every job would be the only ones playing a significant role in our industry. What fun would that be?

It probably says a lot about me, but I usually give software programmers the benefit of the doubt and assume I've made a mistake when something goes wrong. It saves me a massive amount of time as I start trying to work through the problem as soon as it pops up. Here is a trick that has worked for me over the years and seems to be working for many artists working in the industry today. The next time you're deep in production, and the software crashes or doesn't give you the result you're after, ask yourself, "What did I do wrong?" Don't assume it is a bug in the software or blame the computer, even if it turns out that it is.

I've found that 98 percent of the time the problem turns out to be user error. If your first thought is that it's the software or hardware, you have already come to a conclusion without working through the problem. Before you blurt out the knee-jerk reaction of "I didn't do it!" ask yourself, "What did I just do?" It's hard to take the blame sometimes, but give it a try and see if your workload becomes easier. Just remember the term PICNIC (Problem in Chair Not in Computer), and you'll be set.

As CG artists, we need to be problem solvers who are able to think fast and tackle any issues that are thrown our way. With positive thinking and experience, nothing is impossible. These are the tools that allow us to create lovable characters, amazing explosions, and photo-real environments. It's not about the software or hardware. Software and hardware will continue to evolve, and you may find that you jump from one application to another over the course of your career. But the true value of your abilities is your problem-solving skills, not where the Boolean tool is located and what it does.

This philosophy is what has allowed me to accomplish the things that I'm most proud of, and it is my most valuable skill. Take advantage of your problem-solving skills and mix in some positive thinking, and nothing will stand in your way.

So now, let's dive in!

CHAPTER TWO

Understanding a Modeler's Role

To truly master digital modeling, you must be aware of all aspects of production and understand how they are connected. Before I start discussing the modeling process, let's explore the role of a digital modeler in a production environment. With a little help from some of my professional colleagues, I'll also talk about how your work directly affects the other stages and players involved.

It's all about teamwork: In soccer, for example, an individual player can be a skilled star and may be able to outplay many of the defenders on the opposing side, but his skill is greatly enhanced by his team members. They assist by making great passes to set up goals, defending against attacks, and working together to capitalize on every break to turn a game around. One player alone cannot win a game. Individual players may have flashes of genius, but working as a group and knowing the strengths of your teammates is the way to win. As players help enhance the stars of a team by supporting their individual skills, the team works together to reach an end goal.

Projects that require digital modeling come in all shapes and sizes, and can require a team made up of just one artist or hundreds of artists. Working closely with and understanding the needs of your team can only elevate the quality of the texturing, lighting, and animation of your digital models. CG artists at Inhance Digital (**Figure 2.1**), for example, work as a team to accomplish the many tasks that move a single project towards a unified goal.

[Figure 2.1] CG artists at Inhance Digital work as a team to accomplish many individual tasks that move a single project towards a unified goal.

A successful production team is made up of skilled artists who share common goals and a common vision, and have some level of interdependence that requires them to interact with the other members of the production team. The deliverables of each team member may differ, but the means by which each gets there is the same: teamwork!

Production Pipelines: Stages of Production

Depending on the nature and scope of the project, you need to decide the path and schedule that the production will follow from the initial idea to the finished product. This is called a *production pipeline*.

You can liken a production pipeline to a car assembly line. It optimizes production by arranging tasks in a specific order and so that they may be completed before moving on to the next stage. Going back and forth between stages can delay production, leading to a potential missed deadline and blown budget, both of which are frowned upon by all players involved.

A production pipeline for most projects can be broken down into three stages: pre-production, production, and post-production.

These stages are then distributed among several departments, depending on the type of project and what the final delivery method is. No two studios have the same process, but the following are common departments for animation:

- Story
- Visual design
- Storyboard
- Edit
- Audio
- Modeling
- Scene setup

- Texturing
- Rigging
- Animation
- Effects
- Lighting
- Rendering
- Compositing

Incorporating the insights of numerous industry professionals, I discuss each of these in this chapter, and detail how a modeler works with these departments.

If you're the only person working on a project, you are responsible for carrying the workload of all departments for all three stages of production. Larger projects require the collaboration of multiple players, blending the talents and skill sets of the team to produce what would otherwise be a daunting task for an individual. It's important to note that no matter the size of the team or project, you will need a strong production pipeline.

Although every project will go through all three stages of the production process, not every project that you generate digital models for will require all components. A 3D print graphic may not require rigging and animation, for example, whereas real-time 3D games typically do not require the rendering and compositing of image files.

To give you the general concept of where a digital modeler fits into an average project, I'll use the common production pipeline of an animated short as an example. **Figure 2.2** shows a graphical representation of this type of production pipeline.

[Figure 2.2] An animated short's production pipeline involves many stages before its final delivery. This graphic shows where a digital modeler fits into the big picture.

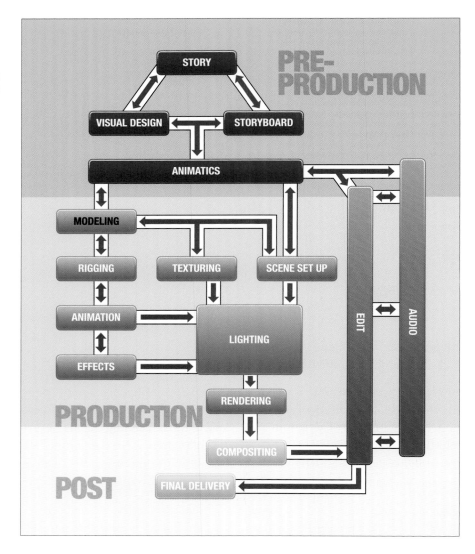

I've called on the expertise and words of several industry professionals whose personal advice is printed throughout this chapter. You may not understand all the terminology they use, and that's OK. If you don't now, you will by the time you've finished reading this book. I encourage you to revisit this chapter after you have completed the other chapters, even if it is just to see how much more you know about these topics.

Stage 1: Pre-production

The pre-production stage is the process of preparing all the elements involved in a production and is the foundation of the project—the blueprint of the entire animation. The story and visual look of a project is developed at this stage, as well as the overall planning of the production. Any shortcuts taken at this stage of the game can directly affect whether a project will be a success or not.

Story

After the initial concept has been approved or decided upon, *writers* develop the story in the form of a script or screenplay. Story is critical. It's my opinion that the success of Pixar films is directly influenced by the fact that it is a story-driven animation studio. The highest production values cannot save a project with an inadequate story. Without a solid story, there are only elements thrown randomly at the screen, leaving the viewer confused, bored, and in most cases, unsatisfied.

In all the stories that I've helped to write, including the award-winning animated short *Tofu the Vegan Zombie: Zombie Dearest* (www.tofutheveganzombie.com/movie), I've found it very useful to use sticky notes during this process to construct a timeline based on key moments in the story. Each sticky note has story points that make it easy to change the order within the timeline. When you're satisfied with the order, you have a solid outline to begin writing your script. **Figure 2.3** is a snapshot of the script from *Tofu the Vegan Zombie: Zombie Dearest*.

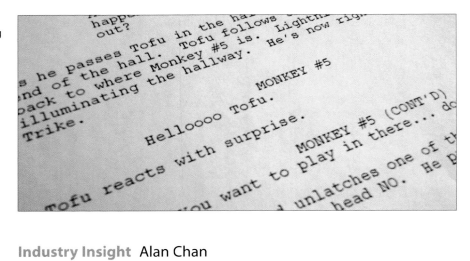

[Figure 2.3] Story is everything. Without a strong story, a project is doomed from the start.

Industry Insight Alan Chan

Writer/director Alan Chan shares his thoughts on the story development process:

> Having worked on feature films such as *Green Lantern*, *Alice in Wonderland*, and *Beowulf* over the years, I've always kept my focus on staying true to the director's vision.
>
> Before it exists anywhere else, the story lives in the director's head. A good director should have the entire movie already playing in the theater of the mind, and the director's job is, quite simply, to transpose what he sees in his mind onto the screen. Having directed indie features and award-winning short films, I can tell you that this is easier than it sounds.
>
> The first step in this process is the development of the screenplay. When we developed the screenplay for our short film *Postcards from the Future*, we knew only that we wanted to share the wonder and inspiration of space exploration with the audience from a human perspective. From this we developed the perspective of the storyline, which was to tell the story from the point of view of an engineer sending video postcards to his wife back on Earth. It is from this seed of the idea that we then develop the world that our story will inhabit. Since this world does not yet exist, it is up to the modeler to build it. **Figure 2.4** shows a basic breakdown of a shot from *Postcards*, including the virtual set created by a digital modeler.

[**Figure 2.4**] Director Alan Chan confers with actor Robb Hughes on the set of *Postcards from the Future*.

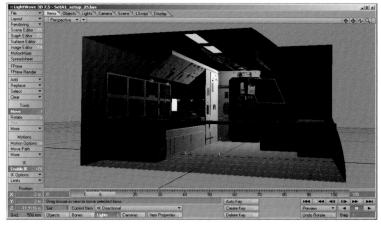

A 3D virtual set was created by digital artists…

…and composited together for the final shot.

As a director and visual effects artist, I've had a chance to experience the production pipeline from various positions on the production chain. My role as a director requires that I work closely with the modeling and visual development team to create a world that holds true to the spirit of the story.

The modeler's role in this context is to help the director design and shape the characters and the stage on which the story will take place. To do so, the modeler must understand the needs of the story and ensure that the models fit together in look and spirit to create a believable world for the director to work in."

Visual Design

The *director* works closely with the *art director* to develop concept art for all elements in the production. Working under the art director's supervision, concept artists in the Visual Design department create multiple versions of these elements, which usually include characters, props, environments, and any asset that will need to be created during the production stage. **Figure 2.5** shows just a portion of the material artists created for the award-winning *Teddy Scares* animated short (www.teddyscares.com/movie).

[Figure 2.5] The production crew worked from an extensive collection of resources on the *Teddy Scares* animated short, including the collectible plush bears of each of the main characters.

Visual designs are usually in the form of traditional sketches and paintings, as well as clay sculptures, often referred to as *maquettes*. These designs begin loosely and are refined over time, and turned into model sheets for the modeling and texture departments. **Figure 2.6** shows examples of a model sheet and maquette from the film *Zombie Dearest*.

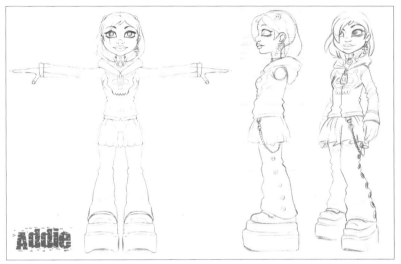

[Figure 2.6] A model sheet of the character Addie from *Zombie Dearest* was passed off to the modeling artist as reference (left). A physical maquette of Addie was sculpted by toy sculptor Rocco Tartamella as additional reference.

Industry Insight Kory Heinzen

Kory Heinzen is a visual development artist for TV, film, and games. **Figure 2.7** (on the following page) shows an example of how Kory might visualize a scene in a movie. He has this to say about visual design:

> A visual development artist can go by many names, including *production illustrator*, *concept artist*, *sketch artist*, *color stylist*, or even *viz-dev artist* for short. No matter what we are called, it is our job to bring into the visual world what has only been described in a script.
>
> When a scene is in the early days of pre-production, or the "blue sky" phase, where there are no crazy ideas and there are lots of artistic exploration and research. That's the honeymoon.

[Figure 2.7] This location study from Kory's animated project *Retro-Active* is an example of the first visual stage of a production.

There comes a point where some practical things need to happen in order to actually make a movie. Character designs need to be finalized, sets and props need to be designed, and color and lighting theories have to be conceived and approved. There are a lot of ducks to get in a row before things can go into production, and it's our job to help the production designer, art director, producers, and director answer the big questions before anything starts.

Films can be green-lit or sent back into development hell. Production budgets can be increased or decreased, characters can be cut or made into stars, and entire sequences can be thrown out or expanded; all of this is based on what we illustrate.

When working on the *Shrek* and *Madagascar* series of films, if I could turn my concept-to-onscreen ratio into a batting average, I would have been sent to the minor leagues. But that's not the point. Meticulously designing a set for three weeks is still cheaper than sending a bad idea into production where dozens or even hundreds of people will work on it. Our ideas are expendable; it's up to us to never run out of them. Simply put, changes are a normal and expected part of production. Ideally, changes are minimized, but there is just no way to avoid them in the creative process. Knowing this will save lives or at least your sanity.

Once a movie is moved into production, the art department is still working ahead of the other departments, feeding them more specific designs that are needed. Typically, characters at a stage like those in **Figure 2.8** are the first to go into production.

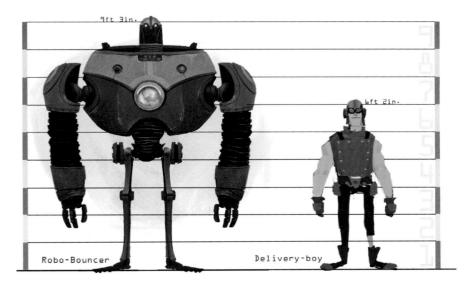

[Figure 2.8] Two character concepts from *Retro-Active*.

In my experience, characters are the hardest to do and take the longest to get approved. There is often a close collaboration between the character designer, modeler, rigger, and texture artist during this point in the process, with frequent input from the director. The transition from 2D to 3D is not always smooth.

There are some designs, especially "cartoony" or stylized ones, that can prove to be nearly impossible to achieve in 3D. Modeling straight from a drawing can be a disaster. Once perspective is introduced, proportions change and what looked good on the page is no longer appealing. A gifted modeler that can translate the feeling of a design is invaluable.

Sometimes there are modelers in the art department. These half-designer/half-modelers can work on designing sets or help create rough assets for previsualization or animatics. One thing to keep in mind if you find yourself in this type of position is to know how your model will be used. Typically, film assets can be amazingly detailed. But for pre-vis and set design, I approach it more like creating a game asset where I rely more on textures than geometry for the details. This keeps the models light for quick changes and helps to increase the interactive speed for the animatic artists. Once the cameras and the designs are locked, the models can be passed on as reference for the final models.

When designs are ready to be passed on, most likely there will be some sort of kick off meeting, formal or informal, where the art directors or directors explain the ideas behind the set and what they hope to see. Modelers receive a "model pack" for a set or location. Individual modelers are assigned props and environments to create. The art department will have broken out props and set designs—pages and pages of illustrations of everything associated with a particular location from the biggest building to the smallest grain of sand. Although there has been a handoff, this is by no means the last you will see of the art director or concept artist. In some studios, you will interact with the art director exclusively or sometimes the artist who did the original design. You will work closely with them to bring the designs to life.

Having worked on games like *Uncharted* and *Uncharted 2* and in TV and film as a concept artist and art director for over 15 years, I can tell you that it never stops being a magical experience when I see a design of mine given dimension by a skilled modeler. Seeing that first turnaround of something as simple as a minor prop still sends a bit of electricity down my spine. The best relationships you can forge at a studio are when you are working with other artists who just seem to "get it." Ask questions and always be willing to make it better.

Storyboard

With the script approved, the director will work with *story artists* to continue to flesh out the story in the form of *storyboards*, or sequences of images that help previsualize the story. **Figure 2.9** shows a storyboard sequence from the animated *Sifaka World* pilot. The storyboarding process, in its form today, was developed at the Walt Disney Studio during the early 1930s.

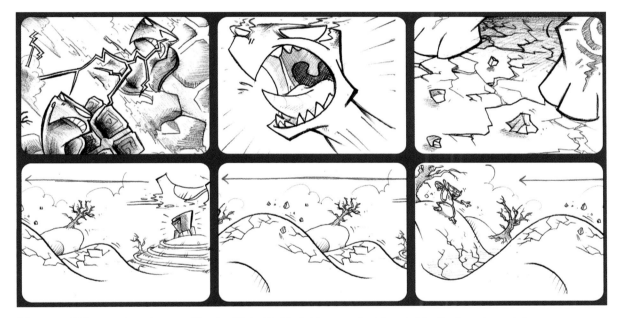

[Figure 2.9] The storyboards created for the *Sifaka World* pilot became the blueprint for the team to work from.

Storyboards are more than just sketches of what is described in the script. They play a role in how shots are framed and can help set the pace of the entire animation. I often direct artists to refer back to the storyboards during a production to ensure that they don't stray too far from the original goal. **Figure 2.10** is a photo of me talking over the opening shot with one of the crew, taken during the production of the animated short *Runners*. Some of the best elements of any story are conceived during this stage of production. Skipping the storyboarding stage can prevent you from further refining the story and can delay production.

[Figure 2.10] Storyboards are very similar to comic books, and in the case of the *Runners* animated short, we actually used the *Runners* comic book as our original storyboards.

Industry Insight Joe DiDomenico

Joe DiDomenico, art director at Applehead Factory, shares some insight on storyboarding:

> First and foremost, my job is to aid the director, to see his vision become a reality.
>
> When a team of artists is working on an animation, it is impossible to get started animating from the script alone. Animation relies heavily on the storyboard process: These drawings help to organize the story and match the visuals to the scenes within the written script. A storyboard is a visual shot-by-shot representation of a script, created in a series of panels that show the concept of the sequence of action, staging, and camera shots.
>
> Beyond what is written, a storyboard artist fleshes out what isn't on the page. I become a writer, artist, and actor all in one. I add visual puns in expressions and actions. I create action in a story when the script is vague. Storyboards help to cut production costs by giving production teams a

better way to understand fights, stunts, the timing of a comedic gag, special effects, and anything else that involves costly and complicated parts of a production.

I put together something that looks like a comic book of the entire film, scene by scene. This art becomes the basis of the whole production process that will follow. A storyboard is really just a foundation—a 2D blueprint. It isn't exactly how the movie is made, but it becomes a guide for what a scene may look like before it's animated.

Some people confuse storyboards with a series of illustrations. It's important to understand that storyboards speak more to the content within the frame than the drawing itself. My job isn't to "render" each frame, but instead try to capture a moment. I need to consider the framing or length of the shot, the angle of the shot, and if there is any movement involved. Usually, color is unnecessary for 99 percent of all boards (unless you are in advertising).

Also, having too much attachment to a sequence or to any one drawing makes for a bad storyboard artist. Everything changes; your best ideas can be thrown out at the drop of a hat. Because of that, when working in this medium, it is important to be able to draw quickly.

It is also extremely important to know the ins and outs of film terminology as a storyboard artist. You need to know the difference between a *cut-in* and a *cutaway*, to avoid crossing the line, and to know the psychology of different camera angles.

In storyboarding the biggest assets are the ability to draw quickly and equally as important, clearly. This job is simply one of visual communication.

Audio: Scratch Voice Recording

Before moving on to the animatic phases of pre-production, temporary voices called *scratch tracks* or *scratch voices* are recorded by the audio department. These are just stand-in voices performed by any willing member of the production crew.

Scratch voices provide the director and editor with placeholders for the final dialogue. They can also be useful in testing how shots play out with audio before committing to final dialogue and the pacing of scenes.

Although scratch voices are almost always replaced later in production, sometimes they don't need to be. If the director enjoys one of these early performances enough, the scratch voice could end up being used in the final. 3D artist Greg Young, shown in **Figure 2.11**, recorded a scratch track for one of the characters in *Runners* and later went on to do the same role for the final performance used in the movie.

[Figure 2.11] 3D artist Greg Young recording a scratch track of one of the characters for the *Runners* animated short.

One of my favorite examples of scratch track casting is Pixar's *Ratatouille* for which Lou Romano, a production designer at Pixar, provided the scratch voice for Linguini. Later it was decided that he would be cast as the character. Lou wasn't alone. Peter Sohn, a storyboard artist and animator for *Ratatouille*, was asked to do a scratch track for the character Emile (Remy's brother), and the directors liked it so much they decided to keep it in the movie.

Animatics

Using previously approved storyboards and scratch tracks, an *editor* works directly with the director to create a story reel, or animatic. An *animatic* is basically a 2D preview of the entire film. The pacing of the story and the story itself are still being refined at this time. The entire movie can then be screened in this format to ensure that all of the story elements work as a whole.

Animatics allow the director to experiment and work out any issues with the story before things get costly. Animation is a time-consuming and expensive process, and this phase of production allows for all levels of changes at little or no cost. It is important to know that if a movie doesn't work in this raw 2D format, no amount of CG polish will help.

Once the 2D animatic has been approved and locked, *layout artists* begin constructing a 3D animatic while working alongside the director. This is yet another level of the story that is refined to ensure that the project has a strong foundation to build on before production begins.

The layout artist places and animates a 3D camera and works with low-resolution, temporary models called *proxy models*. **Figure 2.12** shows a 3D animatic scene using proxy objects as placeholders for the animated short *Zombie Dearest*. Depending on the production pipeline, these proxy models are either created by the layout artist or artists in the modeling department.

[Figure 2.12] This 3D animatic scene from *Zombie Dearest* shows an example of several proxy objects.

Industry Insight Aristomenis Tsirbas

Aristomenis Tsirbas, director and founder of MeniThings, offers more insight on animatics:

This is where the 2D story reel is given a new dimension (literally) and becomes the template for 3D production. From my experience working both on my own films and for other directors, there are essentially two ways you can approach animatic modeling: stand alone or integrated.

The stand-alone approach is typically used in pre-visualization houses and large productions with separate animatic divisions. Here modelers work from the production designs to create models and environments that are light enough to be manipulated in real time with the director present. The modeler needs to be fast, and the results need to look good and read clearly. But since these models won't be used in production, the modeler is free to take shortcuts and spare things like micro-bevels and proper topology flow. The best layout modelers know how to cheat expensive things like smoke and water, and need to be open to frequent and often radical changes on the fly. Also needed is a decent grasp of basic rigging and texturing since animatic teams are often small and value artists with multiple skill sets. The key here is speed and flexibility. Since this is still technically the story stage, everything is up for change, so the modeler needs to keep up with this hectic but very creative part of the pipeline.

The alternative is a method I use for many of my projects. It involves an integrated approach where each model is essentially the first pass of the final asset. In other words, whatever model is created for the animatic is carried over and continued to be worked on into production. This way the animatic models, environment, lighting, and camera all represent the groundwork for each final shot. This approach requires all the skills of the preceding method with the exception that all animatic models must have clean, continuous geometry that can be polished to final production quality. It represents a bit of extra work, but in the long run can save huge amounts of time because modeling work isn't done twice.

In either case this can be the most enjoyable and creatively rewarding form of modeling, since it affords the artist the ability to produce more models in less time with less fussing over the small stuff.

Audio: Voice Recording

At the voice recording stage of production, the story and animatics have been locked, and the producer and director should already have actors cast for all the voices.

As shown in **Figure 2.13**, each actor is recorded separately—although I have found that it is helpful to schedule the voice talent recording so that the actors can interact with each other before they perform.

[Figure 2.13] Actor Dave Shoemaker records final audio at Sound-o-Rama in Orlando, Florida.

For the *Teddy Scares* animated short I directed, it was fun having Rick Baker, Clive Barker, and Linda Blair all in the same place for a short time before the recording took place. It gave them a moment to relax and meet the other players.

Once recorded, the voices are later assembled into the edit so that the timing can be locked, and the audio files are delivered to the animators.

These recordings directly influence the timing in the scenes and help drive the performance the animators will create in the final frames of the animation. It can be extremely helpful to record video of the voice recording sessions to help aid the animators when they are trying to capture the characters' expressions at key moments.

Stage 2: Production

The production phase of the project is where final elements of the animation are initially created based on the work developed by the pre-production crew. It is the production crew's job to stay true to the blueprint in place and to maintain the director's vision. It's also where the digital modeler comes into play in most production pipelines.

Modeling

You didn't think I'd ever get to you, but here we are. Although you've had to wait your turn, believe me, it's definitely worth the wait. The longer it takes to get to this stage of production, the more likely you will be generating digital models for a successful project.

Modelers work under the art director and/or a *modeling supervisor* to generate the 3D models for all elements of the project based on the model sheets (refer to Figure 2.6) created by the visual design department.

Modelers are responsible for the delivery of production-ready *meshes* (also called 3D models) that are ready to be rigged and textured by the other departments. This involves open communication between departments to ensure as little back and forth as possible takes place. Having a model sent back to the modeling department due to issues with the mesh can delay the production, which in turn could lead to a missed deadline. **Figure 2.14** shows the entire cast of *Zombie Dearest* modeled and ready for the other departments to take over.

Depending on the type of work or studio you want to be involved with as a modeler, you may be required to handle multiple stages in the pipeline. Some studios don't have a modeling department. Instead, they have *technical directors* (TDs) that create the models and then see them through to articulation (rigging). As TD, you may also be required to generate UV maps (2D texture coordinates for points) for the texture department, weight maps (a value that defines a bone's influence on a point) for the rigging department, and selection sets (which store a single state of a point, either selected or not selected) for the effects department.

[Figure 2.14] The *Zombie Dearest* character models were modeled and prepped before they went to the next stage in the production pipeline.

Industry Insight Glen Southern

Glen Southern, 3D artist specializing in creature and character creation and the managing director and creative director at SouthernGFX Limited, explains how a 3D modeler is an essential part of any CG production pipeline:

> The 3D modeler is one of the pillars that supports any CG project. To be successful in the role, a modeler needs to be flexible, adaptable, thick-skinned, assertive, a team player, and much more. As one of the primary creative roles in most pipelines, the modeler generally takes his steer from a 2D concept artist who has usually created a set of images defined by an art director. Whether it is for games, film, or TV, the modeler is generally given very specific turnaround images, or accurate side, top, and front profiles to match. It then falls on the modeler to accurately create the required model. Depending on the size of the team, the modeler could also be asked to give the model a set of UV coordinates and possibly even create all the required texture maps.

With advancements in modeling software, a lot of modern digital modelers are required to sculpt a model to a high level of detail in programs like ZBrush or Mudbox. They may then have to re-create the entire model again with better polygon flow for animation using retopology tools. Whether the project dictates that you start a model by box modeling a base mesh or sculpting a high-frequency mesh, you must always be thinking ahead and problem solving on multiple levels.

Taking feedback and criticism from art directors and technical directors is a skill in itself. When you are an integral part of a pipeline, you will at some point have your work critiqued. It is important to keep in mind that you don't always receive positive feedback. What you may think is a fantastic piece of work may have missed the mark in some way and may need revising. In extreme cases the work will need to be shelved and something new created in its place. This is perfectly normal in most projects. The skill comes in taking the feedback onboard and understanding why the changes were necessary. Asking the right questions before ever beginning to model can minimize issues like this, but changes do happen regularly on live projects.

Also, well-planned and laid-out 3D models are easier to unwrap in a UV package. If your model is a mess of badly laid out polygons, it may look OK when subdivided, but when you unwrap it, there could be problems. Another important stage further down the line is the rigging of a character. As a 3D modeler, it is essential that you have a solid understanding of good topology, primarily because good topology allows a rigger to efficiently rig and weight a model for animation. Creating amazing-looking models is one thing; creating amazing looking characters that deform well and have all their joints working correctly is quite another. The best 3D modelers can all rig. This gives them the understanding of where to put accurate edge loops.

Although the 3D modeler begins early on in the production pipeline, good communication between the different disciplines is essential. As I've mentioned, the modeler sits between the concept artist and the artists doing the texturing and the rigging. Technical directors and programmers will also have a say in a model's creation; they will be handling things like dynamic cloth, hair, muscles, liquids, fur, particles, and lighting. The modeler needs to have good communication skills, and this is where being a team player is crucial. If you don't keep those lines of communication open, there will be bottlenecks and you really don't want to be the cause of that delay.

Rigging

Once models have been created and approved by the director, the assets move to the rigging department where *character technical directors* or *rigging artists* design and create rigs (bones and controls) for characters and any other model that requires any form of animation or effect.

If modelers have delivered efficient work, they have given full support to the rigging department and, in turn, will have helped keep the production on schedule and within budget. The rigging artist does justice to the modeler's work by giving the animators the tools to turn a statue of an object into something that can move and react to its environment. **Figure 2.15** shows an example of a rigged character with both body and face controls for the animators to pose the mesh with.

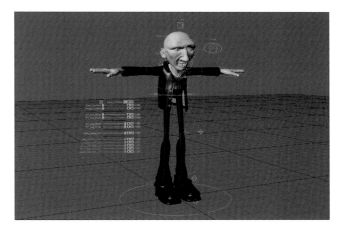

[Figure 2.15] This rigged character gives animators control of the body (top) as well as the face (bottom) with easy-to-use controls.

Industry Insight Kurt Smith

Kurt Smith, a rigging artist at Pixomondo explains rigging further:

As a rigging artist working on shows like *Terra Nova*, my role is to create the hidden mechanics that drive the models animated by the animation department. As a rigger in a production pipeline, my goal is to quickly and efficiently create powerful and highly responsive rigs. An important part of what I do is talking with the animators to make sure that they have the functionality they will need to animate. These conversations ensure that the model is deforming and moving in the way it was designed to.

During any production, I am in constant contact with the other departments. Good communication is essential to the success of any production. This is especially true when the rigging department works with models. Dealing with modeling changes, ensuring that the model has working topology, and that the rigging department will be able to achieve good deformation on the model means the modeler and rigger must be communicating back and forth as much as possible.

Two key areas a modeler should be mindful of are *clean topology* and a *proper base pose*.

Clean topology: It is crucial that a model has excellent topology before it is delivered to the rigging department. This means that the modeler must have an understanding of what makes for good poly flow and has an acute attention to detail. Having an accurate understanding of anatomy and how muscle structures work (in both humans and animals) is an extremely useful tool in a professional modeler's toolkit. Without good poly flow, the model will never deform properly regardless of how much time and effort the rigger puts in to make up for an inefficient mesh.

A modeler can help the rigging department achieve good deformations in more ways than having a working polygon flow. There are some simple adjustments that can make a model a rigger's dream to work with. Avoiding stars (a point with five or more polygons connected to it) in areas that have a wide range of motion is desirable for good deformations.

In hinge joints, such as the elbows and knees of a character, if the "rule of three" is modeled so that the outside edges are angled wider where the bend occurs (the inside of an elbow) and thinner on the opposite end of he joint (the outside of an elbow), the deformation and intersection in those areas becomes better without much effort on the modeler or rigger's part.

Proper base pose: It is also extremely important that a modeler understands what makes a good base pose to send to the rigging department. The model should be resting on the ground plane, centered on the origin, and facing forward. For characters, the base pose that is most often used for rigging is the T-pose, although a rigger might ask for the relaxed pose instead. It is important to have a discussion before committing to one setup or another.

Having a good base pose also means the modeler must make sure that the scale of the model is accurate before handing it off to the rigger. If a base pose is out of place or scaled incorrectly, the rig may have a broken rotation axis or bad deformation and may be extremely difficult for the animators to pose as a result, thus slowing down the entire pipeline.

Anyone interested in modeling for animation should have a basic knowledge of the rigging process. Modelers with an understanding of rigging will be able to diagnose and avoid potential problems as soon as they begin a model, which saves time and effort, and speeds up any production pipeline they are a part of.

In closing I'd like to add that it is just as important for a modeler to have an understanding of rigging as it is for me as a rigger to have an understanding of animation. To be honest, I think every artist should have an understanding of the entire production pipeline, as it will only make them better at their craft.

Scene Setup

As soon as models begin getting approved, either *layout artists* or *set decorators* will start populating the 3D animatic scenes with the final elements based on the concept art and animatics generated by the other departments. This is more than just a paint-by-numbers process; these skilled artists use a keen eye to generate densely populated environments. **Figure 2.16** shows an example of finished models being placed in one of the locations in the *Zombie Dearest* animated short.

[Figure 2.16] This image shows the set decoration underway for Professor Vost's lab in *Zombie Dearest*.

Set decorators take a modeler's environmental models and give them a purpose.

Industry Insight Ed McDonough

Ed McDonough, digital artist at Rhythm + Hues Commercials' boX unit, talks about set decoration:

> As a layout artist, my responsibility is to take the models that are created for the environment (including buildings, vehicles, plants, and any prop items) and set them up to make the storyboard background come alive as much as possible in 3D space. My goal is to populate the scenes with objects that help make the backgrounds more believable, but not too distracting from the main action of the shot. This is done by either adding or adjusting details and props to help fill gaps in the scene or guide the eye to where you want the viewer to be looking. The addition or alteration of even one single rock could change the entire feeling of a shot in the sequence.

Using the storyboards and animatics as reference, I create a list of assets that are needed to mimic the initial animatic. Working with the modeling team, I populate the scene with all the necessary objects. This process goes through many phases during the progression of the project, including model adjustments or additions, taking into account any additional camera choreography changes that may show an alternate view of the set. The environment gets pieced together while trying to be as economical as possible with poly-count (the quantity of polygons that make up a 3D model). This is accomplished with the help of the modelers by supplying low-poly objects for some items in the far background along with models with multiple levels of detail (determined by the distance from the camera) that are able to be swapped out with the final meshes.

While working on the cinematics for the game *Saboteur*, the team was able to start out with some of the video game assets that were then converted for our use in the scenes. This helped by letting us start with all low-poly objects in the scene, and then after determining where the action would take place —including all the camera angles—the modelers were able to clean up the models and textures as needed to fit them into the environment. This was also the time to up-res any models or even remodel them for higher resolution using the original models as scale reference.

It has been my experience that layout artists tend to wear a lot of different hats throughout production, especially in smaller teams. This enables them to model, texture, and animate above and beyond the traditional set design responsibilities. Multitasking works well because the layout artist already has a vast knowledge of the sets and the props that occupy the area. While working on scene layout during the *Crackdown 2* trailer, I was also able to model and texture background assets to help fill the scenes, as well as create the camera choreography. The modelers supplied me with the main assets that were then propagated into the scenes. Before finishing the setup of the scene, the camera was positioned to show what areas of the environment needed more focus. It was very advantageous to be able to jump back and forth between roles, which made it more efficient for the fast turnaround of the trailer.

Communication between layout artists and modelers is a must. The layout artist may need a new model or an adjustment to a model at a moment's notice. Since at any time in production a new item could be required, the modeler's speed, time management, and efficiency are great resources.

Texturing

Using meshes generated by the modeling department, *texture artists* bring these cold, gray assets to life with detail and color.

Texture artists enhance the surfaces of models by generating texture maps from photographs, creating *shaders* that mimic real-world materials as well as customized textures that can only come from a creative imagination. **Figure 2.17** shows Tofu from *Zombie Dearest* (an animated short) receiving skin details courtesy of an image painted in Photoshop and applied using a UV map.

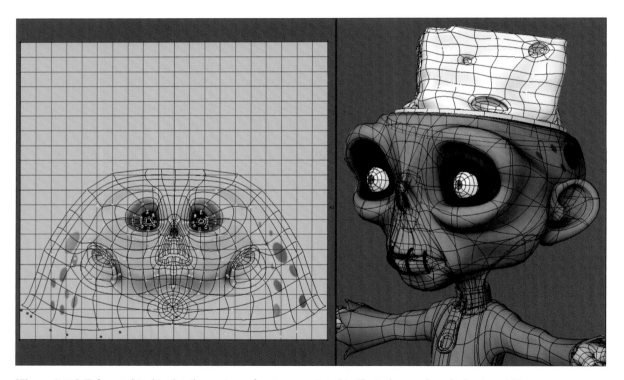

[**Figure 2.17**] Tofu gets his skin details courtesy of an image painted in Photoshop and applied using a UV map.

These highly skilled artists have mastered the art of observation. They have a keen eye for detail and the ability to reproduce materials based on the references they have been provided by the visual design department—or that they have gathered based on the direction they have been given by the director and art director.

Industry Insight Angel Nieves

Angel Nieves, now 3D Lead at MTM, has the following advice about texturing:

> One of my many responsibilities at Hi-Rez Studios was working as a texture artist. This involved a variety of tasks, including:
>
> - Unwrapping and laying out UVs
>
> - Breaking out the mesh into multiple surfaces
>
> - Outputting ambient occlusion and normal maps
>
> - Painting texture maps for the various attributes of each surface
>
> - Finalizing the textured mesh for the production
>
> As a texture artist, I check every model for n-gons—polygons with five ver- tices or more. I also check for stray vertices and polys. Both can cause prob- lems when unwrapping and later problems for the rigging, animation, and rendering departments. If any of those errors are found, the model is sent back to modeling to be fixed before texturing gets started.
>
> Once a model is unwrapped and laid out, a texture artist begins the texture painting process: Diffuse, specular, reflection emissive, normal, and so forth are painted, and then a material is made out of every texture map.
>
> Clean topology is essential for the texturing process as it gets rid of guess work concerning where to separate the mesh for unwrapping, which helps reduce or completely eliminate stretching and distortion in a model's texture. Mechanical meshes like robots, helicopters, and tanks are good examples of where a modeler can assist the texture department. Those kinds of assets usually have parts that a modeler has to duplicate and place correctly on the model.
>
> It is more efficient for the modeler to unwrap one nut and bolt and then duplicate it as necessary than to have the texture artist unwrap each nut and bolt in the whole model, one at a time. If a modeler plans ahead for tasks like this, he can shave hours and sometimes days off of a texture artist's work- load, which is always welcomed.
>
> I would say to anyone who wants to become a professional digital modeler that it is essential to have UV unwrapping skills. Even if you don't create the UVs, it will give you insight on how the texture artist will proceed when

unwrapping the mesh. It also helps with replicated geometry, which directly affects the job of the texture artist.

It is fundamental that communication between a modeler and texture artist is open and frequent throughout production; working together to find solutions allows both artists to be more efficient with their workloads. It saves time, money, and lots of unneeded headaches for every artist in the pipeline, and the resulting modeled assets will be at a higher level of quality.

Animation

Without a doubt, *animators* are the rock stars of the animation industry. Modelers should be their biggest fans, because the animation department breathes life into a modeler's otherwise lifeless mesh. The animation department, working with the handiwork of the rigging department, takes the assets generated by the modeling department and give them motion to tell the story.

Animators match the digital model's actions to the animatic and audio provided by the editor under the watchful eyes of the animation director and the director. **Figure 2.18** consists of three frames pulled from an animated sequence of Addie delivering dialogue in *Zombie Dearest*.

Just like the other artists within the production, animators work from reference materials like stills, video, and real-life observation such as studying the movement of people or animals. They not only deliver a character's movement, but the character's emotions as well, providing the illusion of life.

[Figure 2.18]
An animated sequence of
Addie in *Zombie Dearest*.

Industry Insight Johnny Gordon

Johnny Gorden, founder and animation supervisor at Zero Gravity
Entertainment, explains animation further:

> By the time a model reaches the animation department, it's been through a
> few check points and possibly back to the modeling department a few times
> already; so you might think that it's clear sailing from here. However, there
> are still some issues that present themselves in animation that are difficult to
> detect any earlier.
>
> The rigging team has checked the model, put it through a number of test
> poses, and tested facial expressions, but animators don't always play by
> the rules.
>
> As an animator, I often want the model to move in a way that the rigging team
> never imagined. This will inevitably create unforeseen problems, whether it's
> a pose that pushes the limits, an extreme facial expression, or a combination
> of facial expressions that weren't designed to go together.
>
> It is useful to understand what the different stages are for animating a scene:
>
> • Stage one is the layout, which is either done by a dedicated layout team
>   or by the animation team. This stage usually uses temporary models, or
>   stand-ins.
>
> • Stage two is the blocking stage. This is usually done with low-resolution
>   representations of the models that can be posed quickly, or specially
>   created segmented models that are parented to the joints.
>
> This enables the animator to work efficiently and play the scene at full
> speed. Because the final models aren't being used, problems aren't usually
> encountered in this stage.
>
> Depending on the needs of the production, the director or animation
> supervisor may require a check of the blocking using the final models
> before signing off to identify any problem areas as early as possible. The
> results of this check may identify some problems in the model or rig that
> need fixing.

- Stage three is facial animation and lip sync. This is often where the first problems are seen. The animator will create an expression that is too extreme or combines expressions that weren't tested together, and the model will tear or deform badly.

- Stage four is the final pass, including secondary animation, offsetting the timing of motions, and a final check to make sure there are no intersections. Usually by this stage, a few problems have already been caught, but a few more may be identified.

When problems appear during animation, the director or animation supervisor will decide whether to modify the animation to accommodate the limits of the model or rig, or to revise the model or rig.

Whether or not a modeler communicates directly with the animators can depend on the size of the production. Usually, if the model is to be revised, it is first sent to the rigging team to check whether it's the model or the rig at fault. If the model still needs revision, it will go back to the modeling team.

In some productions, the animation team will only go to the rigging team when there are problems. That way the rigging team can determine whether it's the rig or the model causing the problem, and only bring in the modeling team when necessary.

Effects

An *effects artist* creates all the non-model elements in an animation. These include things like hair fibers; elemental effects like water, fire, and smoke; as well as fabric dynamics. **Figure 2.19** shows an image sequence that an effects artist created of a Hummer being crushed by a robot character from the award-winning, animated short *Spoonman*. Many details had to be worked out to get the car's hood to cave in and the windows to blow out, making it a perfect task for a problem-solving effects artist.

[**Figure 2.19**] This sequence from Spoonman is an excellent example of a type of shot an effects artist would be tasked with.

Effects work is usually based on a performance-driven motion or event. To have the most impact, effects need to be lit a specific way as well. For these reasons, constant communication with the lighting and animation department is a very important part of this process.

Effects artists are elite problem solvers that help transform a mundane visual into the unforgettably spectacular experience.

Industry Insight Jarrod Davis

Emmy Award–winning, visual effects artist Jarrod Davis adds:

> At the most basic level, an effects artist is responsible for animating all of the "other" things in a scene. It's the stuff that the primary animators don't handle—things like simulated effects for cloth or debris, smoke, fire, dust, or even water spray from a boat. Also included are effects that are added to the primary subject after the animation is finalized, like feathers or fur.
>
> When working as an effects artist on shows like *Firefly*, *Battlestar Galactica*, and *Eureka*, the best gift I could receive from a modeler was nice, clean geometry. Like every other stage in the production pipeline, effects artists deal with departments both upstream and downstream from them. But there are a few areas that set effects apart and make it very reliant upon a modeler's skill and attention to detail.
>
> **Cleanliness:** Often, the effects department will be called upon to take an asset and smash it to digital bits. And even though a model may have gone through the rigging and animation processes without problems there, slicing and dicing it into a thousand pieces can very easily expose hidden flaws. A good, clean poly-flow and efficient geometry with no extra or hidden stray pieces are a major boon to the effects artist.
>
> **Efficiency:** I mentioned this before, but it's worth mentioning again, because much effects work revolves around simulation—often of particles, fluids, or other dynamics that can be extremely computationally intensive. The more geometry the computer has to push through the calculation, the longer the process takes. Now, you don't want to cut corners, but making sure that only what's actually needed is modeled is something you'll want to build up experience with. Also, the effects department will sometimes request low-polygon "hulls," simplified objects to use in simulations where the full level of detail for interaction is not required. Being able to make a low-polygon version of your master asset is another skill worth mastering.

Consistency: The simulations that the effects department handles are often physically based. This means, among other things, that units matter. Explosions that are 5 inches across behave very differently than those that are 50 feet across, and it will show in the work. Most modeling departments will require it, but even if yours doesn't, be in the habit of building your items to scale whenever possible. There's rarely a downside, and the major upside is that it will behave much better in every way, especially in an effects simulation.

The better a modeler understands how the mesh will be used by the effects department, the more efficient and clean the digital models will be, which makes for happy effects artists.

Lighting

In most pipelines, the *lighting technical directors* pull all of the elements from the pipeline to finish off the scene before they actually begin placing lights into the environment. Lighting plays a massive role in the final look of the production, setting the mood, color, and atmosphere of each shot. **Figure 2.20** shows a scene from *Teddy Scares* (an animated short) in which a lighting technical director is placing lights.

Lighting artists ensure that there is a consistency in lighting between shots, and that the final look of the animation matches the director's vision as defined by the visual design department.

The lighting department also works closely with the rendering and compositing departments to ensure that their elements are properly prepared for the next stage of production.

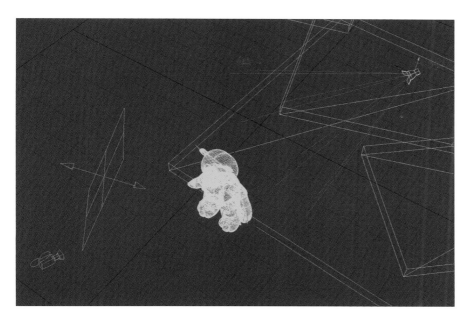

[Figure 2.20]
Lighting artists work in several display modes to place lights, including wireframe (top) and an interactive real-time preview (bottom).

Industry Insight Nicholas Boughen

A VFX supervisor at Method Studios, Nicholas Boughen shares his insight on lighting:

As a lighting artist, I have two areas of responsibility: technical and aesthetic.

My technical responsibilities involve:

- Ensuring that the desired elements of the scene are properly illuminated

- Fulfilling the requirements of time, place, and weather

- Ensuring continuity with other shots in the sequence

My aesthetic responsibilities include:

- Setting or supporting mood

- Assisting composition through lighting, such as determining viewer focus through variations in light intensity across the image

The true artistry comes through combining both the technical and aesthetic into a clear, powerful composition.

In my role as a visual effects/lighting supervisor, I deal with the modeling team almost every day. In the lighting department, lighting artists will sometimes discover errors or glitches in geometry that may not have been obvious at the modeling stage, such as light leaks, flipped normals, or edges that need a microbevel (a small beveled edge connecting two surfaces). Since the asset is public, it is not up to the lighting artists to make repairs; it must go back to modeling so they can make the fix and publish a new version to the studio. After this comes the lighting TD. The lighting TD is in charge of breaking down a shot into render layers, ensuring that the shot renders properly and within production specifications, such as render times and RAM usage. The lighting TD may ask for a model to be split up in certain ways to accommodate different render passes, such as mattes and holdouts.

The interaction between lighting and modeling is constant and fluid as we work together to create perfect shots.

Rendering

Render wranglers, also referred to as *queue managers*, take the approved final shots and break them out into individual passes that will allow compositors full control to refine the final look of the sequences. They then generate the final renders of all the combined passes for each shot, taking advantage of multiple render nodes (processors) that make up a render farm. Without these forgotten soldiers, there would be no movie. **Figure 2.21** shows just a small portion of the render nodes used at Inhance Digital to pull off amazing work on time and within budget.

[Figure 2.21] A close look at a few of the nodes that make up the render farm at Inhance Digital.

Industry Insight Farrah L. Welch

Render artist Farrah L. Welch provides an inside look at her time within the rendering pipeline on *Battlestar Galactica*:

> My core responsibility was to break out approved shots into individual passes and render them out for the compositors to reassemble.

> This started with replacing proxy geometry, lighting, and effects with the correct and final versions, and optimizing the scene so it would render as

quickly as possible without monopolizing the render farm. From there, I would break a shot into render layers, anticipating what the compositors needed in order to have maximum control over the final product. This included multiple diffuse, specular, reflection, refraction, effects, and matte passes for different lights and elements in the scene. Taking shot priority into account, I had to make sure that passes rendered correctly and in a timely manner, especially since a single shot could have 30 or more passes. I also maintained communication with the compositing department to facilitate corrections and make sure it had everything it needed to complete the shot as directed by the VFX supervisor.

I had to confer with the artists, compositors, coordinators, and supervisors to make sure that shots I was responsible for ran through the pipeline smoothly and on time. Each artist's role in the pipeline directly influenced my job on a daily basis, including the modeler. It was important for geometry to be clean and ready for production without holes, polygons on polygons, and other problems that would cause render errors, slowing down production and costing valuable stack time. Mesh density was very important as well. If the geometry was unnecessarily dense, render time would be too high, slowing down the entire pipeline. This often resulted in having to spend time cutting up models and removing detail unseen by the camera. If a model was faceted in-camera, lacking adequate detail, or had obvious UV seams, I would then either have to stop my work and take the time to fix it or send it back for repair.

All of these situations put a bottleneck in the pipeline and slow down production. Ideally, to minimize this bottleneck, models that will be reused again and again should have low, medium, and high-resolution versions with *nurnies* (small technical details added to break up the surface of an object to add visual interest) that are easily removable. Also, good naming convention is key! If someone has already spent time cutting up a model and removing detail, it needs to be saved in the correct location with an appropriate name so another artist doesn't waste valuable production time reproducing another version. Continuity between these versions is very important as well. If you have a low-res model and high-res model in back-to-back shots, they'd better look the same! You can't have a viper with battle damage in one shot and see it without a few seconds later. If you create high-quality models from the start and communicate effectively, you will save valuable production time and make the others on your team happy by creating less work for them.

As a render artist, communication between different departments is essential.

Stage 3: Post-production

Post-production is the part of the process that may take the longest due to the refinement of all of the aspects of the final product. Although this is the last step in the production of an animation, it is key to a project's success. Images get enhanced by compositing, the sound track and dialogue get tighter, and the edit gets tweaked for the most effective presentation of story and pacing. This is the point of the project that can make or break it and should not be taken lightly. It is what the production team loses the most sleep over.

Compositing

Compositors start work towards the end of the production process, combining the rendered elements created by the render artists into a finished sequence.

Most professional compositors have an understanding of color theory and an artistic eye. This allows them to enhance the lighting and color of the shots, maintaining the established look from the director and visual design artists, but refining it with a final layer of polish. **Figure 2.22** shows shots from *Zombie Dearest* receiving this final layer of polish by applying color correction, using an ambient occlusion pass to help add realism to the shading of an object, and taking advantage of depth passes to add depth of field and environmental effects.

[Figure 2.22] Compositors add the final tertiary details to each shot, including things like color correction (top), using an ambient occlusion pass to help add realism to the shading of an object (middle), and taking advantage of depth passes to add things like depth of field and environmental effects (bottom).

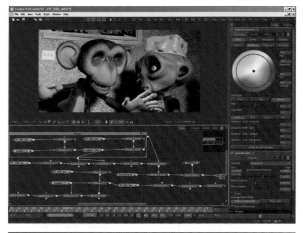

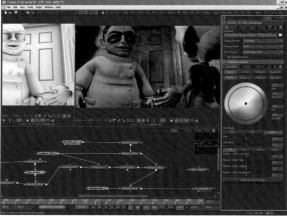

Industry Insight Lee Stringer

Lee Stringer, Emmy Award–winning visual effects supervisor, shares some insight on the role of a compositor:

> These days, compositing includes many new tasks. Gone are the days of simply combining several elements to create the final image. Yes, that's still a major part, with live action green-screen footage being combined with computer generated locations and effects elements. More and more compositing is used to actually light and texture many of those CG images.
>
> Having a good eye for color is key. Color correction is a major part of the compositor's job and although it's always ideal to have the textures of all the CG elements adjusted to the environment they will be rendered in, this can be tweaked much quicker in a comp.
>
> A great example of how compositing can be used within an all-animated film or TV series is the workflow used on *Star Wars: The Clone Wars*. In Lucasfilm's pipeline, just about all the lighting is actually done in the compositing stage. When a scene is lit, no real consideration is given to the color of the light and little to its intensity. (Only the position and direction of the light are adjusted.)
>
> Instead, the scene is generally lit with three lights giving the key (example: sun), fill (opposite of the key), and bounce (under fill), and then rendered with each light set to red, green, and blue respectively. Once in the comp, these three lights can be quickly separated, and each light can be colored with its brightness adjusted almost in real time. Additional passes provide rim (edge) lighting in a similar way along with environmental lights. Not only can the lighting be adjusted and refined far quicker, but one render pass can provide three separate light passes. It's a very efficient workflow but requires much more attention in this stage of the pipeline. This same technique can also be used with live-action productions and was used on the new *Battlestar Galactica* series.
>
> Advances in software are opening even more control for the compositing stage of production with the new use of normal maps generated at render time (this shows us the direction each pixel is facing). It's even possible to add new lighting in the comp phase. Also, mattes can be generated to isolate just about any component, enabling the compositor to adjust all the properties from color to specular highlights or reflection.

By far the biggest change in the compositing phase for modelers these days is the ability of compositing programs like the Foundry's Nuke to load 3D objects into a comp. With an accurate camera track also loaded, the compositor can not only move items around in a 3D space (very handy for stereoscopic projects), but also project new textures or matte paintings onto that geometry. Generally, these 3D objects are of lower detail than the ones used earlier in the pipeline. This technique is being used to great effect at Energia Productions on *Iron Sky* where landscapes that would require extensive modeling and texture painting can be built fairly quickly and then painted on, adding detail, once in the shot.

With these advances in technology and the changes in production pipelines, it's now more important than ever for a compositor to have open lines of communication with the rest of the team. It's also the best time for someone interested in creating the final look of a shot to get into compositing.

Audio

In most cases *audio engineers* work simultaneously with the rest of the crew by starting to develop the music and sound effects as early as the animatic has been locked. These masters of sound open up a whole new level of awesome into an animation.

I'll explain the importance of good audio in an animation by pointing out that sound contributes 50 percent of what makes an animation a success or a disaster. I've been fortunate to work with talented sound designers throughout my career, and one such audio guru, K. C. Ladnier, owner and lead sound designer of Sound "O" Rama, has helped several of the projects I've written and directed become award-winning animations.

Industry Insight K. C. Ladnier

K. C. Ladnier is shown in **Figure 2.23** working on the audio for the *Zombie Dearest* short.

[Figure 2.23] Sound designers play an extremely important role in the production pipeline by opening up a whole new level of detail into an animation.

Read K. C.'s thoughts about how sound relates to an animation production and to the work of a digital modeler:

> I was first exposed to sound design for animation at Walt Disney Studios in 1982.
>
> Early models (characters) were simple and hand drawn—interesting but just pictures. If the character artists were fortunate, they had access to sound recording and editing equipment. If the character artists were very fortunate

(or good), they were able to add music. It was not uncommon to see a character artist lurking around with a sound recorder, searching for something to record that would transform the character into something more than just pictures. Sadly, over time, I have seen less and less of the character artist's involvement with sound.

The ear is a terrible thing to waste.

The ear is connected to the brain from which the mind receives information that it processes and uses to make decisions about the world we live in. For eons humans have relied on this ability as a survival tool. Smart people tell me that the brain has many amazing abilities, including one where it combines multiple sound reflections like those that occur inside a cave or racquetball court. Sounds that arrive at the ear and are within a certain time interval of each other are combined into a single sound. The single sound is sent to the mind. This gives humans much greater ability to determine the location of predators or prey and to communicate in an ambient environment. The result is a much greater chance of survival.

The brain is constantly processing sound arrivals and sending information to the mind, even when you are asleep. You are completely unaware of this yet it happens in every theater that has adequate atmosphere.

My job as sound designer is to provide the brain with sound that makes sense and adds to the telling of the story. I use sound and music to lead your mind and your emotions. This increases the likelihood that you will experience suspended disbelief in the theater.

Let's say a modeler makes a character that wears a swinging chain and has flat feet that slap onto a marble floor. If I show you this animated character with good sound design, the information sent from your brain to your mind will be completely different from one presented with bad sound design.

With good sound design, the brain sees with your eyes that the chain is made of links and has motion. With your ears it knows the chain emits a metallic rattling sound. This information is passed on to the mind, and you think: check, one metal chain.

Everything makes sense.

Then the brain reports that the flapping sound and the image of feet hitting the marble floor appear to go together. The mind takes in all this information and might decide that this character is a duck. Oh! There is a quack sound, yes, must be a duck.

Without good sound design, the mind is not sure about anything. The chain emits no sound. Is it made of cotton? Is it in a vacuum? *I don't know!* And that is the information that gets passed along from the brain to the mind, lowering the likelihood that you will experience suspended disbelief in the theater.

This is the dynamic that flows through great productions. It flows between the group of artists that makes the pictures and the group of artists that makes them live. The more thought and imagination that is put into a digital model when it is created, the more life can be given to it using sound design and music.

Final Edit and Delivery

With all of the elements in the edit, the director, working with the editor, fine tunes the movie before putting it to bed. **Figure 2.24** shows editor Joseph Schneider putting the final edit together for an animated clip. Although much of the refinement in the edit of an animated piece happens during the creation of the animatic in the pre-production stage, the director and editor may still need to tweak the film for many reasons. Sometimes shots that seemed necessary in the animatic may have to be cut out for reasons of either pacing or budget. Once all of these issues have been resolved (or maybe time just runs out—it happens) and the sound track is finalized and added to the edit, the film is finally complete and ready for mass consumption.

[Figure 2.24] Editors work closely with the director to put final tweaks on the project. They are also the final artists to work on a movie, giving it a final polish.

Evolution of Production Pipelines

Although the basic structure of production pipelines is usually the same, the pipelines are different depending on a studio's idea of what the most efficient setup will be to produce the type of work it sets out to deliver. In most cases, pipelines evolve over multiple productions based on experience gained from past productions, keeping the components that work and removing or replacing the elements that were the weakest. Over time, a studio's production pipeline becomes solid and efficient for that particular studio's way of working.

Every once in a while, pipelines take a massive leap in evolution that can forever change how a studio or the industry as a whole approaches a production, introducing new stages and/or positions and departments.

Two perfect examples of this type of pipeline evolution are the virtual art department and the stereo department.

Virtual Art Department (VAD)

The *virtual art department* (also sometimes called *virtual art direction*) is now a fully recognized area under the jurisdiction of the ADG (Art Directors Guild) and is widely accepted as a major new area of the craft of filmmaking and television production.

Conceived by Rob Powers and his team of digital artists for James Cameron's *Avatar*, the virtual art department enables a unique, real-time, interactive system that combines different technologies for virtual production. This efficient workflow gives a director a real-time workspace, allowing for the flexibility to make important changes on the fly—something every director dreams of in movies that require heavy use of CG elements.

As live characters on the motion-capture stage are being shot, a director can see CG representations of characters and environments in real time and in-camera, and they can be used for composition and blocking. **Figures 2.25** and **2.26** show two examples of this setup in action.

[**Figure 2.25**] The virtual camera, virtual environment, and performance-captured actors all combine to provide the immersive virtual production experience.

[Figure 2.26] The virtual art department process allows for virtual location scouts and shot blocking very early in the modeling and design phase of production.

Artists working in the virtual art department are responsible for creating low-poly environments, props, and occasionally characters that serve as a foundation for final assets. These representations can vary widely, ranging from gray-shaded primitives for rough layout to modeled environments complete with detailed textures and matte paintings.

This new time-saving system is so efficient that it's being adopted by many studios working on productions such as *The Adventures of Tintin*, *A Christmas Carol*, *Mars Needs Moms*, *Jack the Giant Killer*, and many more.

Industry Insight Rob Powers

Rob Powers, virtual art department supervisor and virtual art director in the ADG, shares his firsthand experience of working in the virtual art department on *Avatar*:

> With the industry's first virtual art department on James Cameron's *Avatar*, I was in a position of problem solving in areas that had never been previously attempted. The bleeding edge requires quite a bit of "out of the box" thinking

and a willingness to approach problems with an open mind. The VAD is essentially a very fluid and flexible hub where many departments on the product can collaborate in a real-time "sandbox" to achieve the most compelling final result in the completed film, television show, or video game. It allows everyone to work out all types of potential problems long before they become critical, and the VAD workflow can often change a production for the better through this collaborative discovery process.

The impact of the VAD workflow on modelers and the area of asset creation in general is profound. To facilitate the required flexibility and interactivity required by the virtual production process, VAD modelers must think of many different challenges that might face a director on set and build in to the assets as many options as possible. For example, where previously a pre-vis workflow may have just modeled a tree, the VAD modeler would break a hero tree down to its most basic components and design a hierarchy to allow maximum flexibility on the set. The tree trunk, branches, roots, and leaves would all be carefully considered and flexible enough to give the director the creative freedom on set to actually redesign the tree for a shot.

All of this would also have to be done within the constraints of a real-time display engine so it requires a fairly high level of creativity to maintain the integrity of the production design provided by the art department while keeping polygonal counts and overall data optimized. A modeler must also deliver "clean" assets consisting of tri or quad polygons only. Delivering an asset with n-gons (polygons with more than four sides) can often create shading errors and causes extra overhead for the render engine.

At its core, the VAD process applies a real-world director's camera perspective to all phases of design, development, and modeling. This simple but important new approach has a huge impact on the final resulting assets. Assets created with the VAD process are more specifically geared toward the director's intent and are more "camera-ready" than they would have been with traditional approaches. Using asset creation software with a strong, integrated render engine and an included texture baking workflow, like that offered in NewTek's LightWave software, allows the artist to "bake" in beautiful lighting and textures, which go a long way toward increasing the visual impact of the virtual assets.

Another very unique aspect of the VAD modeling process is the art of manufacturing 180 degrees of a setting not represented fully in a concept painting. Of course, the key locations will often provide many angles, but more often than not, there are a significant number of sets or locations that have only a single-angled concept painting as the guide. Working with a virtual art director, the VAD modeler must invoke the look and feel or "spirit" of the concept art, but often actually creates many new assets that are not already designed. This can often prove to be quite a challenge, but also offers a very high level of creative freedom for those modelers who have a knack for design. The final result transforms a single-angle concept painting into a full 360 degree virtual environment or set that is ready for the director to shoot on.

The virtual art department process and virtual production workflows are really like a merger of real-time gaming technology with film and television production. This new, innovative resulting workflow enhances overall team collaboration, facilitating the director-centric production process that has guided film and television production for over a century.

Stereo Department

Stereoscopic 3D is a technique used in production that creates or enhances the illusion of depth in a 2D image. It's important to understand that it is an illusion—a trick of the eyes. Two images of the same subject, each from a different position, are used, which when wearing special glasses, trick the brain into merging these into one.

Stereo artists convert 2D films into blockbuster 3D experiences, as well as 3D assets into stereoscopic 3D. Although both methods achieve (mostly) the same result, the processes behind creating these images are very different.

In CG films like *Up*, *How to Train Your Dragon*, and *Battle for Terra*, the characters and situations all exist in a digital 3D space. This 3D space is calculated in Z-depth (the third dimension toward and away from you when looking down at a flat X and Y axis) and can be represented in a second eye by either using the Z-depth information to convert the film or by adding a second camera and rendering out that second eye. **Figure 2.27** shows a scene from *Zombie Dearest* being converted to stereo 3D.

[Figure 2.27] This shot uses a single-camera stereo setup using a grid-shaped null to measure convergence (the focal point of the shot).

In 2D to 3D conversions of live-action films that were not shot with two cameras, the Z-depth information has to be artificially created by an army of rotoscoping (tracing over live-action film movement frame by frame), depth, and compositing artists.

Industry Insight David Maldonado

David Maldonado, depth artist at Stereo D, has had the benefit of working in both stereoscopic methods and shares some of his experience:

> While working as a depth artist on the 3D versions of *Thor*, *Captain America*, and the fifteenth anniversary version of *Titanic*, I had to approach Stereo D's proprietary procedure of 2D to 3D conversion with a certain amount of delicacy. I had to be mindful of this new way of presenting film, respecting both the creators of the films' visions as well as the eyes of the potential audience. Although stereoscopic viewing has been around for a long time, this new method of presenting it hasn't and is still in a stage where it needs to prove its worth to the general populous.
>
> We have to make the stereoscopic viewing experience not only comfortable to the eyes, but also an enhancement to the movie-going experience. New methods of presentation are developed every day, and it helps when those who are developing these methods have a legion of cooperative artists behind them to help make these experiences possible.
>
> There are specific challenges that the roto artists, depth artists, edge clean-up artists, and stereoscopic compositing artists face every day, and no one department is more important than another. We all have to work as a cohesive unit to make sure that the film gets delivered on time, and that can only work if we remain in constant, respectful communication.
>
> When I worked on the 3D conversion of the animated feature *Battle for Terra*, I was part of a team that was going into each shot's scene and adding an additional camera that would be the second "eye." Setting this second camera in a place that truly enhanced the original vision of the shot while being mindful of how much or how little things were popping out of the screen plane was an exciting challenge and important to the success of the film. Each shot was populated by several digital models with baked-in animations, preset lighting, and visual effects. Knowing the proper naming conventions and paying attention to studio protocol was just as important as setting up each shot, and an attribute you learn to value in your coworkers.
>
> In the end, it doesn't matter which method of stereoscopic is being used to present the material. The audience doesn't care *how* it got up there, the audience just wants to see something amazing, and it is up to the stereo artists to make that experience possible.

You should now have a better understanding of the production pipeline and where a digital modeler fits into the big picture. Although you may only have interest in modeling, I have found that the more I learn about the other aspects of production, the more efficient my models become. Another benefit that most artists don't think about is the development of their professional reputation. The more aware you are of your place in production and how you interact with everyone involved, the better chance you have of doing a good job and getting more work based on positive word of mouth. As huge as this industry may seem to you now, in reality it is very small, and news travels fast within it. Keep that in mind with every project you lend your talents to.

CHAPTER THREE

Preparing for Modeling

Throughout my career, I've tried to pass on my knowledge and experience to as many people as are interested. It's my philosophy that no information is too priceless for me to keep locked away for my use only. I love when new artists ask questions, because it gives me the opportunity to share any and all tips and tricks—many of which I wish I had known when I was learning how to model. I am asked questions of all sorts, ranging from networking ("How do I use my artwork to break into the industry?") to the technical ("How do I drop my selection in Photoshop?"). The questions neophytes ask of me all follow a continuous theme, and whether they are aware of it or not, the real question they are asking is: "How do I make my work look like what the pros are doing?"

Every artist who wants to make it in the industry has asked this question. I've done it, my colleagues have done it—heck, the reason you are reading this book is probably because you've also asked it.

My answer to this question (and its various forms) is always the same, and it will completely blow your mind. Here it is:

Use as much reference material as possible and hone your observational skills.

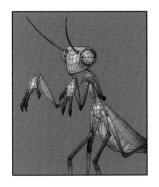   

Not exactly what you were expecting, huh? But yes, that is the mind-blowingly simple trade secret of the pros. It's what separates a hobbyist from a professional. Remember that the sooner you come to the realization that there is no magic "Do My Job" button, the sooner you can start down the road of creating professional CG work.

The biggest problem I see for new artists is a lack of reference and observation. It immediately shows up in their work. Not only is it obvious to me, but most importantly, it's obvious to those doing the hiring. To help you avoid this common problem, let's take a closer look at using the tools of a professional digital modeler to prepare for modeling.

Tools of a Digital Modeler

When most modelers think of the term *tool*, it's usually in the literal sense. They think of the many options of the modeling tools in their chosen application—tools like Edge Bevel, Extrude, and Lathe. But the true tools of a professional digital modeler can be broken down into three important tools that are *not* a part of any package:

- Reference
- Observation
- Problem solving

Using and honing these three fundamental tools will allow you to raise the quality of your digital modeling from hobbyist to professional standards. Let's explore these tools in greater detail.

Reference

Good reference material coupled with attention to detail is the key to any successful project. Professional artists use any and all resources they can to attain the level of quality they produce in their work. Using reference is like using a cheat sheet in school—except the teacher doesn't care! *Not* using real-world reference for modeling is like washing your clothes without laundry detergent. It's like Batman fighting crime without his utility belt, or a person mowing the lawn with scissors. You get the idea. To put it simply: *Using reference makes your job easier, period.*

Don't fall victim to your faulty memory. Although eyewitness accounts can aid in the conviction of guilty parties, they can also lead to the conviction of the innocent. Artists that work from their "photographic" memories usually end up with mediocre work at best. You cannot imagine all of the little details that go into making up the simplest of items, such as the screws shown in **Figure 3.1**. Take note of the Phillips head on these screws and the shapes that make up the inset area. Without good reference, there's no way you could make up the fine minutiae, and those details would be overlooked.

One of the first modeling projects I usually start off new modelers with is to work with real-world items, like a standard key. **Figure 3.2** shows a few examples of keys. It's interesting to watch new modelers as they realize just how detailed the shape of a key can be, and that it isn't just a flat, extruded shape. As I stated earlier, their work made it quite obvious to me which students chose to use reference and which ones didn't. I can't say this enough: To make something look real, you need to reference something real.

I used to give my students weekly practical modeling quizzes that required them to create a model in a certain amount of time using the reference material that I supplied. It always amazed me how many students would leave the material unopened and proceed to model without ever using the reference! This would happen even after they listened to me go on and on about the importance of reference material. I don't think I need to describe in detail how inaccurate their models were.

[Figure 3.1] Good reference material provides details that your memory leaves out, like the details in the head of this screw.

[Figure 3.2] This photo shows the intricate details that make up common keys.

It's very important that you constantly reference the material so that you never lose sight of what you are trying to create. Professional artists use reference material for every project they work on. This includes everything from photo-real work to highly stylized work. Even when I'm designing and modeling cartoon-style characters, I always have reference on the screen and at my desk. For example, when I was working on a cartoon version of *Praying Mantis* for Animation Factory, I contacted Chris O'Riley, a friend who has an amazing collection of insect photos he's taken over the years. Fortunately, he had some great images he'd taken of a praying mantis. I displayed them on my reference monitor while I worked on the character to make sure I captured the qualities that make that insect look the way it does. I also added elements to the model that I didn't even know about before studying the photos, and these extra details added to the overall personality of the character.

Figure 3.3 shows the 3D model and one of the photos I worked from. You can check out some of Chris's other photos on his site (www.chris3d.com/photos).

[Figure 3.3] No matter what style you plan to work in, reference plays a substantial role in the success of a 3D model. The photo of the praying mantis (left) provided details for the stylized 3D model (right).

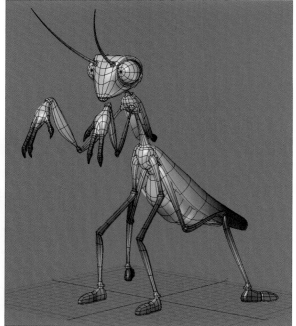

Even when making something abstract or completely from your imagination, it's generally a good idea to base it on real-world objects so that the audience can relate to them easily. Industry veteran and director of *Postcards from the Future*, Alan Chan, once told me to not think of it as creating whole new worlds, but to think of it as repurposing different parts of reality to paint what you see in your mind's eye. When working in a more realistic style, it's important to pay attention to all the small details but not to get caught up in them.

Observation

It's not enough to just have a collection of reference material. You need to increase your observational skills so that you can study and compare what you're working on with the reference you have. Your job is not only to match the reference, but to also figure out what makes the reference look real. Don't just duplicate the object; duplicate what makes it look like the object.

Observation is a continuous process of learning. It should never be skipped. In the case of digital modeling, the model becomes a "problem," and you can use your observational skills to come up with an answer. The reason there are so many inferior digital models in the 3D community is that the artist has solved the problem without ever truly understanding what the problem was. It's like trying to assemble a plastic car model kit without the instructions, not ever knowing what kind of car you are building, what color it should be, or most importantly, why you are building it in the first place! The finished model will only ever be the potential of a great one, doomed to be forever unfinished.

Before you ever launch your favorite 3D software, you need to think about what it is you're going to model and fully understand it. Ask yourself questions about your subject so that you can formulate the problem and devise a solution.

Some questions you might ask include:

- What is the scale of the object?
- What is the object made of (wood, metal, living tissue)?
- What is the surface of the object like (rough, smooth, sticky)?
- Is the object seamless or is it composed of sub-objects?
- Does it have cracks and fissures?

- How does the object's surface interact with light?

- Does it have an organic or hard-edged shape?

- Where do parts meet or overlap?

- Are there hidden recesses?

- What is the volume of the object?

- Has the object been damaged, or is it in pristine condition?

- Is the object symmetrical or asymmetrical?

- What is the mass of the object? Is it that of a balloon or a boulder?

- How does it interact with its environment?

- How would the object behave in gravity?

- Is the object manufactured by man or born in nature?

You can never ask too many questions about your subject, and each subject matter will probably lead to different questions that you'll want to have answers for. To model a character, I'd want to know the character's name, how old it was, where it was from, whether it was an introvert or an extrovert, and whether it prefers Ginger or Mary Ann. Some of those questions may not apply to observing a vehicle, but asking how the vehicle articulates, its mode of mobility, or its fuel source could be important.

Learning to observe your subject matter can transform you into a better digital modeler and is a requirement for professionals.

Problem Solving

Reference and observation are crucial in deciding exactly which tools and techniques to employ during the modeling process. Digital modeling is simply the process of solving visual problems and the art of devising a strategy that you will use to see the model from start through to completion.

Visualization

Want to model quicker and more efficiently? Simply *see* it modeled before it happens. One great technique that I learned when I was a teenager on the school's track team was the power of visualization, which means envisioning the race in your mind (and your success) before performing at the actual event. Professional athletes use visualization to see the basketball going through the hoop, the bat connecting with the baseball, the perfect pass being thrown between defenders, or the soccer ball being kicked out of reach of the goalie's hands without missing the goal.

This may sound like a silly and complete waste of time, but it's not. It simply works and is a powerful problem-solving technique. Another great benefit of visualization is that you can hone your skills throughout your day, even when you're not in front of a computer.

Find a quiet space, preferably away from the computer. Take some time leading up to the modeling session and visualize yourself constructing the mesh. When visualizing, be as specific and detailed as possible. Imagine yourself sitting at your workstation and launching the software. Imagine creating the first element all the way to the last. Spin the model around to take a good look at how true you stayed to your reference. The more specific you can be with the details, the more calm and confident you'll be when you actually start modeling.

Visualization is the process of creating a blueprint of how you go about modeling, and this preplanning will go a long way toward making efficient use of your time.

Another technique for increasing your problem-solving skills is something I call *modeling pilates*. Yes, you read that right—modeling pilates. I've done it for years and continue to do it to this day. All you need to do is look at the environment around you, select any object you see, use your observational skills, and work out how you might construct it in 3D. You may never actually build that object, but the fact that you're giving your brain a mental workout will increase the speed at which you'll be able to develop solutions for modeling challenges. Do this throughout the day when you're commuting to work, waiting in line at lunch, or anytime that you have a free moment.

Practice, practice, practice

Of course, there is the old advice for any art form: practice, practice, practice. It may be cliché, but the simple fact is that it's true. The more modeling experience you have behind you, the more prepared you will be for what's to come.

You now know the secrets of creating stunning digital models. Always remember that the first step of any new production is to gather reference material. Then you need to study the reference and make mental and written observations so that you can develop modeling solutions and apply them to your work.

Gathering Reference Material

Knowing that you need good reference material, the next step is gathering as much of it as possible. You can never have too much. So where do the professionals get their reference material? Let's explore the most common resources.

Physical Reference

The best source for good reference is usually sitting right in front of you. If you're trying to model a realistic lamp, simply grab one from your home or office and take it to your workstation. **Figure 3.4** shows a few of my anatomy figures that I constantly reference when modeling both realistic and stylized characters.

Now I know this one will be hard for some, but you may need to leave your workstation to gather reference material. I can't tell you how many times I've seen artists working on re-creating something in the real world that may be just outside their door, yet they never get up to go look at it firsthand. I've also seen character modelers trying to work out the polygon flow of a character's hip without getting out of their chair and moving their leg or asking someone nearby to get into a particular pose to get an idea of the way that area might deform.

There are a few other tools you can use to aid you in collecting reference, and every digital modeler should have them at their side as often as possible.

[Figure 3.4] Anatomy reference is key to any digital character modeler wanting to produce quality meshes.

Digital Camera

A digital camera will blow away any human's ability to remember details. Digital cameras have come a long way over the years, and the best thing about their evolution is price. You may even have a perfectly good one in your phone.

You don't have to get the latest and greatest camera to get good reference material. I've purchased several cameras over the years and will still use the Canon PowerShot that I bought in 1999 when I leave my newer camera at work. I use my phone's camera when I'm in a pinch. Although I envy some of my friends' high-end cameras, I typically stick with point-and-shoot cameras because I usually just need clear reference images, and I'm not using the camera in the same way a professional photographer would. I do find it interesting that most of the artists I know in the industry have a high-end camera and have taken up photography as a hobby. This can be very valuable when it comes to rendering your work; knowing how a camera works should never be overlooked.

Although a camera can help you obtain a great deal of information to work with, there are a few more tools that I would suggest as well.

Tape Measure

A perhaps surprising must-have tool is a standard tape measure (**Figure 3.5**). The information you can get with one can sometimes be even more useful than the photos you take with your camera. If you want to model something as accurately as possible, you should record its dimensions. A tape measure can't be beat in this regard. You can even include the tape measure in your photos for later reference, as the measurement of the antique chest in **Figure 3.6** shows. Some tape measures are quite small (and even fit on keychains); most usually have a convenient belt clip—so you have no excuse to be without one.

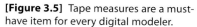

[**Figure 3.5**] Tape measures are a must-have item for every digital modeler.

[**Figure 3.6**] Including a tape measure in your reference photos can be a great way to determine the scale of a reference object later.

By including the tape measure in the actual photo, you can use it as a way to measure items in the image by comparing it to the size of the tape measure. I've also used business cards, credit and ID cards or even money for the same reason. If you know that a standard business card is 2 inches tall by 3 ½ inches wide, credit cards and IDs are 2 ⅛ inches by 3 ⅜ inches, a U.S. dollar bill is 2 ⁷⁄₁₂ inches tall by 6 ⅙ inches long (Canadian bills are 6 inches long by 2 ¾ inches tall), or that a one cent coin is ¾ of an inch across, you can easily figure out how large an item is in comparision placed next to it in a photo. **Figure 3.7** shows an automotive carburetor. The business card placed in front of it gives you an idea that this carburetor is about 10.5 inches long. This is a handy trick that has helped me avoid having to go back on location to get measurements after I'm back at the studio.

[Figure 3.7] Placing a business card in a photo is an easy way to determine size later.

Sketchbook

You'll also want to have a sketchbook or notebook and a writing utensil to record as many notes as you can. A smartphone can also give you the ability to take notes (or dictation) without needing to carry a pen and sketchpad (and some apps even allow for full-color sketches). Details to make note of will differ from reference to reference, but get down as much information as you can. Some specifics to make note of may include

- The dimensions you collected with the tape measure
- The number of sides the item has
- The type of material the item is made out of
- Whether the item looks new or old
- The time of day when you took photos of the item

If you don't have a camera, you can do rough sketches to refer back to when you're back in the office. I do this every week on my commutes from Philadelphia to New York. People on the train seem to take issue with you firing off photos of them, but I've never had anyone complain when they've seen me obviously sketching them in my sketchbook. Some of my favorite character designs have been based on sketches from my commute. **Figure 3.8** shows a few quick sketches of some interesting-looking commuters from my morning trips to New York City.

[Figure 3.8]
Rough sketches can make for great reference material when you're unable to get a snapshot with a camera.

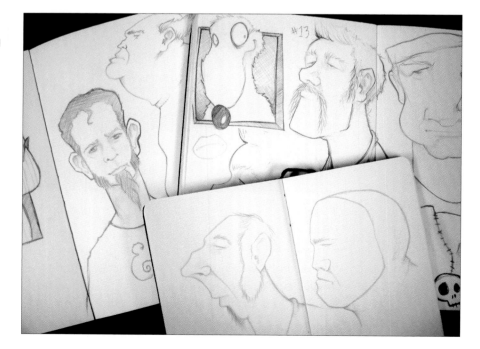

Digital Reference

What if you can't get your hands on the item you need to re-create, even to take a picture? The next best resources are reference images that others have made available to everyone. You have a ridiculous amount of resources at your fingertips thanks to the Internet. You can find images of just about anything online if you know where to look. My biggest online resource for reference gathering is Google (www.google.com). Within seconds, you get a large collection of reference images without ever leaving your seat.

Another great tip I picked up from artist Jamie Clarke when I was visiting the crew at Zoic years ago is to use Ebay (www.ebay.com) to collect reference images. Sounds like a strange idea, right? It is actually a brilliant one that has proven to be invaluable. When people try to sell something on Ebay, they usually take loads of large pictures of it from many different angles. I introduced Ebay to my searches a couple years ago, and it has made a massive impact on my ability to gather good reference of any given item.

Printed Reference

You can still gather great reference material at the bookstore, even though they are a dying breed. Libraries can also supply a wealth of material for just about any subject matter. Most of the artists I know have large libraries of books and magazines at their houses or studios. One of my friends—a digital modeler who owns a tattoo shop—has an impressive collection of books that I usually get caught up in when I visit.

My personal collection of books and magazines has become so large that it can be found all over the studio at Applehead Factory. A portion of my collection is shown in **Figure 3.9**. I look for any reason to grow my collection, because I have learned over the years that good reference books come in handy on almost every project, especially my anatomy books.

[**Figure 3.9**] You can never
have too much reference
material. Most artists I know
have impressive book and
magazine collections to pull
from.

Movie Reference

Movies are also great sources for reference. With the growing collection of
clips on sites like YouTube (www.youtube.com), it's now easier than ever to
pull great clips together for reference. It's also extremely important to have
a wealth of knowledge of movies in general, because directors and supervisors reference them all the time. Do your homework on this one, especially
because all it requires you to do is *watch movies*. Being able to communicate
with directors or supervisors is incredibly important to your job, and getting
a film reference (particularly a very obscure one) will give you a leg up on
the competition, possibly even making you their go-to artist. This seems
to be a weak area for many of the new artists coming into the industry. I'm
always shocked when I'm talking to someone in this field who has not seen
the movies that have helped shape this industry. *Star Wars: The Clone Wars*
CG supervisor, Lee Stringer, and I were teaching a class a few years ago, and
no one in it knew who the legendary stop-motion animator Ray Harryhausen
was. How can you think you can master your craft if you haven't studied how
the greatest artists did it?

Copyrighted Material

An extremely important judgment needs to take place when it comes to using reference material and whether it's okay to use copyrighted material as reference for your digital models.

In this case, copyrighted material includes photographers' photos, artists' illustrations and paintings, movies, and animation, as well as someone else's concept or likeness.

Although digital modeling is quite different from traditional art, the same copyright laws apply when working from copyrighted material.

Basically, if you're only using someone else's material as reference, you can simply collect the information you need and apply it to your digital model. On the other hand, if you intend to *essentially re-create* a specific image in 3D, you need permission from the copyright holder of that material.

There is a big difference between using an image for reference and copying the image. Think of it like this: If you show others the reference material and an image of your model and they say the model is clearly based on the reference material, assume it's a derivative use of the other person's work, not just a reference use. Simply put, if your model looks "exactly" like the copyrighted material, you've broken the copyright laws.

Many copyright-free resources are available online that you can pull from if you are questioning whether or not you should use a copyrighted image. 3D.sk (www.3d.sk) has been a favorite of mine for years; it has more than a quarter of a million royalty-free images available for instant download.

Disclaimer: The information given here is based on U.S. copyright law and is given for guidance only; you're advised to consult a copyright lawyer on copyright issues.

References to Avoid

With the wealth of amazing reference materials available to a digital modeler, you should know that there are some you should stay away from beyond the copyrighted material I discuss in the preceding section.

Inadequate reference

Common mistakes modelers make when gathering reference are selecting images that lack detail. Their imagination fills in the missing element, which in turn means they are no longer working from reference but their interpretation of the reference. Which image in **Figure 3.10** gives you a better idea of the details that make up the engine of the boat? Personally, the image with the boat in the water tells me more about the environment than the boat.

Try to find reference material with clear detail and that is easy to explore. Photos taken from newspapers or photocopied pictures are notorious for not having enough detail.

[**Figure 3.10**] The boat in the image on the left is too far away to gather proper details, whereas the engine details in the image on the right are very clear, making it ideal for reference material.

Having a blurry image is also one of the worst types of references you can use. It distorts the shape of an object and makes it difficult or even impossible to differentiate details. **Figure 3.11** shows an example of how a blurry image makes it difficult to work out specific details on this toy truck.

It may seem obvious, but I've seen many an artist trying to work from thumbnail-size reference images. Just as with blurry or low-detail images, if you can't make out the detail, you're no longer working from reference; instead, you're just working from your interpretation of the reference. **Figure 3.12** is a perfect example of an image you'd want to avoid because it's too small.

[Figure 3.11] Blurry images don't provide enough information and should be avoided when gathering reference material.

[Figure 3.12] Small images don't provide adequate details and should be avoided.

Illustrations

Illustrations created by the visual design department for the project you are working on should be good reference, but you should avoid using art created by others artists as reference for your own work. It's like making a photocopy of a photocopy. Eventually, some attributes will get lost in translation, and you'll be relying on another artist's interpretation of the subject matter.

Figure 3.13 shows a 2D sketch of a horse by Graham Toms. Although it appears to be true to life, it's still his interpretation of reality. You'd be better off working from a photograph of the real deal.

[Figure 3.13] Illustrations aren't ideal reference material unless they were created either by or for you.

If I were going to model a horse, I would probably have ten or more real horse photos open on my secondary monitor instead of someone else's interpretation, no matter how accurate it may appear to be. Also, keep in mind the information covered earlier in the "Copyrighted Material" section.

Digital models

For reasons similar to avoiding illustrations as reference, using another artist's digital model as reference, such as the CG strawberry in **Figure 3.14**, is probably not the best road to travel. First, you have to assume that it's copyrighted material; second, once again you are relying on that artist's interpretation of the subject matter.

[Figure 3.14] Chris O'Riley created this amazing 3D strawberry model, and although it appears to be accurate, you'd be better off working from a photo.

Photos with extreme lighting conditions

Whether the shadows in an image are hiding details or the lighting is blowing out or clipping the material (losing image detail due to maximum brightness), bad lighting conditions can ruin an otherwise perfect reference image. Look for images that show even lighting. Remember that these images don't need to win awards—your model work does.

Figure 3.15 shows the same teapot photo taken using both ends of the bad lighting spectrum. Both distort the important details that make up the shape of the object. Modeling from either of the images would result in a 3D model that isn't 100 percent accurate.

Note that if you're the one taking the photos, the best time of day to get even lighting outside is just as the sun is coming up and just as it's going down. At those times, the sun isn't high enough to cast those pesky harsh shadows. You avoid strong shadows and get a nice even light over everything, which is exactly what you're looking for in good modeling reference.

[Figure 3.15] The bright teapot has areas that are clipping and blending into the background.

The darker image has areas that blend into the shadows. Both are far from ideal to work from.

Preparing Reference Material

Once you have all of the reference material you feel you need for a modeling project or you've simply run out of time to gather it (which is usually the case for me), you'll want to prepare the content.

If your reference is a physical object, make sure it's in an ideal spot where you will be working. You don't want to have to get up every few minutes to go examine it for details, because it will most likely break your concentration and workflow, which leads to an inefficient use of your time. Most digital artists I know prefer to work in a dark environment, but make sure your physical reference is well lit. Being able to glance over at the reference and back to your model without even turning your head is ideal.

When dealing with images, the following sections suggest some common tasks you may want to perform before you launch your 3D software.

Scan or Transfer

Even though you can place books, magazines, and photographs at your workstation, I've found it to be more efficient to have them onscreen (this is another time when a second monitor comes in handy). That usually means scanned. The higher the resolution at which you scan your reference material the better. As a general rule, 300 dots per inch (dpi) usually does the trick. Good resolution allows you to zoom into areas for closer inspection of details.

If you've captured your reference photos with a digital camera, transfer them to your system. Believe it or not, I've seen artists using their tiny LCD screen on their camera to view their reference while they model! At that point, it doesn't matter which resolution you used to take the picture, because you are viewing it at postage-stamp size. Put it up on a big screen so you can get a good look.

Adjust Color and Levels

Using image manipulation software, such as Photoshop or Paint Shop Pro, you should adjust the images' color balance and levels to optimize their quality. Often, an image that is too dark can be salvaged with a few tweaks to Brightness and Contrast or Levels. Some artists prefer a lower contrast and/or a grayscale image for backdrop images they plan on modeling on top of, because it can be easier to read a model's wireframe when displayed over the images.

Avoid overprocessing (making too many adjustments to) your images while editing them, or they may fall into the references-to-avoid category. It's also a good idea to save any and all changes to a new file so that you can always return to the raw source file when needed.

Rotate, Size, and Crop

If the camera was tilted when you took the photo and the object you are modeling is crooked, it is good practice to rotate the image and level the object to straighten it as much as possible. Although most 3D applications have this option built in, it's usually quicker to handle it before ever opening the 3D program.

Rotating and sizing your images is extremely important when preparing multiple views of the same object. For example, I always prepare the front and side images when modeling a human head from reference, making sure they are the same size and that they line up with each other. **Figure 3.16** shows reference photos that I prepped for a CG model of my friend Sam.

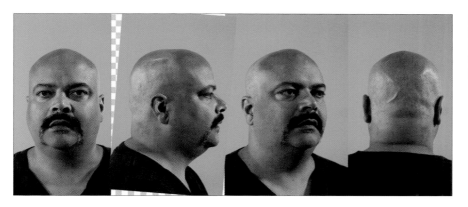

[**Figure 3.16**] Taking the time to align reference images in the beginning will speed up the modeling process later.

It's usually OK to size down an image, but you want to try to avoid sizing up an image larger than its original size. There is a safe tolerance for sizing up photos without losing too much quality, but it's a fine line—so be careful not to destroy on otherwise perfect reference image. It's usually best to just zoom in and out of the picture without ever having to scale the image permanently.

You can also crop your reference images to display only the required details you need from that particular image, which will not only decrease the file size, but you'll avoid having to zoom in each time you access the image.

Composite

A task that I've done for years that I find very useful is to composite reference images into one large image. Merging these images allows you to quickly load one image onto your second monitor without needing to load several separate images and organize them each time you prepare to model. **Figure 3.17** shows the composite I created for the modeling session of Sam.

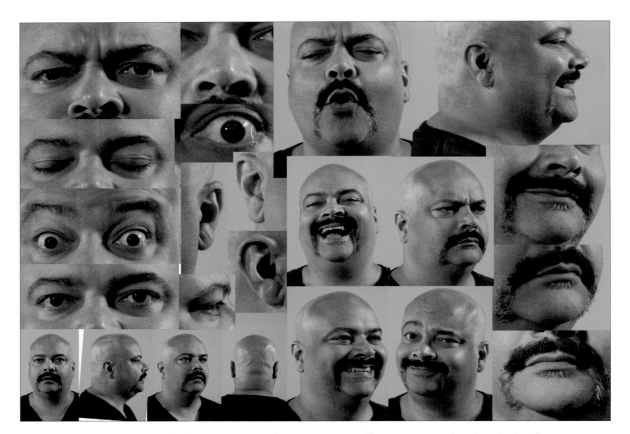

[**Figure 3.17**] Compositing multiple images into one large image is an efficient way to work with multiple references.

Rename and Organize

Renaming and organizing are steps most artists skip in their race to start modeling. By default, most digital camera naming conventions are those of a mindless robot. Which name best describes an image: 2079033 or Sammy_Head_Front?

Giving proper naming conventions to your reference material will make them easier to recall at a later time. You should also save them in organized directories. Taking shortcuts with your reference's naming and organization may save you time up front but will always come back to bite you in the digital rear later on.

CHAPTER FOUR

Fundamentals of a Digital Model

Before we go too far down the rabbit hole, I want to introduce some of the elements of digital models and the terms you'll encounter throughout the book. If you have some experience already, you may be inclined to skip this section, but I recommend you at least skim through it just to make sure we're on the same page. You can think of this chapter as a refresher course of 3D models 101.

A Model's Anatomy

Digital models can be broken down into three types:

- Polygonal models are made up of a collection of points, edges, and polygons.

- NURBS surfaces consist of a network of curves with smooth surfaces between them.

- Subdivision surfaces are similar to polygonal models because they are made up of points, edges, and polygons but also share some of the benefits of NURBS surfaces, placing them into their own category.

In this section I explain some of the terminology used in the creation of all three types of digital models.

Points

A *point*, also called a *vertex* (plural: vertices), is the lowest-level component that makes up a 3D model. Each point exists in 3D space with a specific X, Y, and Z coordinate. Because points alone do not have height, width, or depth, they cannot be rendered.

When two points are connected, a *line* is drawn. When three points are connected, they can become corners of surfaces on a model called a *polygon*. Without points, there would be no polygons. A triangle, for example, consists of three points and one polygon, as shown in **Figure 4.1**.

[Figure 4.1] The three points (shown here in pink) define the shape of the triangle and its placement in 3D space.

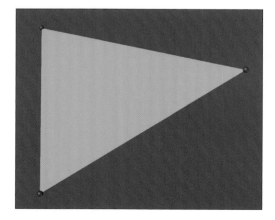

Multiple polygons can share the same points when used on a *contiguous* (seamless) mesh. The tessellated sphere in **Figure 4.2** shows individual points being used to define the multiple polygons that make up the object.

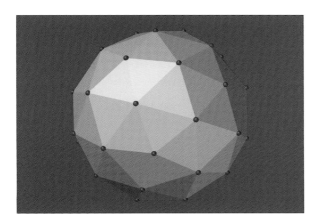

[**Figure 4.2**] Polygons that share a common edge also share points to define their shape.

Vertex Maps

Every point in an object stores information about its position and rotation, although you normally don't access the rotational values of an individual point. Points also have the ability to store a variety of additional information using vertex maps. Simply put, a *vertex map* is information saved to a point.

The most common types of vertex maps include:

- Texture (UV)
- Weight
- Morph
- Color
- Selection

Texture (UV)

Texture, or UV, maps store texture placement information and are the most common vertex map. UV mapping adds two extra coordinates to the points in your object; those on the U (horizontal) and V (vertical) axes, running horizontally and vertically through the flat plane of the texture map, on which you can paint your texture. UV coordinates are a 2D representation of 3D space. They set up a relationship between a two-dimensional image and the three-dimensional surface the image will be applied to.

Points can have as many UV maps assigned to them as you'd like. **Figure 4.3** shows three UV maps that were created for the Spiderbait character that you can download from my site at www.pushingpoints.com/2011/07/spiderbait-rig.

[Figure 4.3] Three separate UV maps were assigned to the points that make up the character mesh on the right.

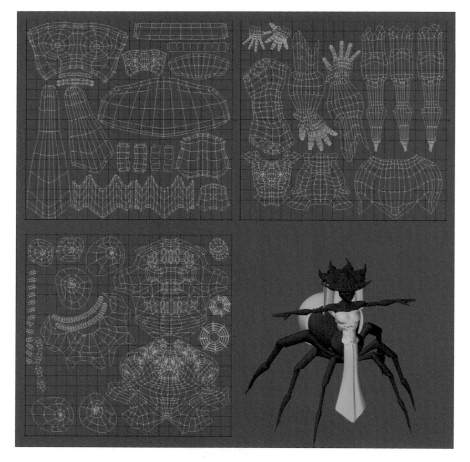

Weight

Weight maps store a single value, usually between -100 and 100 (although in some instances lower and higher values are possible). The most common use of a weight map is for defining a bone's influence on a point when *rigging* (placing bones and controls to allow a model to be deformed for animation). **Figure 4.4** shows positive weight values applied to the points that make up the character's jaw. When the weight map is assigned to the jaw bone, the points will move when the bone moves. This allows for seamless organic meshes to deform in localized areas.

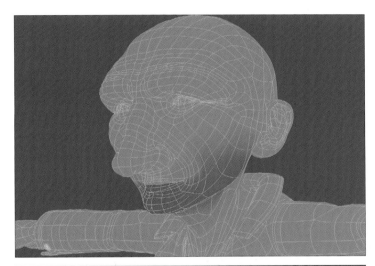

[Figure 4.4] Weight values assigned to points in the mesh (top) can be assigned to a specific bone (bottom) during the rigging process.

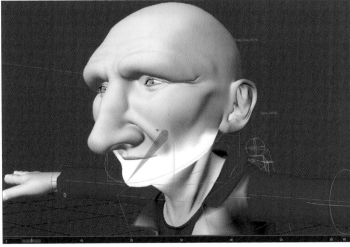

There are far more uses for weight maps than rigging. For example, you can use weights to mask a surface when texturing, influence dynamic simulations over an object, aid during the modeling process, and do much more.

Morph

Morph maps store offset information (alternate XYZ values) for a point's position and are commonly used for creating morph targets for animation. **Figure 4.5** shows several morphs applied to the base mesh. Each morph relies on multiple points being moved to new coordinates, and that information is saved to each vertex.

[Figure 4.5] Morph maps are commonly used to create facial poses for animation.

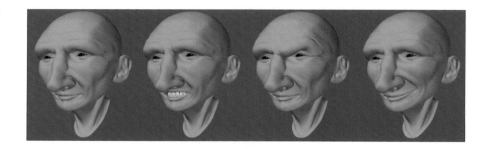

Similar to weight maps, morph maps have a variety of uses during the modeling and texturing processes.

Color

Color maps hold values for Red, Green, Blue, and Alpha (RGBA) color information. I often use color maps on my character models to add color variation to the object's surfaces, like adding blush to a character's face. **Figure 4.6** shows an example of using a color map to add a five o'clock shadow and some color to a character's face.

[Figure 4.6] A color map was applied to the character's face (right) to give the appearance of a five o'clock shadow.

Selection

A *selection map*, also referred to as a *selection set*, stores a single state of a point—either selected or unselected. Selection maps allow a modeler to recall a selected group of points quickly and can be extremely useful for defining which points will be affected by dynamic simulations.

Edges

An *edge* is a one-dimensional line that connects two points in a polygon. Another way to describe edges would be to say that they are the line segments that border a polygon. A triangle, for example, has three edges, three points, and one polygon, as shown in **Figure 4.7**.

Similar to points, multiple polygons can share the same edges when used on a contiguous mesh. The tessellated sphere in **Figure 4.8** shows individual edges bordering the multiple polygons.

[Figure 4.7] The polygon in this image consists of three edges, shown here in pink.

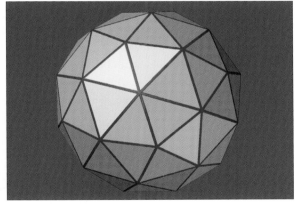

[Figure 4.8] Each polygon shares common edges in this mesh.

Edge weights

Edge weighting increases or decreases the sharpness of an edge between two subdivision surface (SubDs) polygons, allowing for harder or softer corners without additional geometry being added (**Figure 4.9**). The main issue with edge weights is that there is no universal, widely supported format that allows you to transfer edge weights from one 3D application to another. In today's mixed software pipeline, this can be a showstopper. Most modelers I know avoid edge weighting and opt for additional geometry to accomplish the same end goal.

[Figure 4.9] Edge weighting has been increased to 100 percent to the four edges on the top of the SubD object on the left to produce harder edges.

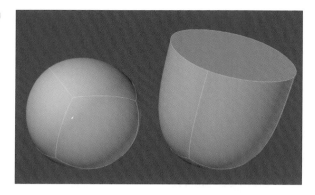

Polygonal Models

Polygons, often shortened to *polys* and commonly referred to as *faces*, are geometric shapes consisting of a number of points that define the surface of a 3D object. A polygon is what you actually see in a render, and a typical 3D model will consist of hundreds or thousands of polygons (**Figure 4.10**).

[Figure 4.10] This head mesh consists of over 6000 polygons.

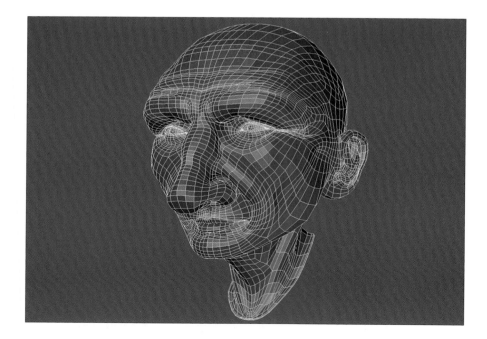

Although some 3D applications allow the creation of one- and two-point polygons, it's more common that a polygon be made up of at least three points. Three-point polygons are commonly called *triangles* or *tris*. Polygons made up of four points are called *quads*, and a polygon that has more than four points is usually referred to as an *n-gon*. The term *n-gon* means a polygon with *n* sides, where *n* is the number of the polygon's sides. For example, a polygon with six sides is a 6-gon. Examples of a triangle, a quad, and an n-gon are shown in **Figure 4.11**.

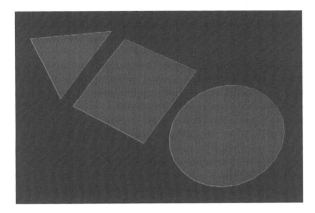

[Figure 4.11] Polygons come in all shapes and sizes. The triangle (left) consists of three points, the quad (middle) is made up of four points, and the n-gon (right) is made up of 24 points.

NURBS

A *Non-Uniform Rational B-Splines (NURBS)* surface is a smooth mesh defined by a series of connected *splines*, which are polynomial curves. This smooth surface is converted to polygons at render time, so NURBS surfaces can contain an arbitrary number of polygons. NURBS can be converted to polygons or subdivision surfaces and are useful for constructing many types of organic 3D forms because of the minimal nature of their curves. NURBS geometry is smooth by default and doesn't need to be subdivided to "become" smooth like polygon geometry does.

Non-Uniform refers to the parameterization (defining the parameters) of the curve. Non-Uniform curves allow, among other things, the presence of *multi-knots* (a sequence of values that determines how much and where the control points influence the shape), which are needed to represent Bézier curves.

Rational refers to the underlying mathematical representation. This property allows NURBS to represent exact conics (such as parabolic curves, circles, and ellipses) in addition to free-form curves.

B-splines are *piecewise* (a function that changes) polynomial curves (splines) that have a parametric representation. Simply put, a B-spline is based on four local functions or control points that lie outside the curve itself.

The best way to understand NURBS is to see them in action. **Figure 4.12** shows multiple examples of the splines that define the NURBS surfaces.

[Figure 4.12] Each of these three NURBS surfaces are defined by a series of splines, shown to the left of each object.

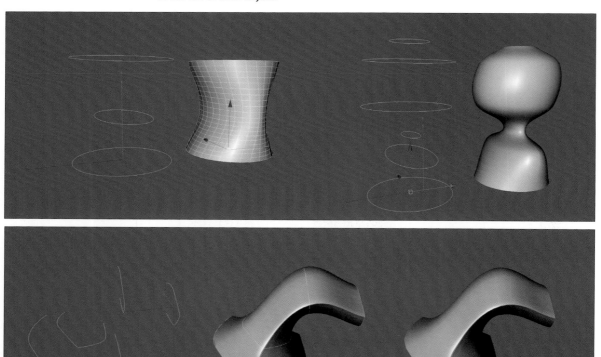

NURBS are most commonly used in computer-aided design (CAD), manufacturing, and engineering. Although they were once used heavily for organic objects (see the forthcoming section "Model Classification: Hard Surface and Organic") in the film and broadcast markets, subdivision surfaces have since replaced them in almost all instances in movies and television.

Splines

A *spline* is a curve in 3D space defined by at least two points. The most common spline used in digital modeling is the Bézier curve. *Bézier curves* are used to model smooth curves using far fewer points than a polygonal model would require. *Control points* make up the curve and can be used to dramatically manipulate the curve with little effort. Also, splines are resolution independent, unlike a polygonal mesh, which can appear faceted when you zoom in close enough to a curved surface.

Splines in 3D applications can be likened to vector curves in software such as Illustrator, Flash, and Photoshop. Splines are similar to NURBS in that they can create a "patch" of polygons that extends between multiple splines, forming a 3D skin around the shape (**Figure 4.13**), a feature which is extremely useful when modeling. Unlike NURBS, the splines must be converted to polygons before rendering.

Splines are also useful in many other modeling techniques, including but not limited to, *extrusion* (adding depth to a flat surface) and *cloning* (duplicating) along a spline and deforming a mesh based on the curves of a spline.

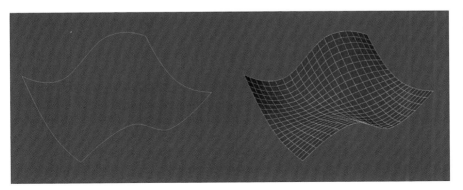

[Figure 4.13] The four splines on the left were used to patch the polygonal mesh on the right.

Subdivision Surfaces

Subdivision surface (*SubD*) is a refinement algorithm that creates a smooth curved surface from a coarse *polygonal mesh* (also called a *base mesh*). This process takes the base mesh and creates a smooth surface using the original vertices as control points, also referred to as the control cage. **Figure 4.14** shows the polygonal mesh (left), the control cage (middle), and the resulting SubD mesh (right).

[Figure 4.14] Subdivision surfaces allow you to work with a very light and simple polygonal mesh to create smooth organic shapes.

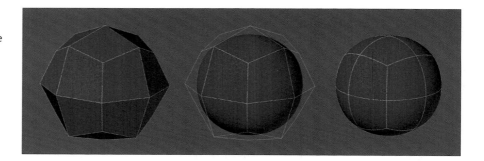

The number of polygons, or subdivisions, generated from SubDs can be adjusted to a varying level of density, and complex smooth objects can be created in a fast and predictable way from simple base meshes, as shown in the character model in **Figure 4.15**. This makes SubDs a popular option for most digital modelers.

[Figure 4.15] This character was created with a very simple polygonal mesh (left). But with SubDs applied (middle), a smooth, high-poly mesh was generated (right).

Model Classification: Hard Surface and Organic

When 3D was still in its infancy, digital modelers were usually put into one of two distinct groups based on the type of meshes they constructed. Although the lines have become blurred, these groups still exist today and play a role in how modelers define themselves in the industry. Also, the distinction of the types of meshes a modeler creates makes it easier for studios looking for talent to find the right digital modeler for their specific modeling needs.

Every 3D mesh can be grouped or classified as either a hard surface or organic. What's the difference? What defines an object as hard surface? What defines an object as organic? So many objects nowadays seem to blur the lines between the two. How would you make a distinction between these classifications?

What may come as a surprise is that if you ask 20 professional digital modelers what the difference between these two classifications is, you'll receive 20 different responses. I did just that before writing this section of the book and was quite surprised at some of what I heard.

How can something so seemingly clear-cut bring about so many different ways to classify a 3D model? Before coming to a conclusion, let's explore the most common responses.

Production Driven

Many artists felt that a model would be classified by how it would be used in a production. A static object, such as a stone statue, gas pump, or street sign, would be considered a hard surface object, whereas objects that would deform or animate, such as an animated human character, flag, or animal would fall into the organic category.

The same item could be classified two different ways depending on what the object is called to do for the shot/project. A statue is made of stone and doesn't usually deform; therefore, it is a hard surface object. But if it becomes a moving statue, as in the world of Harry Potter, it is organic.

Although a gun has moving parts that can be animated, it is still a rigid object, which makes it a hard surface object, unless of course, someone with super human strength comes along and bends (deforms) the barrel—then it becomes organic.

If the mesh is going to deform in some way, it needs to be modeled differently and it should then be classified as an organic object.

Attribute Driven

Some believed that it was a model's *attributes*, or what an object looks like, that defined whether it was hard surface or organic. So if the mesh had flowing "organic" curves where any shape could smoothly transform into any other, like a character, ornate piece of furniture, or a sleek sports car, it was an organic mesh.

Hard surface objects would be defined as meshes typically involving tight edges or simpler shapes joining together with distinct edges, even if the shapes were soft or sleek, like guns, power tools, and retro robots.

Also, if the object's surface attributes were that of stone, metal, or glass, it would fall into the hard surface category, whereas objects made up of living tissue, like animals, plants, and people, would be considered organic.

Construction Driven

One artist defined the two by focusing solely on the modeling aspect. Objects that require a more "organized" topology could be classified as an organic mesh and easily created using "organic" modeling tools and techniques. He believed that organic meshes tend to have more polygons and could benefit from SubDs more than hard surface objects. Hard surface objects don't require an organized, semi-regular topology and could be created with fewer polygons with less concern about the object's underlying mesh.

Model Classification Evaluation

Although each of these schools of thought has valid arguments and may work for a particular artist, we simply can't classify an object based on how it is constructed, will be used in production, or by its appearance. To do that would cause confusion, because every object could find its way into each category.

Take, for example, my dog Jack. He's a chocolate lab, which is classified as being part of the *Canidae* family. For the most part, Jack acts like your average dog, wanting to eat, play, and sleep most of the time. He does, however, show attributes of a cat at times, and every now and then he will scratch at the ground after he urinates, like a cat pawing at its litter box. Although this is common in cats, it doesn't make Jack part of the *Felidae* family.

Organic modeling goes beyond the fact that the shape of the model is rounded. Many hard surface objects have organic shapes, like cars, cell phones, and robots, whereas organic objects can have rigid shapes like rocks, insects, and crustaceans. Industrial design has moved more towards organic shapes over the years, and the entertainment industry is taking things that were traditionally hard surface, static objects and deforming them in animation—having gas pumps dance in commercials, for example.

Also, modeling something to perform well when animated is just good modeling technique and shouldn't determine whether something is hard surface or organic. For example, look at a mesh sculpted in ZBrush, or modeling with metaballs or voxels. You can create something very organic, but these modeling techniques will make the model nonconducive to animating. Would that then be considered hard surface modeling? Of course not.

Most modelers don't limit their tool and technique use based on whether a model is organic or hard surface. Generally, they use good modeling techniques, which include building a model that'll hold up if deformed, even if it's not intended to, and apply those same techniques regardless of whether the model is hard surface or organic.

You hear the terms *hard surface* and *organic modeling* all the time in the 3D modeling community, and artists are often defined as one or the other. If you make mostly characters meshes, you are an organic modeler. If you make more architectural or mechanical objects, you are a hard surface modeler. I usually describe myself as an organic character modeler, but it is simply not that straightforward, because I create products and vehicles that are defined as hard surface too.

So back to the point: What's the difference between hard surface and organic models, and how do we define the two? I suppose, essentially, there is no difference at all, and it is a question of semantics. For the purposes of this book (and based on my personal philosophy), I use the following distinction: Characters, creatures, plant life, and more naturalistic environments are organic models, and architectural environments, vehicles, and mechanical products are hard surface. This is very loose as a definition, and as I've tried to emphasize, the lines between the two are indeed very blurred.

Hard surface

Hard surface objects are anything man-made or constructed. Architectural structures, vehicles, robots, and anything machined or manufactured could fall into this category. The robots from FunGoPlay's *Grid Iron Gladiators* (www.fungoplay.com), shown in **Figure 4.16**, would fall into the hard surface category.

[Figure 4.16] Although these robots have smooth organic shapes, they still fall into the hard surface category.

Organic

Organic models are subjects that naturally exist in nature. This would include humans, animals, plants, trees, rocks, boulders, terrains, clouds, and even lightning bolts. The nonplayer characters that roam the world of FunGoPlay (**Figure 4.17**) would be considered organic models.

[Figure 4.17] These characters from FunGoPlay would be classified as organic models.

Model Styles

As with a model's classification, a mesh usually has a specific style associated with it. A *style* refers to a specific philosophy, goal, or look. Realism, impressionism, abstract expressionism, and surrealism are common styles found in traditional art. Although a digital model could easily fall into any of the traditional art styles, the 3D industry usually places them into one of two different model styles: photo-real and stylized.

Photo-real

When a model depicts an object with realistic accuracy, the term *photo-real* is applied. Digital artists use photographic reference and their observation skills to transfer the realistic properties to the details that make up their models.

It's important to understand that the subject matter is not required to be a real-world object, like a car, human, or architectural structure. Models of robots, dragons, and other fictional subjects can also be modeled in a photo-realistic style using real-world reference as a guide.

Stylized

When a digital model consists of artistic forms and conventions in a non-realistic style, it is referred to as a *stylized* model. Simply put, a stylized model is one that is not photo-real. Cartoon characters and environments are classic examples of stylized models.

The best stylized modelers I know still gather and use just as much real-world reference material as a photo-real modeler. The only difference is how they interpret it and apply that information to the model.

Choosing a Style

Although many artists would argue otherwise, I don't find either style of modeling to be more difficult than the other. Both styles require the same attention to detail, and the same care needs to be put into the poly-count and topology of the mesh. At the end of the day, the only real difference between the two styles is where the points are arranged on the model, as shown in the head models in **Figure 4.18**.

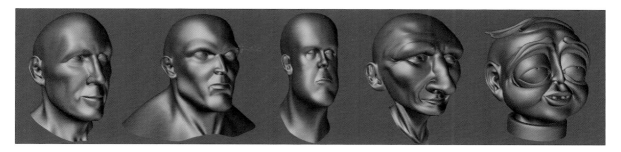

[Figure 4.18] Each of these head models consists of the same elements, but only the head on the far left would be classified as photo-real.

Most artists gravitate towards a particular style. I prefer creating stylized models and creating meshes that have otherworldly proportions and attributes, but I also tackle photo-real models on a regular basis. My modeling toolset and techniques don't change depending on the style of the mesh I'm tasked with. Digital modelers' goals should be to hone their observational skills and to have the ability to work across styles.

Learning to work in both styles will only enhance your ability in the style of your choice and will open up more opportunities to you as a professional modeler.

CHAPTER FIVE

Digital Modeling Methods

An interesting fact in the digital modeling world is that no two artists use the same techniques when creating a digital model, even when the two modelers are working from the same reference material, producing the same final mesh. Consider this example: When I had classes of thirty students working on the same robot model, I never saw any two working with the same method. This just goes to show that there is no set way to work, and that artists are free to work with whatever method(s) they feel most comfortable with.

When first introduced to 3D software, I began creating digital models by building everything using common primitives like boxes, spheres, discs, cones, and so forth. Using this primitive modeling method, I was always able to successfully create just about anything I was tasked with, but I still felt there had to be a better approach for the organic meshes I was making.

 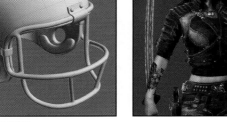  

I began exploring alternate modeling methods and eventually discovered box modeling, which I then dubbed the Holy Grail of modeling. Adding box modeling to my bag of modeling tools opened up all sorts of new possibilities that forever changed the way I tackle creating digital assets. If adding one new technique could make such a difference to my modeling efficiency, what other techniques existed that I wasn't aware of? I continued to learn as many techniques as I could to hone my skills as a digital modeler. Over the years I've discovered that each modeling technique I pick up inevitably paves the way to solving a multitude of modeling challenges, big and small.

Getting locked in to a particular way of working is easy. However, it's important to understand that limiting your toolkit can come at the price of modeling efficiency. I never felt I reached my maximum potential as an artist until I armed myself with a wide array of modeling techniques. With this arsenal, choosing the right tool for the specific task at hand has become a matter of instinct.

In this chapter, I cover the most popular techniques used to generate digital models, providing insight on their strengths and most common uses. Adding these techniques to your modeling toolkit will give you more options to pull from when your next big modeling challenge pops up.

Build Out

The build out approach to modeling is the oldest method of digital modeling and is still widely used throughout the industry. This technique involves constructing the tertiary details of a model from the very first polygon created. Once one portion of the mesh is complete, you simply build towards another area of the model and continue this process until the entire mesh is constructed.

For many, the build out method is the easiest modeling technique to grasp. It is a great method for both new and seasoned users to build everything from stylized to realistic models. The two most common modeling tasks performed by artists using the build out method are creating realistic head models and performing *retopology* (the process of rebuilding the topology of an object). Using a preexisting mesh consisting of millions of polygons—usually created in a sculpting program such as Mudbox (www.autodesk.com) or ZBrush (www.pixologic.com)—the process of retopology creates a lower-poly, clean model that deforms properly when animated.

Two primary techniques fall into the build out category: point by point and edge extend.

Point by Point

The technique's name says it all. With the point by point technique, you start by generating points to define the shape of the mesh you want to produce and then create polygons from those points. I know a few modelers that use this technique to model all their low-poly models for games. I find point by point to be the fastest way to generate custom letterforms for 3D text and logos when a font is not available. **Figure 5.1** shows a custom *W* that was created by placing multiple points, selecting those points, and generating a polygon from the selection.

[Figure 5.1] Placing individual points to use to create polygons is the oldest form of digital modeling.

Edge Extend

The edge extend method of modeling usually starts with the creation of a flat polygon created either using the point by point method or by using a primitive object. Once the flat polygon has been created, an edge is selected and extended to produce a new polygon. This step is repeated until the entire mesh has been formed. Digital modelers use this method to create just about any subject matter, including vehicles, weapons, and more. The most common use of this technique is the creation of a realistic head. **Figure 5.2** shows the edge extend method used to create a boot with an embossed design, starting with a single four-point polygon.

Primitive Modeling

Primitive modeling, in simple terms, is combining multiple primitive geometric shapes (like boxes, spheres, discs, and so on) and modifying their shape to form the desired final object. **Figure 5.3** shows a few examples of the most common primitives.

All 3D software packages offer a wide range of tools to manipulate and combine custom shapes from primitive objects, making this method of modeling very popular with digital modelers. Although artists have used this method of modeling to create an endless variety of models, its primary use is on hard-surface, mechanical meshes like the scout robot in **Figure 5.4**, which was created by Deuce Bennett for military visualization.

If you look at the items around you in your environment, you can start to see how you might model a majority of them using primitive geometry. Most tables, shelves, and even your keyboard and monitor could be created from simple boxes. When I first started modeling, I constantly thought about how I would model whatever was in front of me using nothing but primitive objects. Although I work with several modeling methods, primitive modeling still plays a major role in the construction of my polygonal models.

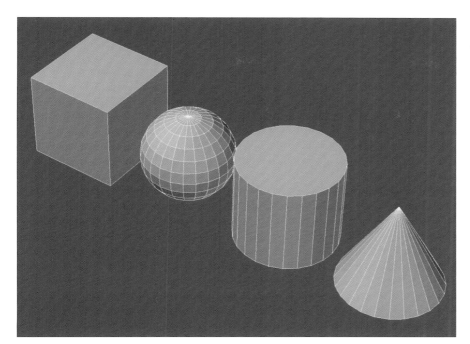

[Figure 5.3] These common primitives can be found in most if not all 3D software available today. From left to right: box, ball (sphere), disc (cylinder), and cone.

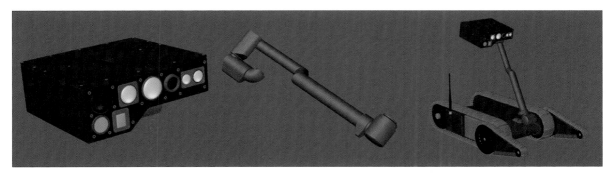

[Figure 5.4] This robot, created for military visualization, was constructed from primitive geometry. The two components on the left could be made from multiple boxes and discs.

Box Modeling

The box modeling technique can be likened to primitive modeling, because the first step in the process of box modeling is starting with a primitive shape—usually a box (hence the name). Instead of using multiple primitives to generate the final mesh, the digital modeler "grows" additional geometry from the single primitive to create an entire seamless mesh. This additional geometry is created by extending or beveling individual or groups of polygons, giving the artist more geometry to help shape the model.

Although working with subdivision surfaces isn't required when box modeling, the two are usually used in tandem. Box modeling is an extremely fast way to create complex, smooth objects from simple base meshes. Modelers use box modeling as a way to quickly create a low-poly, rough, polygonal base shape and then apply SubDs to smooth out the shape, all the while using the original polygonal mesh to control the overall shape.

Box modeling is most commonly used to create organic meshes, although artists use it to create everything from weapons to vehicles. **Figure 5.5** shows two models I created for Pixar's animated short film *Partly Cloudy* using the box modeling method. I made the shoulder pads from several box primitives, and the helmet started off as a sphere primitive.

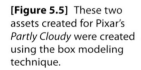

[Figure 5.5] These two assets created for Pixar's *Partly Cloudy* were created using the box modeling technique.

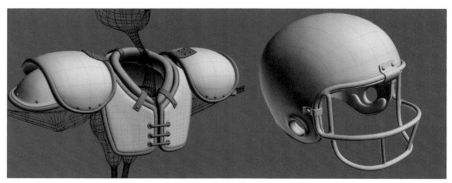

© Disney/Pixar

Box modeling is without a doubt my go-to modeling method for creating character models. **Figure 5.6** shows a cartoon animal head being box modeled. I prefer to start with a box so that I begin with as few polygons as possible and only add additional geometry when needed. With that said, I never discount the other primitives and have found them quite handy at times.

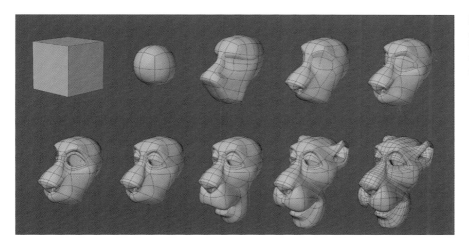

[Figure 5.6] Starting from a box, this cartoon animal head takes shape quickly using only a handful of modeling tools.

Patch Modeling

When it comes to patch modeling, whether you're creating them using NURBS (Non-Uniform Rational B-Splines) or polygon patches from splines, the process is relatively the same. Using curves, you create a wire cage to define the surface of an object. The surfaces created between the intersecting curves are known as patches. These patches are controlled by the points that make up the curves and are commonly called control points. When multiple patches are combined, you can create complex organic shapes with minimal curves. **Figure 5.7** shows an example of NURBS defining the surface of a bottle.

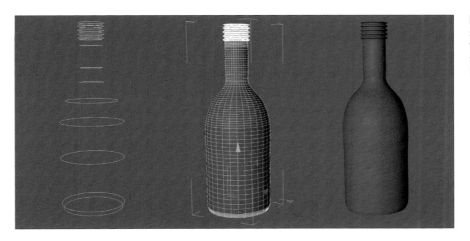

[Figure 5.7] The simple set of curves shown on the left defines the NURBS surfaces that make up the bottle (right).

NURBS patch modeling is commonly used in computer-aided design (CAD) and manufacturing. The best vehicle modelers I know use spline patch modeling, almost exclusively. **Figure 5.8** shows an example of a car model created by my friend Lewis (www.lewis.tomsoft.hr) using spline patch modeling to generate a SubD mesh. Don't let these examples limit your use of this powerful modeling method. Digital artists use patch modeling to create characters, clothing, and more. I've used patch modeling to create everything from the membrane in bat wings to the hull of a boat.

[Figure 5.8] Splines were used (left) to create polygonal patches (middle) that were used to generate a base mesh. This mesh served as the base to create this detailed muscle car (right).

Digital Sculpting

Although all digital modeling is, in a sense, digital sculpting, the name has been recycled for the newest method of modeling to be introduced to 3D artists. Digital sculpting is a method of modeling that is the closest an artist can get to traditional sculpting.

With the ability to use millions of polygons, a modeler manipulates a base mesh using a brush-based system that allows for the creation of photorealistic, highly detailed meshes that weren't possible until recently. The base mesh can be anything from a simple ball primitive to an object consisting of any number of polygons. **Figure 5.9** shows a digital creature maquette sculpted by Glen Southern (http://southerngfx.co.uk). He created this mesh in a fraction of the time he would have needed to model it with traditional polygonal modeling methods.

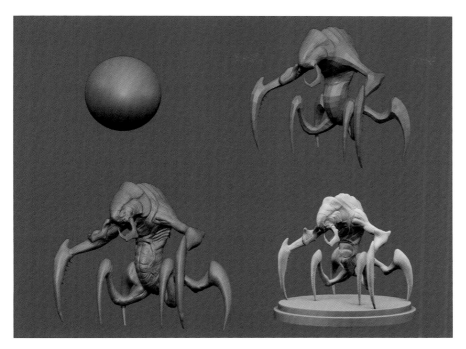

[Figure 5.9] Starting from a primitive sphere, this creature maquette was sculpted using millions of polygons, producing fine details that would be difficult to accomplish with other modeling methods.

Once limited to organic subject matter, digital sculpting has recently evolved, allowing digital modelers to easily create all manner of models, including hard surface. One of the reasons digital sculpting is so attractive, besides the ability to achieve high levels of details easily, is the freedom an artist has when it comes to the meshes' topology. No consideration to the layout of polygons is needed when digital sculpting, leaving the artist's focus on the shapes, not the underlying geometry.

This method of modeling is used throughout the 3D industry, and you'll see it in feature films, illustrations, prototyping, and more. It has virtually replaced traditional sculpting in the toy industry and has completely changed the face of the gaming industry. The high-poly meshes are used as source material to enhance low-poly models used in real-time games with the use of normal maps. This mapping option uses pixels containing the high-res mesh data to fake the lighting of raised and recessed areas on a surface, which allow for low-resolution game models to display the details of a high-poly sculpt. **Figure 5.10** shows the elements that were generated by Jon-Troy Nickel (www.kalescentstudios.com) to create a next-gen game model.

[Figure 5.10] The details shown in the high-poly digital sculpt (top) are mapped onto the low-resolution mesh (middle) using a normal map (lower-right corner).

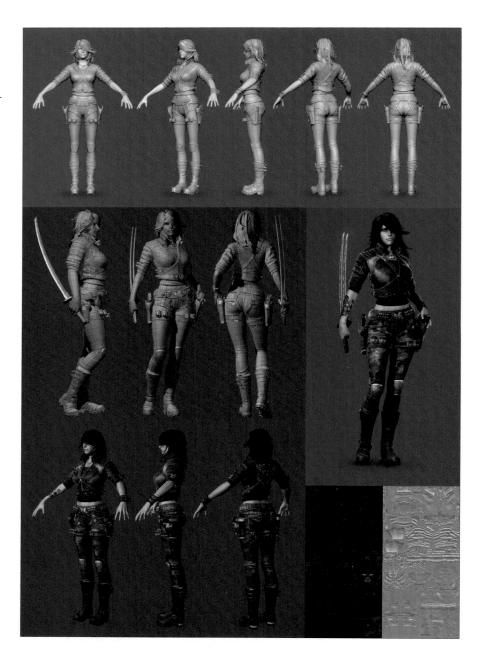

3D Scanning

3D scanning allows for the collection of surface data from a real-world object. This recorded information is then converted into a digital mesh, usually consisting of millions of points (vertices). It's the 3D equivalent of a flatbed scanner, or a camera for capturing 2D images. Everything from small traditional sculpts, whole bodies, buildings, and even landscapes can be scanned. This technology is used throughout the 3D industry for markets like medical visualization, film, games, industrial design, and more.

3D scanners are available in small desktop units, such as the NextEngine 3D Scanner (www.nextengine.com), to large scanners like the Whole Body Color 3D Scanner by Cyberware (www.cyberware.com), which can scan an entire person, capturing not only the surface shape, but the color information as well.

Once limited to only a few different technologies, there are now many options available for 3D scanning. The variety of scanners available today can be placed in one of two categories, contact scanners and noncontact scanners:

- **Contact scanners** require the scanner to physically touch the object being scanned. The MicroScribe G2 (www.emicroscribe.com), shown in **Figure 5.11**, is an example of a contact scanner.

[Figure 5.11] The car's surface data is captured by using the tip of the articulated arm to trace over the contours of a physical object.

To capture the dimensions of a car, for example, you simply take the tip of the arm and trace points along the outside of the car's body. Sensors at each joint in the arm are used to calculate the precise 3D position of the tip at any given point. The recorded information is then translated into data points and processed by your 3D software, and a 3D mesh appears on your screen. The 3D model can then be manipulated using any of the modeling tools you prefer. One benefit of contact scanners is that they can capture surface data from objects made up of any material type.

- **Noncontact scanners**, also called active scanners, emit light, X-ray, or ultrasound to capture the surface data of the object being scanned. The light or radiation emitted from the scanner is reflected off the object being scanned and sent back to the scanner, recording the distance of the surface.

Although noncontact scanners are more popular than contact scanners, one key limitation is that noncontact scanners have difficulty scanning reflective and transparent objects. This can sometimes be overcome for objects that are expendable by spraying the object with white or light gray paint. Objects that are one of a kind or irreplaceable can be dusted with white powder that is easily removed after the scanning process is complete.

The artists at Varner Studios (www.varnerstudios.com) use a noncontact 3D scanner that uses light to capture surface data from traditional sculpts. The scanners Varner uses are a Minolta Vivid Laser scanner and a Steinbichler Comet 5 White Light scanner. The captured data is converted into a digital mesh and further sculpting is done to the model using digital sculpting programs, such as ZBrush and Freeform. **Figure 5.12** shows a clay sculpture created by Steve Varner being scanned by the in-house scanner and the resulting digital model.

X-ray computed tomography (CT) produces volume data in the form of 2D slices that can be stacked together and converted into a digital mesh using specialized software, such as Volumedic (www.volumedic.com). This process is called *image-based meshing* and produces extremely accurate models. Volumedic is mostly known as a tool for medical illustration and visualization but is also used extensively in neuroscience, biology, and the Earth sciences. I've used Volumedic to generate medical illustrations,

and for several years it has been instrumental in the creation of Zoic's
Emmy award–winning visual effects for shows like *CSI: Crime Scene
Investigators* and National Geographic Channel's *Inside the Living Body*,
among others. **Figure 5.13** shows CT scan data being used to create a
digital mesh of a skull using Volumedic.

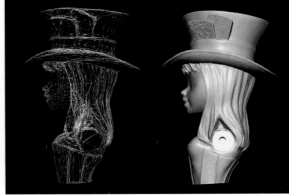

[Figure 5.12] Using a 3D scanner, Varner studios takes advantage of its 30-plus years' experience of traditional toy sculpting
to create digital meshes. The physical sculpt (left) is scanned with the 3D scanner, producing a digital mesh (right).

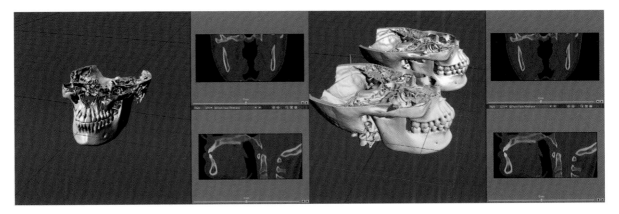

[Figure 5.13] The volume data rendering from CT scan data (left) can be automatically converted into a polygonal mesh
(right) using Volumedic.

Modeling with Texture and Animation Tools

Many 3D programs with modeling capabilities also have the ability to perform other areas of production. You can take advantage of the tools normally designated for texturing and animation to aid in the modeling process. There are a wide variety of tools to pull from. Some of the popular tools digital modelers have adopted for modeling are texture displacement, bones, and dynamics.

Texture Displacement

Using images and procedural textures to drive mesh displacements can be extremely useful modeling tools, allowing for the creation of detailed geometry with very little setup time. When applied to a 3D object, textures can displace the geometry, manipulating the points that make up the model into an endless variety of shapes. **Figure 5.14** shows a simple SubD plane with several different procedural textures being used to displace the mesh.

[Figure 5.14] The subdivided plane (left) can take on many different shapes when procedural textures are used to displace the points within the mesh (right).

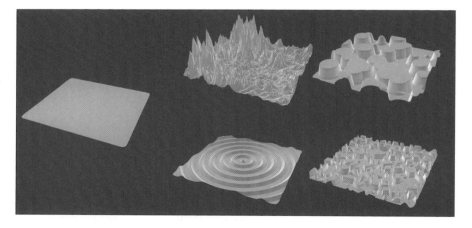

I've used texture displacement to model realistic landscapes, rolling ocean waves, and more. I recently used this technique to create details in a character's hair for the FunGoPlay (www.fungoplay.com) virtual world. A procedural texture was used to displace a simple hair mesh, producing the hairstyle the art director was looking for and making light work of what could have been a more challenging task to model traditionally. **Figure 5.15** shows the character with and without the procedural texture applied.

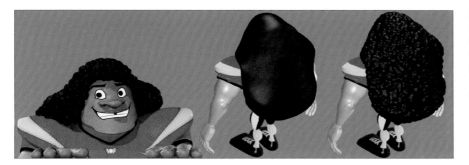

[Figure 5.15] The details in this character's hair were easily created using a procedural texture to displace the geometry. The model in the middle shows the base hair mesh without displacement.

When a modeler uses texture displacement to manipulate an object's surface, it allows animators to work with a low-resolution mesh when animating and then increase the object's polygon density before applying the displacement at render time. Animating with a lower-resolution object speeds up viewport playback, allowing the animator to work faster.

Bones

The standard method of animating a seamless 3D mesh is the use of a *skeleton rig*, which consists of a series of virtual *bones* that are similar to their real-world counterparts. This hierarchy of interconnected bones is assigned to a mesh and deforms it based on each bone's position, scale, and orientation. Although bones are usually set aside for rigging meshes for animation, I've used bones in my modeling toolkit for several years to speed up complex tasks, such as deforming a wire, hose, or tube around a complex shape. **Figure 5.16** shows a ribbed hose that was rigged with bones and posed to conform to the shoulder pads of a robot character. Using bones allowed natural bends in the hose that would have required far more time to accomplish with traditional modeling methods.

[Figure 5.16] The ribbed hose (right) was rigged with bones and posed to easily conform to the shape of the robot's shoulder pads.

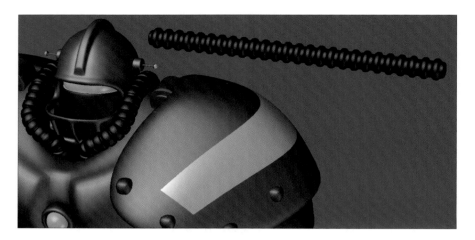

Dynamics

In 3D software, *dynamics* collectively refers to any physics-based simulations that enable you to animate virtual objects with realistic physical movements. This can range from soft deformable objects (soft body), like hair and cloth, to rigid simulations (rigid body), such as a glass shattering or a building crumbling. Digital modelers can take advantage of these powerful simulations to aid in the modeling process. For example, you could create a segmented flat plane and run a dynamics simulation on it to create a sheet draped over a table or bed, producing natural folds and wrinkles with the click of a button.

I employed dynamics to model a microphone that was used on a Ludacris album cover (*Battle of the Sexes*). The microphone itself was quite trivial, but the woven mesh posed a major challenge. Using dynamics, I took what could have been a nightmare modeling assignment and turned it into a few minutes' worth of work. I created a flat woven mesh and used cloth dynamics to conform it to a spherical shape. This made the perfect, wire-woven mesh needed to top off a microphone model. **Figure 5.17** shows the process of using dynamics to create the wire-woven mesh on the microphone.

[Figure 5.17] A flat woven mesh was modeled (left), draped over a collision object using cloth dynamics (middle), and then used as the wire mesh on a microphone model (right).

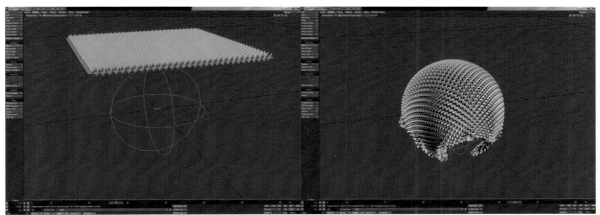

The Importance of Mixing Methods

Don't limit yourself to just a few modeling methods. Every professional digital modeler I know gravitates to a particular method of modeling for the majority of the meshes each is tasked with, but each modeler is quick to use other methods when needed. The more techniques you become proficient in, the more efficient you will become.

Adding new methods to your toolkit will not only broaden your ability to solve problems, it will improve your ability with the methods you are already familiar with. For example, I found that I became faster at box modeling a character head after I became proficient with the edge extend method.

Also, none of these modeling techniques is mutually exclusive, and they can actually be extremely complementary. When modeling a given object, you don't have to choose one and only one method to use on the entirety of that object.

I've always looked at every model as just a collection of simpler shapes. The robots in **Figure 5.18**, for example, are made up of several different components. Each part is trivial to create on its own. When you're comfortable connecting different shapes together, you can model each shape separately using the method best suited to that shape and then combine all the shapes into the single final object.

For example, you could use spline patching to generate a portion of an object and then merge the resulting polygonal patches into a different section of the object that you used the point by point build out method to generate. You could then take that object into a sculpting program to add finer details and then use the edge extend build out method to handle the retopology.

When you're comfortable with several modeling techniques, you can choose the most efficient method not only for a given object, but for each part of a single object as well.

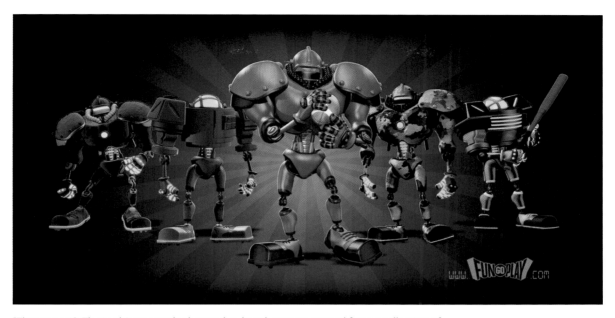

[**Figure 5.18**] These objects may look complex, but they were created from a collection of simple parts combined to create complete robots.

CHAPTER SIX

Professional Modeling Practices

Becoming a professional modeler requires more than just a knowledge of points, polygons, and the various modeling techniques. Modelers must be organized, pay attention to details, and gain full control over the mesh. Polygon count, flow of the geometry, and other attributes of an object should be dictated by the modeler, not the software or tools used to create the mesh. Knowing proper object preparation for the other departments in the pipeline is another skill often overlooked and is what separates a professional from a hobbyist.

This chapter focuses on the important skills most digital artists overlook: naming conventions and directory structures, clean modeling, and preparing a model for production. Mastering these skills is essential to a successful career as a digital modeler.

Naming Conventions and Directory Structure

All the artists I know have their own way of labeling and organizing files. When working alone, you can work any way you choose, and in most cases the production will run like a well-oiled machine. However, when working with a group, failing to use the same naming conventions and directory structure will bring production to a grinding halt every time.

I've worked on quite a few productions where the team wasted hours trying to locate files in order to move on to the next stage of production. The artist responsible for the files either chose a poor name or location for the files in question. Currently, I'm working in New York on a production where one of the artists, let's call him Cesar, insists on saving files to his local desktop instead of the project content directory on the server. We've yet to break him of this bad habit that has diminished the efficiency of our team. Even giving Cesar the nickname "Desktop" hasn't seemed to work.

My friend Lee Stringer uses the "hit by a bus" scenario to explain to artists the importance of organization on a production. If you were hit by a bus on your way to work tomorrow, would your team be able to pick up where you left off to finish the job? Lee's really not that callus towards his coworkers, but it is an easy way to help explain the importance of good naming conventions and directory structure. (Note to self: Find out if Lee has ties to any local bus companies.)

Content Directory

One of the most difficult areas of production for a new artist to grasp is a studio's content directory structure, especially if the artist has never worked on a project with a team of any size.

Don't let the name fool you. *Content directory structure* is merely another term for the organization of the folders where your project's assets are saved. They're quite easy to manage, make common sense, and will definitely make your job easier. Having a central location for all assets and a system that everyone follows allows the entire team to know where all assets are located without ever having to ask.

Something I used to do that helped instill good directory structure in my students was to load that week's deliverables for critique directly from the project's directories. If the file wasn't in the correct place, they'd receive a zero for the week. It didn't matter if the students' assets were the best in the class. If the work wasn't in the right location, it was as if they had never done it. Needless to say, they usually didn't make that mistake twice. Although that may seem harsh, it's a lesson better learned in school than at a studio on a production.

Content directories in action

Let's step through the process of setting up a directory structure for a new project. Imagine that I just landed a toy commercial with Applehead Factory for its popular Teddy Scares line of stuffed bears. I need to create a master directory for this project and want to stay as organized as possible—not just for the current production, but for years to come. Because I hope to get more work from the company in the future, I'll create a directory named Applehead.

In the Applehead folder, I'll create a subfolder named Teddy_Scares. To stay even more organized, I'll create a subfolder named CG_Content in the Teddy_Scares folder. This is where I will tell my 3D applications to look for all items associated with this project.

So why don't I just save all the files in the root of the Applehead folder? If I plan on working with Applehead on future projects, I want to be able to organize each project separately and avoid any confusion between projects. That makes sense, but why not just save all the 3D object files in the root of the Teddy_Scares folder?

If this project is like any of the other projects I've worked on, I'll probably have files that are not used by my 3D applications but are important to the project. These files can be almost anything, such as reference images, story-boards, documents about the project, and so on.

It's easier to track down 3D content if I keep the files separate from everything else. I've used a CG_Content folder for many years, and it seems to prevent confusion among the other artists working on the project.

[note]

Documents, Reference, and Storyboard folders are optional but extremely useful.

Before I ever open my 3D software, my directory structure looks something like this:

```
\AppleHead
        \Teddy_Scares
                \Documents
                \CG_Content
                \Reference
                \Storyboards
```

Unless I'm only required to create objects for the project, I'll need subdirectories to stay organized. I'll add directories for any other file types needed in the production. A common project folder that I work with starts off looking something like this:

```
\AppleHead
        \Teddy_Scares
                \Documents
                \CG_Content
                        \Animations
                        \Dynamics
                        \Envelopes
                        \Images
                        \Motions
                        \Nodes
                        \Objects
                        \Previews
                        \Rigs
                        \Scenes
                        \Sounds
                        \Surfaces
                \Reference
                \Storyboards
```

Many of the projects I work on only call for Objects, Scenes, and Images folders. You're not required to use a set number of directories per project, and each project will need a specific setup. If you start each production with a clearly defined directory structure, you'll be setting a strong foundation for your project. But remember that it's only foolproof if all the artists on the team save their files in the appropriate location.

One of the biggest showstoppers is when an artist is working on a portable drive or in the wrong content directory. You don't want to be that artist. You'll be amazed at how much more efficient the project becomes when no one is asking where a particular file is located.

Naming Conventions

You know how to set up a directory structure that will keep you organized and keep your production humming along, so it should be smooth sailing from here, right? Well, close. Naming conventions are equally as important.

Bad naming conventions are another production showstopper. Naming conventions should apply to anything that can have a name: folders, images, objects, scenes—everything! A few years ago while working on a project with a team of artists who were under a tight deadline (is there any other kind?), we were going through the edit and one of the artists started screaming at me because I had used the "wrong" object in one of the shots. We loaded the last scene that I had worked on, and the object in question was called Carrot_016_Final.LWO. That sounds like the right file for working on a "final" shot, right? Well, it turns out that the artist wanted me to use the file called Carrot_013_UseThisOne.LWO.

Both are horrible names. I've seen worse, but let's not go there. Almost every project you work on will involve other artists, and most if not all like their own naming conventions. The best bet is to standardize the naming conventions at the beginning of the project. The tricky part, as always, is having everyone follow the rules.

Naming directories

When naming directories, use a logical title that is pertinent to the content. If you're working on a model of a carrot, a good name for the folder would be Carrot. If the carrot model is just one vegetable of many that will be used on the project, maybe the Carrot folder should be located in a Vegetables folder. So the directory structure might look like this:

```
\AppleHead
        \Teddy_Scares
                \CG_Content
                        \Images
                        \Objects
                                \Vegetables
                                        \Carrot
                        \Scenes
```

If other artists went looking for a model of a carrot, they should find it without having to ask where it is. Are you starting to see how good naming conventions come into play? I could get hit by a bus tomorrow, and my team members would still be able to make deadline. But how would they know which carrot object to use once they accessed the Carrot folder?

Naming objects

When naming your object files, you should use the same logic used for folders with one addition: version numbers. I've seen all sorts of naming conventions used in production, but none is more efficient than using version numbers. Using the carrot example, the first model you make is named Carrot_001. After you've worked on the model for 10–15 minutes or feel you've made significant progress, save a new version named Carrot_002. The latest version of the object should have the higher number tacked on at the end of its name.

If you went looking for a carrot model that I created, you'd know that the last file in the folder, the one with the highest number, would be the correct one to use. If everyone uses this naming convention, there will be no confusion, and you will save massive amounts of time not having to decide whether you're using the right files.

Another good practice when naming folders or objects is to avoid using spaces. Spaces can easily be overlooked, and some applications have issues with spaces for areas like animation when using mathematical expressions. Opt for an underscore (_), which is much easier to see and doesn't cause issues later down the production line.

Don't Agonize, Organize

Organization is a required job skill in the industry and should not be taken lightly. Many would argue that organization is more important than any software knowledge or computer skill. Lack of organization is the one problem that I've seen bring a production to a screeching halt more than any other issue.

Good naming conventions and directory structure not only help during production, but they can be a lifesaver if you ever have to return to the production files in the future. I've often had to pull files from archives that I worked on eight or more years prior. With good organization, you can jump right back into the files with little or no hassle.

Whether you're working on a project alone or with a large team, good naming conventions and directory structure are a must. Take the time in the beginning to build an organized foundation, and you will save everyone involved not only time, but an enormous number of headaches. It's all common sense, but you'd be surprised (or maybe you wouldn't) at how uncommon organization can be among artists.

Clean Modeling

Not all models are created equal. Professional digital modelers create meshes that are far more superior to hobbyists, by keeping a model's wireframe in mind during the modeling process. Artists that deliver *clean* models are in high demand and quite rare.

Think about it this way: It's wise to be concerned about hidden details when purchasing a home. You want to make sure the house is built on a good foundation and has a solid underlying structure that will withstand weather, time, and 120-pound chocolate labs named Jack. Like all good houses, 3D models should not only look right on the surface, but they should also have a strong foundation, which makes surfacing, rigging, and animating much easier.

On any online CG forum, you will encounter artists asking to see wireframe images of the models other artists post. This is mainly due to the fact that most professional 3D artists won't call a model excellent or finished unless it has a clean wireframe.

Two core attributes define a clean model: polygon-count and topology. An artist who pays careful attention to these details is more likely to create meshes that deform well when animated and are not overly complex, which saves on production time in all departments of the pipeline.

Polygon-count

In the simplest of terms, polygon-count—usually just called *poly-count*—refers to the quantity of polygons that make up a 3D model. It's important for artists to be aware of and gain control over their meshes' poly-count to reach mastery of digital modeling.

Why count polygons?

The fewer polygons you have in your mesh, the easier it is to work with throughout a production. Fewer polygons equal fewer points, which means fewer points to weight and assign to bones. It's also easier to create UV textures on a low-poly, clean mesh.

Probably the most obvious reason to be mindful of a model's poly-count is the effect it has on rendering, both offline and real time:

- **Offline rendering** is used for film, broadcast, print, and other markets. It affords artists higher-quality rendering options—such as the ability to use shaders (a set of algorithms that determines how 3D surface properties of objects are rendered) of unlimited complexity—than real time but requires the rendered frame or sequence of frames to be saved to an image format. These prerendered images are displayed at a later time, which allows artists to create images with as high a quality as time allows. Offline rendering also allows the use of CPU-intensive effects and can take advantage of massive render farms (clusters of computers) working together to calculate thousands of complex images. Simply put, the more complex something is, the less likely it will be possible to process it in real time.

- **Real-time rendering** refers to the process where the images are generated on the fly with a goal of displaying them to the viewer as fast as possible. It's primarily used by the gaming market. Image quality is traded off for interactivity, and shortcuts are used to quickly generate the displayed images. An example of this is your 3D modeling software's viewports displaying a 3D model.

It is important to create optimized meshes with the lowest possible number of polygons to improve rendering performance using either rendering method. Digital modelers who are mindful of their meshes' poly-count respect the entire production process and understand how their models directly or indirectly affect everyone involved.

How do you count polygons?

Many artists misunderstand how to properly determine a model's true polygon count. It's important to understand that all render engines at their core, both offline and real-time, work with triangles or three-point polygons. Real-time render engines need the geometry to already be converted to three-point polygons because all modern graphics cards work only with these simple polygons. Most offline render engines can perform a conversion to triangles at render time.

So really, poly-count refers to a model's triangle count. A mesh that consists of 120 three-point polygons has a polygon count of 120. However, a mesh containing 120 four-point polygons actually has a poly-count of 240 when converted to triangles (two triangles are produced when a quadrilateral is bisected).

N-gons can be the trickiest, because they can be very misleading. A single polygon with more than four points can range anywhere from as few as 3 triangles to as many as 1,200 or more.

Figure 6.1 shows an example of three meshes, each made up of different polygon configurations. The ball on the left consists of 1,280 triangles, the ball in the middle consists of 1,536 quads (3,072 triangles), and the flat plane on the right consists of one 128-gon (126 triangles). It's easy to overlook the fact that the true poly-counts of the middle and right objects are much higher than they first appear. Always remember to count *triangles* when determining the mesh's poly-count.

[**Figure 6.1**] The image on the left shows the three meshes in their original state. The image on the right shows the three meshes as a render engine would see them— converted to triangles.

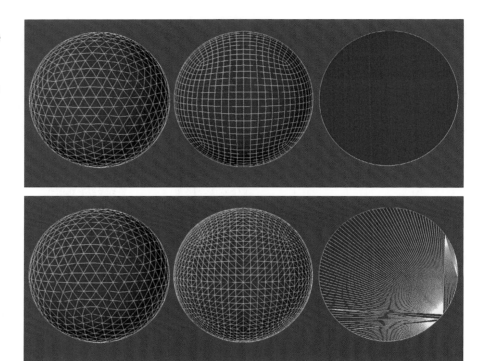

Another mistake artists often make when counting polygons is that when they are dealing with SubD objects, they forget that the SubD cage doesn't truly represent the object's polygon density. I'll use the panda character in **Figure 6.2** as an example. Although the panda was created with 1,942 SubD polygons, that's a total of 31,072 polygons when set at a subdivision level of four, which converts to 62,144 triangles at render time. There's quite a difference between 1,942 polys and 62,144.

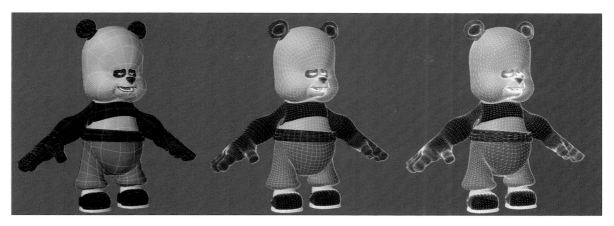

[Figure 6.2] Don't let objects created with subdivision surfaces mislead you when counting polygons. This panda character made up of 1,942 SubDs is actually 62,144 triangles at render time.

What defines a good polygon count?

Artists should always strive to use as few polygons as possible while still maintaining the proper shape to achieve their modeling objective. Simply put, good poly-counts are optimized poly-counts.

Most game artists have mastered the art of poly-count because they are limited to the amount of polygons they can use for their game engines. Every polygon has to have a purpose, and any unneeded geometry is removed. We can learn a lot from this process even when we are working on higher-polygon models for film, broadcast, and other markets.

How many polygons should you use?

When it comes to digital modeling, how many polygons should be used is probably the most asked question. What's the answer? Well, it depends. It's a bit like asking how much paint you need to cover a wall. How big is the wall? What color are you painting with, and will it need multiple coats to paint over the existing color? More details are needed to give a proper answer.

A clean mesh doesn't necessarily mean a low-poly mesh, or the model might not end up with the detail you need to get realistic shapes. The trick is to use only the geometry you need to get the detail you want and only have detailed geometry where you need it. I refer to this technique as having *localized detail*.

Let's use a human hand as an example. The hand, which has complex joints that deform in multiple areas, needs much more geometry than the forearm, which has a much simpler shape and requires little deformation. There is no reason to have the same poly-count for the forearm as you would for the hand. You can use localized detail to manage the distribution of your poly-count to optimize the mesh. **Figure 6.3** shows the polygon layout for a hand transitioning into the forearm of a character.

[Figure 6.3] With the use of localized detail, the forearm can be created with less geometry while still providing proper density for the hands.

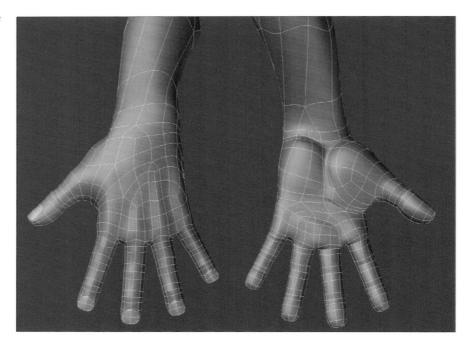

An important factor in determining how much geometry to use when modeling is to know what the object will be used for. A few good questions to ask about the model in this regard include

- Will the object always be in the distance, or will it get inches from the camera?

- Will it be in a well-lit area, or will it always be in shadow?

- Will the object only be seen from one angle or multiple angles?

The more you know about the model's intended use, the easier it is to determine the proper poly-count. Objects that are seen up close are sometimes referred to as a *hero object* and require far more detail and polygons than objects that sit off in the distance.

You wouldn't want a rock made up of 20,000 polygons if it will always be 20 yards from the camera. This may seem obvious, but I've helped optimize models worse than that for movies.

Another consideration is having multiple versions of the same object, each at a different poly-count. I usually label them as *Hero* or *Primary*, *Secondary*, and *Tertiary*. This gives you the ability to swap out a model for an appropriate level of detail and poly-count when a situation calls for it.

To address the original question of how many polygons you should use, my answer is to use as many polygons as needed, but not one polygon more than that. The cardinal rule of professional modeling is less is always more. Albert Einstein said it best: "Everything should be made as simple as possible, but not one bit simpler."

Topology

In modeling terms, *topology*, also called *polygon flow* (or just *poly flow*), refers to the way a 3D mesh is constructed and how the polygons are arranged to build up its shape. Good topology makes for geometry that is easy to select, manipulate, and construct, and is even better for sculpting onto. Also, generating and using UV maps are easier with clean topology. Although topology is important in all models that you create, you might approach a static object's poly-flow differently than that of an object that will deform.

Topology for static objects

Objects that are rigid and require no deformation—such as guns, cars, or houses—have fewer topology restrictions as deformable geometry but can still benefit from clean poly-flow. **Figure 6.4** shows the wireframe for a wireless remote I modeled with clean polygon flow, even though it was never intended to be animated or deformed. This topology made it easier to manipulate the mesh as I worked and allowed me to generate a clean UV map with ease.

[Figure 6.4] Static objects can benefit from good topology when editing or texturing is required.

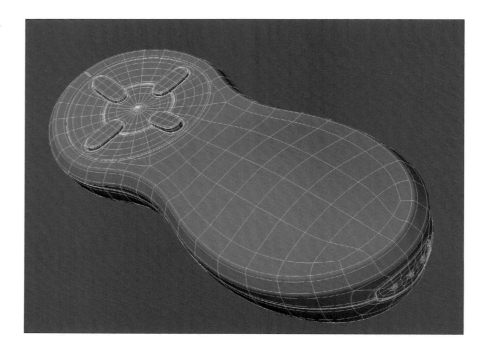

Another example is a vehicle. The topology of a car can determine whether the surface will appear smooth and flawless or has unwanted dents and dings. Also, you never know when you may need to deform a static model for posing, even if it will never animate.

Topology for objects that will deform

Animation of an organic object can be like a hurricane to a house if good polygon flow doesn't exist. Your model will not hold up, and problems like pinching and polygon flipping will occur. It's also easier to predict how an object will animate with clean geometry, and artists down the production pipeline will run into fewer problems compared to dealing with models created by an artist who produces sloppy or heavy models.

Are you in the loop?

Edge loops and limiting a model to all quads are often cited when talking about good topology. They are important in ensuring that the mesh is production ready. *Edge loops* are bands of polygons in a mesh that make models easier to read, select, and manipulate. They are fundamental in creating good polygon flow. Just like having fewer polygons, the use of edge loops makes a mesh easier to rig and animate.

The formation of these distinct loops can mimic major muscle groups, produce more realistic-looking character models, and create more predictable deformations in facial animation and posing. **Figure 6.5** highlights three sets of edge loops in the face of a character that aid in the creation of facial animation.

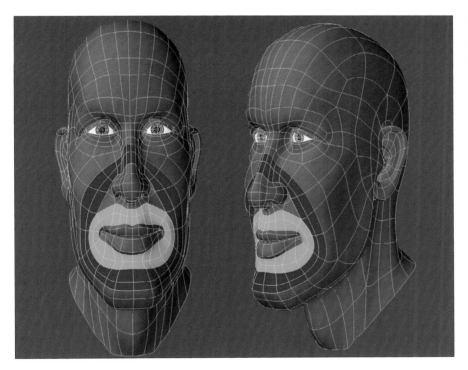

[Figure 6.5] Building edge loops into a character's face can help create more predictable deformations in facial animation.

One detail to keep in mind is that although loops are extremely powerful and you want to use enough to get the shapes you're after, you need to be careful not to have too many loops. Too many can cause pinching and unwanted creases in your object. Using the right amount of loops can be tricky when you first start modeling, but the more models you animate, the easier it will be for you to judge how many to use.

Controlling polygon flow

Part of creating geometry with clean topology is learning to manage and control the flow of the polygons that make up the mesh. This can be a challenging skill to master and will only come with lots of practice. The payoff will come into play on every model you build, so time invested is time well spent.

I've found that the most useful way to control poly-flow is to learn to redirect the flow of polygons either by manually building them point by point with the desired flow or with tools specifically designed for this task. Each 3D application has at least one tool that can perform the same action, but each may call it something different. Some common names are SpinQuads, Flip Edge, Spin Edge, and Rotate Edge. These tools change the dividing edge between two adjacent polygons by spinning (rotating) the edge, so that the two ends of the edge attach to different points while leaving all of the points in the same place.

This process will change the flow of your polygons while maintaining the surrounding mesh. It's good to know that there are only so many options for where this dividing edge can be placed. Usually, after the third use of the tool, your edge will end up where it started. **Figure 6.6** shows the process of spinning an edge to change the polygon flow of the mesh.

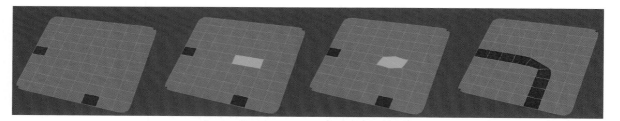

[**Figure 6.6**] To connect the two polygons shown in pink (left), the common edge of the two green polygons is reconfigured by spinning the edge (middle two). With the edge reconfigured, the topology of the geometry allows for the two pink polygons to flow into each other.

Four-point perfection

When modeling an area that will undergo heavy deformation, you will get better results if you resist the urge to mix in any three-point polygons where it may seem convenient and stick to using all four-point polygons (quads).

Three-point polys tend to cause pinching and strange smoothing errors in most cases. Although you can get away with that in certain lighting situations or camera setups, it is good practice to have your models deform nicely no matter what type of lighting or camera placement you may be working with.

N-gons—polygons with more than four points—are also known to cause pinching and smoothing errors in areas with deformation, and they are not supported by all subdivision algorithms, such as LightWave's subpatches.

For this reason, I like to limit organic meshes to all quads. Simply put, quads are superior for meshes that will deform while animated, and working exclusively with quads should be the goal of every organic modeler.

One reason artists may use n-gons or triangles is to try to reduce the polygon count in areas that don't need as much detail, like the back of the head. If you choose n-gons or three-point polygons to help reduce geometry, try to use them in areas that won't deform or be in plain sight. This will reduce the chance of them showing up as errors in your animation.

If you choose to use all quads, you can use a technique I have used for years with much success, which I like to call *four-point triangles*. I've also heard artists refer to them as *pole polygons* or *diamond polygons*.

Four-point triangles are a great alternative to the use of triangles and n-gons, and are basically just polygons that are made up of four points. These polygons are configured in the shape of a triangle or diamond, as shown on the hand and gun in **Figure 6.7**. These polygons not only help reduce poly-count, but can help define edge loops within your mesh.

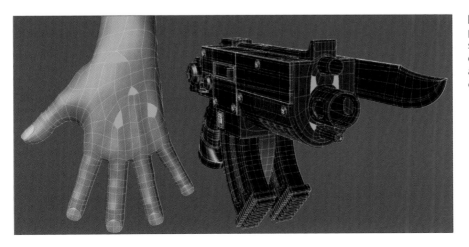

[Figure 6.7] Using four-point polygons that are shaped like triangles or diamonds can be a great alternative to using triangles or n-gons.

The rule of three

Areas on a model that will have heavy deformations need an underlying structure that will support the shapes you have defined. Although there are always exceptions to the rule, it is a good idea to use three segments in areas that will deform heavily. I refer to this as the *rule of three*.

The middle segment is where the deformation will take place, and the segments on either side support the mesh beyond the deformation. Example areas for using the rule of three would be elbows, shoulders, knees, finger joints, wrists, and even laugh lines on faces and eyelids. **Figure 6.8** shows a few areas on the body to which I like to apply the rule of three to ensure that good deformations take place during animation.

[Figure 6.8] The polygons shown in green are some of the areas on a character's body where I like to apply the rule of three for better deformations.

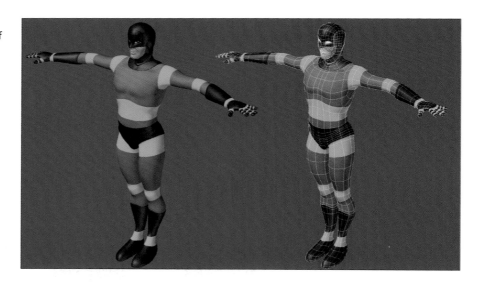

I used to fight areas like shoulders and hips when rigging and animating characters until I applied the three-segment configuration. Now I feel I can predict how those areas will deform with just a quick survey of the mesh.

Although the rule of three can be the solution most of the time, all objects are different. The number of segments depends on the type of deformation you want to achieve. Too many segments or loops can cause pinching in your mesh, as discussed earlier.

All digital artists will find their own path to clean modeling and will have their preferred way of handling topology based on their own experiences.

The lack of good poly-flow, unnecessary use of triangles or n-gons, and excessive numbers of polygons are pitfalls that all modelers should avoid. You can sometimes get away with a disjointed rat's nest of a mesh if you're creating a static mesh, but if your model is going to be animated, those pitfalls will come back to bite you.

Just remember when modeling to keep it simple and smooth (K.I.S.S.) and you'll be on the right track to creating professional, production-ready meshes.

Preparing a Model for Production

The last ten percent of any modeling task is to prepare it for the next phase of production. Whether you're flying solo and plan on handling all aspects of a project or working with a team of artists in a production pipeline, there are some steps you can take to ensure that your model is production ready.

General Production Preparation

The first step in preparing a model for production is to find out the guidelines for the project at hand to ensure that the team will receive the model in the proper condition. Open communication with the other artists involved will prevent the model from getting sent back for adjustments later.

It's also good to have a personal checklist that you use, because at the end of the day every model you deliver says a lot about you as an artist. You want to take pride in ownership and have your models be as prepared as possible. It's as important as proofing an email to an important client before clicking Send.

A good short list of general items that you should check include scale, position/rotation, and giving your model the final once over, or as I call it, giving a model a final pass.

Scale

Many artists build their meshes to real-world scale during the modeling process. When modeling hard-surface/technical models, I almost always model to scale as I go. But on 99 percent of my organic objects, such as characters,

I never model to scale. I usually like to just start modeling and worry about details like the size of an object later.

Regardless of whether you model to scale or not, take a final look, measure, and adjust accordingly. You don't want to deliver a model of a mouse the size of the Empire State Building unless, of course, you're modeling for an Asylum film called *Mega Mouse vs. New York City*.

Position/Rotation

When building a mesh, I always prefer to work with the model centered at the origin. This isn't a requirement, but I find it the most efficient way to work, especially when working with modeling functions like symmetry.

The majority of the time you'll want to position your finished model at the origin, resting on the ground plane (zero in the Y axis) and rotated to face forward (towards the positive Z axis). This not only helps the rigging department, but is quite useful for layout, texturing, and effects artists.

Final pass

Giving your objects a final pass allows you to take one last look at your poly-count and topology, naming conventions, and any other details. Too many artists assume that a model is complete as soon as they've finished putting the last of the polygons in place. This is where they often overlook small issues that would only take a few seconds to adjust. Put in the extra effort and feel confident when passing on a model.

It is good practice to take a break from the model before doing the final pass. When possible, I like to wait until the following day so I can review the previous day's work at the start of the next day. This allows you to review your models with a fresh eye.

Texturing Preparation

Depending on the requirements of the production pipeline, there may be ways that you can better prepare the texture artists before passing on a model. Up to this point in a production, you are the one who has spent the most time with the mesh and can navigate its geometry faster than anyone else, making you the ideal candidate for creating surface names and UV maps.

- **UV layout.** When laying out your mesh on a UV grid, start by placing the portions of the mesh that will need the most accurate textures. These high-detailed areas may include the head and torso of a character, like the one in **Figure 6.10**.

[Figure 6.10] When laying out the toad's UVs, the areas that required more details were positioned first.

The spacing between the polygon groups, or *islands*, as many people call them, should be close enough to not waste space, but not so close that textures will transfer from one island to the next. Be as efficient as you can with the real estate you have to work with.

- **UV seams.** There is no escaping UV seams, but you can minimize their effects by placing them in areas that are more out of sight, like the inside of a character's arm (**Figure 6.11**) or the back of a character's head. On organic meshes, try to use as few polygon islands as possible, creating a continuous island of large polygon groups.

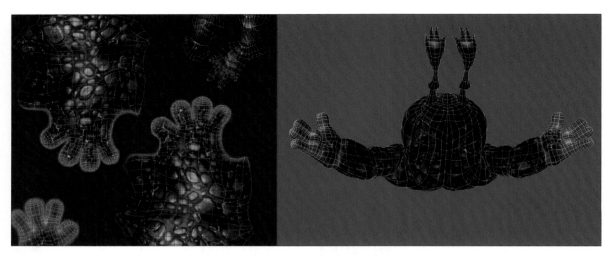

[**Figure 6.11**] Placing the seams of the toad's arms on the inside helped to hide them from the camera at render time.

- **UV options.** There really is no right or wrong when it comes to laying out UV maps, so give yourself and/or the texture artist multiple options if time permits. An object can have multiple UV maps applied to its points, so experiment and see what works best for all involved.

Rigging Preparation

If you've already completed everything on the general production checklist, you're already on your way to making the rigging artists happy campers. All that is really left is to make sure the character object's base pose is ideal for the rigging process.

Base pose

Although many artists have a unique default pose they prefer to work with, there are some industry-standard attributes that most have adopted. When no direction is given, these standards are usually your safest bet. The two most common base poses are the T-pose and the relaxed pose.

- **T-pose.** In a T-pose, the character is standing up straight and its arms, hands, and fingers are at 90 degrees, as shown in **Figure 6.12**. This pose gets its name from the T-shape the character makes and is the most commonly used base pose.

  Positioning the arms and legs straight down a specific axis can make placing bones and controls much easier for a rigging artist. It also puts some distance between the arms and the torso, making them easier to see and access in multiple views.

[Figure 6.12] Modeling a character in the T-pose makes it easier for the rigging department to set up the mesh for animation.

- **Relaxed pose.** In a relaxed base pose, the character's arms are at a
  45-degree angle, and all of the joints (knees, elbows, ankles, hands,
  fingers, and so on) are slightly pre-bent instead of straight, as shown in
  Figure 6.13. These pre-bends can assist in good deformations and IK
  (inverse kinematics) solving, but can make for more work for a rigging
  artist when placing bones and controls.

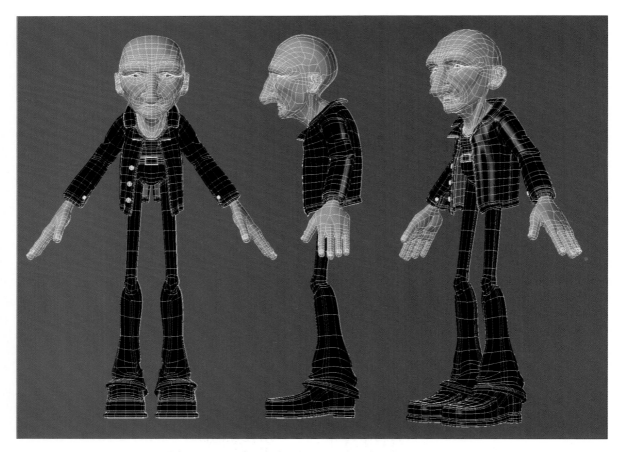

[**Figure 6.13**] Placing the character in a relaxed pose can help create good deformations but can be more challenging for the rigging artist to place bones and controls when creating a rig for the mesh.

Each mesh will call for its own specific needs, and ultimately, you need to fully discuss those needs with the rigging department before locking down any particular base pose. In your career as a digital modeler you'll probably use several different base poses. The important thing is to do what you can to deliver the mesh in the optimal pose for the rigging department, and communication with them will answer all of your questions.

If you've created a clean mesh with good naming conventions and you've gone through your final pass on the model with no surprises, you could be ready to call the mesh complete. My advice at this point is to be proactive and meet with the effects team to see if any of the models will require additional prep work that involves modeling.

If a model is going to explode or break apart, a proficient modeler can be an effects artist's most powerful weapon. Creating multiple versions of a model in various stages of destruction could give a shot that extra level of detail that an effects artist might not have the time for. Anything you can bring to the table with your modeling skills to aid the effects department is usually welcomed with open arms.

CHAPTER SEVEN

Polygonal Modeling

This portion of the book represents the first of several chapters that are designed to sharpen your problem-solving and observational skills, as well as hone your digital modeling skills through real-world digital modeling examples. In this chapter, I walk you through the creation of 3D text and the digital modeling of a complex seam pattern into a mesh with a focus on polygonal modeling.

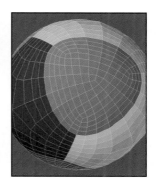

Modeling 3D Polygonal Text

A typical 3D text job is creating a logo. Logos, of course, are symbols or designs used by companies and individuals to help give them or their company an identity. Just about every company has one, and with millions of companies in the world, that means there is a pretty good chance that at some point in your career you'll be tasked to create one in 3D.

3D logo creation is not just limited to entry-level spinning logos created by artists just getting started in the industry. Entire studios have been built and survive off the creation of 3D logos used for print, broadcast motion graphics, and more. The logo for *Sister Act* on Broadway (**Figure 7.1**) is an example of 3D being used for signage in New York City. Also, just about every summer blockbuster film opens with several studio logos that have been created in 3D.

[Figure 7.1] This *Sister Act* logo is a great example of how 3D has spread into new markets.

The techniques used to create professional 3D logo meshes can be a valuable skill set that carries over to other areas of digital modeling. In this section I explore the process of creating a 3D logo from an existing 2D design. I've selected the Applehead Factory logo (**Figure 7.2**) because it poses a few challenges that may come up on future models.

[Figure 7.2] Creating a 3D version of the Applehead Factory logo will be our goal for this section.

Vector and Raster Images

It's common that a client will supply a logo as an EPS or Illustrator file (vector file), and most 3D software has the ability to load these formats.

Vector

Vector graphics use geometrical primitives—such as points, lines, curves, and shapes, which are all based on mathematical equations—to represent images in computer graphics. They are resolution independent, making them ideal for print graphics. The vector data is converted into editable geometry when imported into 3D software, which speeds up the 3D modeling process and can help ensure that the logo is technically accurate by working with a client's file.

Raster

Just as often, a client will only supply you with a raster image. *Raster* files are made up of a rectangular grid of pixels, or points of color, stored in image files with varying formats. Their resolution is based on the number of pixels that make up the image, and when imported into 3D software for modeling, the image is used as a template to build on top of.

In the example in this section, I walk through the construction of a logo from scratch, using a small raster image, so that I can cover some useful techniques that would not be discussed if I used a vector file.

Getting Started

Before I start modeling, I like to study my reference (in this case the logo itself) and come up with a strategy for how I will move forward. For the Applehead Factory logo, the shapes were fairly simple letterforms, but they were not created from an existing font. This meant I would need to model each letterform from scratch. To make the logo 3D, I'd need to give it depth and add details that improved its quality.

I started by counting the number of shapes I needed. Although there are 3 symbols (the factory and two smoke plumes) and 16 letters, there are actually only 18 individual shapes that I needed to construct because the r and the y connect into one solid shape.

At first I thought I could cheat and reuse the p and the e shapes, but after close inspection, I discovered they are slightly different. It would have been tempting to take a shortcut and reuse the shapes, and although most people might not catch it, I can almost guarantee the client would. Shortcuts and cheats are a must in this industry, but make sure you're choosing shortcuts that help you meet your end goal quicker, not those that change your end goal of producing a mesh that is 100 percent accurate to the supplied reference material.

I decided to use a mixture of point-by-point and primitive modeling methods to create these shapes, because I've found this technique to be the fastest way to create custom-shaped polygons. I had a pretty sound game plan, so it was time to get started. Without a game plan, I might have found myself having to back track halfway through the modeling sessions for lack of forethought.

Creating the 2D Base Mesh

I used the client-supplied reference image of the logo in the background as a template to work from. Because the 18 shapes are all independent, I could have started anywhere, but I wanted to get that factory shape out of the way first.

I created 16 points, placing one point at each corner of the shape. I made sure to zoom in as close as possible to ensure proper placement. Once I had the points created, I selected them and then converted that selection into a polygon. **Figure 7.3** shows the result of this process.

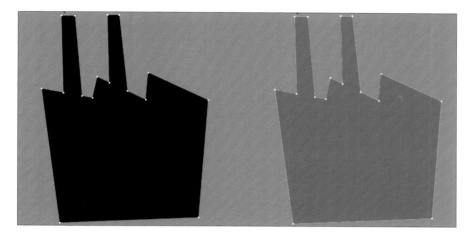

[**Figure 7.3**] Each point needs to be accurately placed based on the reference image (left). This shape was created by the selected points being converted into a polygon (right).

That shape was the easiest of the bunch because it consisted of nothing but straight lines. Every other piece contained curved components that required far more points to produce the proper shapes. Placing each of these points by hand could have been time-consuming and produced undesirable results.

I have a few options available for creating shapes:

- **Placing the points by hand:** This technique is identical to how I approached the factory shape and requires the placement of each point by hand.

- **Using primitives:** These are basic geometric shapes that are the building blocks for many other shapes and forms, and using them to help create detailed curves is a technique that I've successfully applied for years. I usually use a disc primitive (a cylinder shape), and the idea is to create the disc with a portion of its edges conforming to the shape you are attempting to create.

  Once I create the disc, I select and copy the points I need, and then remove (delete) the disc object. With the points I copied still stored in the system's clipboard, I simply paste them back into the model (**Figure 7.4**). I can repeat these steps until I have all the points needed to make up the desired shape.

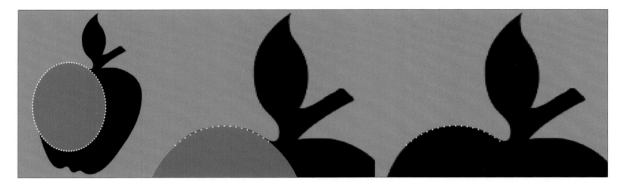

[Figure 7.4] The top portion of this disc primitive has been lined up to the edge of the apple shape (left). The selected points need to be copied to the clipboard before removing the disc (middle). Once the disc is removed, the copied points are pasted back into the object file (right).

- **Using splines:** Splines (curves in 3D space) are probably the most common and preferred way of generating multiple points along a curve. Similar to the primitive method, I simply create a spline based on the shape I'm building. With the spline created, I convert it to a polygon and copy the points I need, paste the points back into the model, and repeat as needed. **Figure 7.5** shows these steps.

  A good idea when working with splines is to create copies before converting them to polygons so that you can always return to the original source at a later time. I never like re-creating something I've already created; it is not an efficient use of my time.

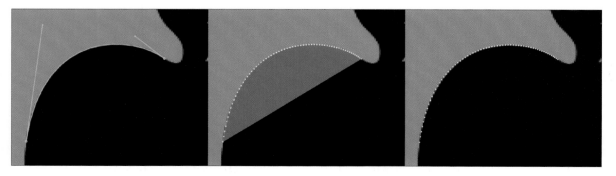

[Figure 7.5] A Bézier spline is used to trace the outer edge of the apple shape (left). The spline is converted into a polygon, and the points are copied to the clipboard (middle). The result of pasting the points for the clipboard (right).

I decided to use a combination of all three of the preceding options because the majority of the letterforms have a mixture of straight and curved shapes. At this point I didn't worry about how I was going to get the apertures (holes in the letterforms) and simply created them as separate polygons.

As I finished the points for a shape, I selected them and converted the selection into a polygon (**Figure 7.6**).

[**Figure 7.6**] All of the necessary points for the apple shape have been created (left). This polygon was created from the selected points (right).

Once all the shapes were created (**Figure 7.7**), I focused on getting the apertures cut into the letterforms that need them. Booleans—modeling tools that let you add, subtract, and intersect one mesh with/from another—are pretty standard fare for this type of operation, so I decided to use them to tunnel the aperture shapes through the letterforms (**Figure 7.8**).

[**Figure 7.7**] The result of all the shapes being created, including the letterform's apertures.

[Figure 7.8] The shapes that make up the holes are selected and used to create the apertures in the letterforms.

[Figure 7.8] The shapes that make up the holes are selected and used to create the apertures in the letterforms.

From 2D to 3D

With the 2D base mesh complete, it was time to add some dimension to this logo. I'm not a big fan of the "Superman logo" effect of a massive amount of depth, so I went for a more subtle depth on this logo. I used the Extrude command to give thickness to the shapes (**Figure 7.9**).

[Figure 7.9] These figures show the before and after of extruding the base logo mesh.

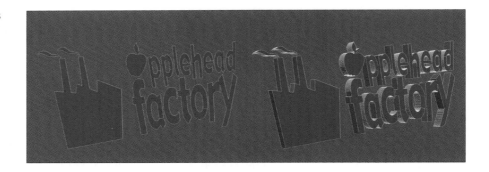

[Figure 7.9] These figures show the before and after of extruding the base logo mesh.

You could call this logo final, if you were a hobbyist. Although I brought this 2D logo into 3D space, it was missing something that most artists overlook that could take their models to the next level: micro-bevels.

Micro-bevels, Chamfers, and Fillets

When most people hear about using micro-bevels on their objects, they immediately think it must be a special tool or plug-in. A *micro-bevel* is a small beveled edge connecting two surfaces. If the surfaces are at right angles, the micro-bevel will typically be at 45 degrees. Although the term micro-bevel is sometimes also used to describe both chamfers and fillets, they are actually quite different from each other:

- A *chamfer* is a beveled edge connecting two surfaces. Another way to describe it is as an angled cut applied to an exterior edge. In **Figure 7.10**, the edges on top of the object are chamfered to create a beveled edge.

- A *fillet* is the rounding off, or beveling, of an interior corner. In **Figure 7.11** the interior edges of the model are given a small bevel.

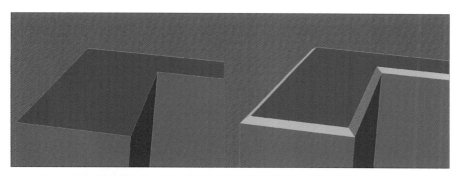

[**Figure 7.10**] The outer edges of this shape are too sharp and need smoothing (left). The chamfer on these edges can help prevent it from looking too CG (right).

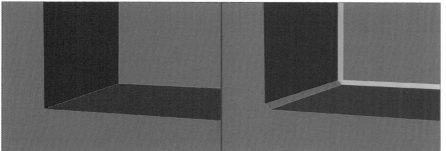

[**Figure 7.11**] The interior edges of this shape are also sharp and need refining (left). A fillet is applied, giving a much more realistic inner seam to this object (right).

You can see why chamfers and fillets fit in the micro-bevel category, but why use them? Look around you and try to find something, anything, that has a razor sharp edge. It's harder than you think. It's quite rare that an edge in the real world lacks some form of rounding. That means adding edge rounding can help you mimic the properties of real-world objects.

Another equally important reason for using micro-bevels is that they catch light on their surfaces and produce a highlight along the edges of the model.

This can not only mimic real-world properties of an object, but can help define the shape in a render.

When you compare an object that has micro-bevels with one that doesn't, it becomes quite obvious why you'd want to use them on your meshes (**Figure 7.12**). Professionals can spot them a mile away, and the lack of micro-bevels usually makes your work look more CG than realistic. It's good practice to add micro-bevels to your modeling checklist and to include them whenever possible.

[Figure 7.12] The object on the left suffers from a very CG appearance. The object on the right has a much more realistic look to it thanks to micro-bevels.

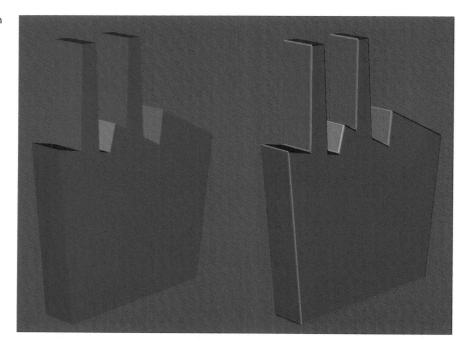

For the Applehead Factory logo, I created these bevels on each letterform individually instead of beveling all of the shapes at once to ensure that they all produce clean results. It was important that I use the same bevel values to produce a consistent look. **Figure 7.13** shows several of the shapes with micro-bevels created.

[Figure 7.13] The micro-bevels added to the edges of these letterforms will increase the quality of the final render by catching highlights along the beveled surfaces.

Clean Up

I chose the Applehead Factory logo for this example knowing it would create a common issue that I could use as an example. Bevels often produce errors in corners with sharp angles caused by overlapping polygons, which can produce render errors and unsightly geometry. Many 3D artists will tell you to avoid fonts that are prone to produce these errors when beveled, but that isn't very useful if you are trying to re-create a specific shape based on a client's logo.

There were a few problem areas on the current Applehead logo that needed to be addressed. The tip of the leaf on the apple shape shown in **Figure 7.14** was a bit of a mess, with overlapping polygons caused by the inset of the bevel operation.

[Figure 7.14] This geometry suffers from a common case of overlapping polygons due to the beveled inset.

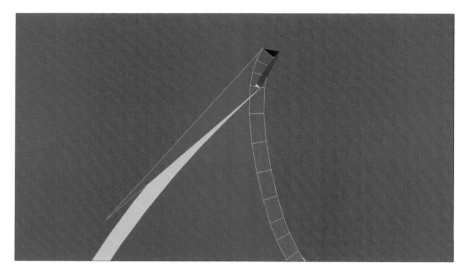

This issue was easy to fix with a few adjustments to the mesh. By moving some of the points, I quickly cleaned up this issue (**Figure 7.15**) and moved on to other problem areas. Don't take the easy way out and either change the amount of bevel you really want or avoid beveling the edges altogether. This issue is an easy fix and worth the time invested.

[Figure 7.15] Simply adjusting the points in the tip solves the issue without having to avoid the desired beveled edge.

Before calling the model final, I always look over every area of the mesh with a fine-toothed comb. If anyone is going to find an issue with my model, I'd rather it be me. With the bevel issues resolved and a detailed survey of the mesh, I had a completed 3D version of the Applehead Factory logo (**Figure 7.16**).

[Figure 7.16] The completed 3D Applehead Factory logo.

Polygonal Modeling Exercise #1

Now that you've seen the production of the Applehead Factory logo, choose another company's logo with a challenging design made up of complex curved shapes and take it through the same process. To get the most out of the experience, avoid using EPS or Illustrator files; create all the letterforms from scratch. The more time you invest in this type of polygonal modeling, the more prepared you will be when working on other model forms, such as robots, buildings, weapons, and more.

Modeling a 3D Polygonal Object with Seams

Years ago, I was tasked by a client to create a detailed 3D model of a traditional soccer ball (**Figure 7.17**). After reviewing the storyboards, I was sure that a *bump map* (an image used to create the appearance of surface detail) on the surface of the sphere wouldn't produce the seams at a high enough level to hold up under the scrutiny of the extreme close-up shots the animation required.

[Figure 7.17] A soccer ball can be a challenging 3D model without a good technique in place to create the seam pattern.

Fortunately, I was lucky enough to come across an amazing tutorial that took what could have been a difficult task and simplified the steps for me. This technique involves starting with a tessellated primitive sphere (a sphere made up of nothing but evenly spaced triangles), and with just a few steps, you end up with a photo-real, fully detailed, traditional soccer ball model (**Figure 7.18**).

[Figure 7.18] A tessellated ball (left) is a great base mesh when starting to model a traditional soccer ball. Each patch on the ball was selected and beveled to create the seams (middle). Beveling each patch and assigning surfaces resulted in a photo-real soccer ball (right).

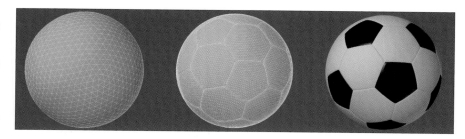

I've used this technique anytime I've been called on to create a traditional soccer ball over the years, and it always reminds me of how good problem solving can make light work of any challenge.

While creating 3D assets for FunGoPlay (FGP), an online virtual sports theme park for kids, I was tasked with creating another digital model of a soccer ball. This time it was a custom version of a traditional soccer ball that would be used for a close-up shot in a commercial showcasing FGP's sports gear product line. Once again I used the same technique that had never failed me, and the resulting mesh was created in short order. **Figure 7.19** shows a final frame from the commercial that ran on Cartoon Network and Nickelodeon.

[Figure 7.19] This CG soccer ball was created for a FunGoPlay commercial using the same technique discussed earlier.

The FGP virtual world also called for several new digital soccer balls, ranging from the 2009 Teamgeist to the 2010 World Cup Jabulani. I loved the seam pattern on the Jabulani ball (**Figure 7.20**), so I gladly accepted the challenge to re-create it in 3D.

[**Figure 7.20**] Our goal in this section is to re-create the paneling of the 2010 Jabulani soccer ball.

Getting Started

As with any digital modeling project, I started by gathering reference material and carefully studying the design of the ball. I find that loosely sketching out the shapes can be a great way to try to get your head around an object. **Figure 7.21** shows how I broke down the ball's paneling, and I discovered that the Jabulani ball is composed of eight panels that are spherically molded. There are two distinct shapes that make up the eight panels. It's important that these shapes be exact so that they connect perfectly together.

It didn't take long to figure out that starting with a tessellated sphere was not the solution for this unique seam pattern. However, after a few hours, I was able to create the pattern of the ball using spline patch modeling. I accomplished my goal but was left unsatisfied because I was convinced there was a more refined solution that would produce a cleaner topology, and to be quite honest, I wanted to take this opportunity to put my problem-solving skills to the test.

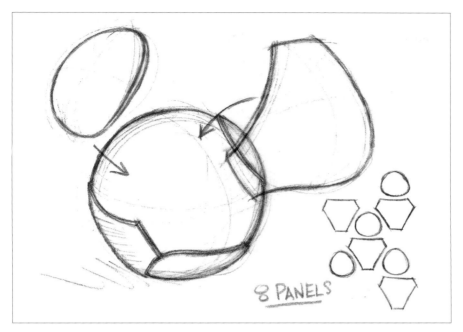

[Figure 7.21] This rough sketch helped to work out a game plan for how I was going to build each of the eight panels.

The procedure that follows is the result of a day's experimentation with the goal of creating easily reproducible results when modeling a 2010 Jabulani soccer ball. By going back and breaking down the model into refined steps, you truly become a better problem solver, and I'd suggest doing the same on your own projects from time to time.

I found that starting with either a segmented or tessellated ball produced undesirable polygon flow, but starting with a tetrahedron (**Figure 7.22**), a platonic solid primitive, could provide a good base mesh for the Jabulani ball. The polygons that make up a platonic solid are all identical, with the same number of faces meeting at each vertex; thus, all its edges are congruent, as are its vertices and angles.

[**Figure 7.22**] Starting with a tetrahedron seems odd, but this platonic solid is surprisingly versatile

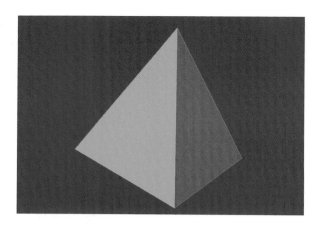

A *tetrahedron* is a type of pyramid consisting of four equilateral triangles with a flat polygon base and triangular faces connecting the base to a common point. My thought was that the four tips of this pyramid could be a good base for four of the eight panels.

Next, I needed to split the tetrahedron into several sections to allow for reshaping. Instead of measuring or guessing where to split the polygon faces, I subdivided the object into smaller faces that made it easier to work with. The resulting mesh gave each triangle face a poly-count of 64 three-point polygons, with a total object poly-count of 256.

To keep the object manageable, I assigned the tips of the tetrahedron to a new surface group and changed their color so that I could easily see the difference between the polygon islands (groups of polygons). **Figure 7.23** shows these tips in blue.

[**Figure 7.23**] The tetrahedron divided into 256 polygons. Changing the surface of the tips makes it easier to define each section of the base mesh.

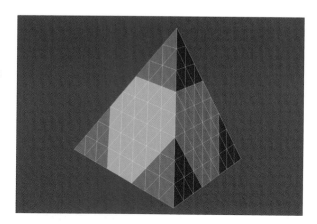

With the tetrahedron sectioned off, I needed to remove the excess polygons. I simply selected the polygons that make each section and merged them into one. It was important to merge only those polygons that were on the same plane, not the entire tip. **Figure 7.24** shows the base mesh after merging each group of polygons.

[Figure 7.24] Each poly-group is merged to refine the mesh by removing unneeded geometry.

I know I just finished making those extra polygons, but that step was only to help create the shapes I now have. It prevented me from having to do any measuring, and I knew that all of the shapes that had been created up to this point were identical.

House Cleaning

Some 3D software may leave unwanted points behind after merging. I like to keep my work area clean as I go, so I always remove any points that are not connected to any polygons when constructing a mesh in this fashion.

There were still a number of points that needed to be removed from the tip portions of the object, so I selected the 12 unneeded points per tip (a total of 48 points), which were located along the base edges, and removed them. The process of cleaning the mesh is shown in **Figure 7.25**.

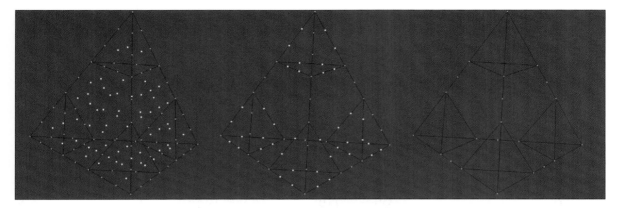

[Figure 7.25] These selected points are no longer connected to any polygons and can be removed (left). Although these points are connected to polygons, they are no longer needed for us to continue on to the next step (middle). The resulting mesh is much cleaner with the points removed (right).

Layout Foundations

To get the base mesh closer to the proper shape I was after, I needed to bring the four points at the very tips of the tetrahedron down to the same edge that bordered the base of the tips. I selected the four tip points and moved them so that they became flush with the tips' base edges. **Figure 7.26** shows the result of the moved points.

[Figure 7.26] The four points at the tips of the tetrahedron are selected in preparation of the next step (left). The selected points are moved flush to the tips' bases (right).

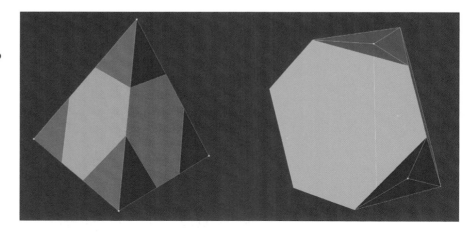

My goal was to end up with the cleanest polygon flow possible, so I reconfigured the geometry that makes up the tips. To do this, I split the edges that
make up the base of the tip sections, working on one tip section at a time.
I selected the bordering edges and added a point in the center. I did this for
all four tip sections before moving on. For each section, I created new edges
that connected the new points to the center point of each tip. **Figure 7.27**
shows these new edges.

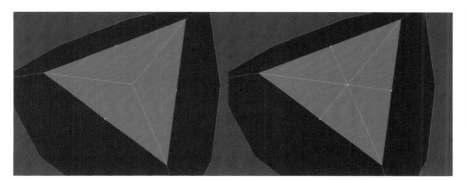

[**Figure 7.27**] The points
selected here (left) were the
result of adding points to
the three bordering edges
of the tip polygons. These
three new edges (right)
were generated to help aid
in reconfiguring the tips'
topology.

All that was left for the tip sections was to merge the polygon pairs, so that I
ended up with a diamond shape configuration (**Figure 7.28**). Reconfiguring
the tip sections may seem trivial right now, but it will drastically change the
final topology of the object for the better. Trust me!

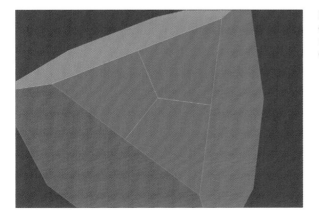

[**Figure 7.28**] Three sets
of triangle polygons were
merged into these three
diamond-shaped quads.

I made sure that all four tip sections had been reconfigured before moving on to the next step. With all of the tips in the proper configuration, I started to create the topology needed for the center sections of the base object.

I knew I wanted to split the center sections into smaller components. Doing this would enable me to control the polygon flow of the final mesh. I started by selecting the two center points and splitting the center sections right down the middle, creating a new edge (**Figure 7.29**).

[Figure 7.29] These two points (left) are selected in preparation of splitting the center polygon. An edge is created, connecting the two selecting points (right).

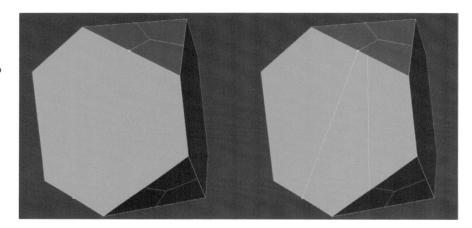

I then selected the new edge that was just created and added a new point in its center. I added the points that were on the edges that border the center section to my selection and created new edges, splitting the center area into four faces. **Figure 7.30** shows the result of the split.

[Figure 7.30] A new point is added to the center of the newly created edge (left). The two points along the border of the center patch are added to the selection (middle). Edges are created to connect the selected points (right).

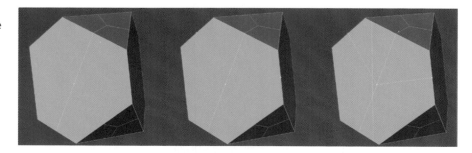

I repeated the steps on the lower portion of the mesh by selecting the center point and the points bordering the tips on the other side of the triangle, creating two more edges and thus splitting the center area into six polygons (**Figure 7.31**).

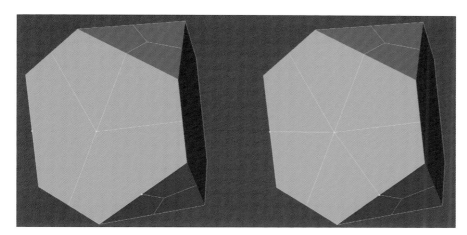

[**Figure 7.31**] The same edges are needed for the lower portion of the mesh. These points are selected in preparation for new edges (left). Edges are created to connect the selected points on the lower part of the mesh, resulting in the center patch being made up of six polygons (right).

I once again repeated the steps until all four of the center sections were identical; each contained six polygons. I still wanted to divide the center areas into more polygons, so I selected the edge loop that bordered one of the tips and split it down the center, creating two bands around the tip. **Figure 7.32** shows the two bands around the base of the tip.

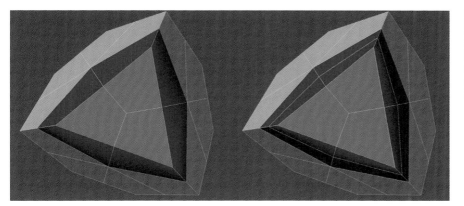

[**Figure 7.32**] The edge loop bordering the tip geometry is highlighted here in pink (left). This band of polygons has been split down the center, creating two sets of loops (right).

Satisfied with the results, I repeated these steps for the remaining tips (**Figure 7.33**).

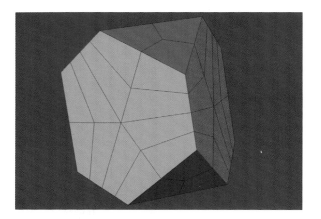

[Figure 7.33] New bands are created around the remaining tips.

Believe it or not, the tedious portion was then complete. What I currently had was a magic configuration that would allow me to create the Jabulani soccer ball I was after. This base mesh consisted of 60 four-point polygons (60 quads).

It was important to go through these steps so that the underlying topology would provide optimal results. There are several ways I could have divided the base object to end up with the current state of the mesh, but I found this to be the most efficient way to ensure that all the segments were evenly spaced. This even spacing guarantees a more refined final mesh, which should be a goal of any model you create.

Final Stages

The finish line was in sight. To speed up selecting individual sections in future steps, I gave each of the center sections its own surface (**Figure 7.34**). Trivial steps like this are often overlooked by artists, costing them lost time on a production.

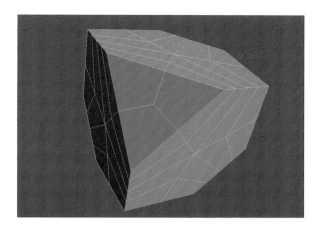

[Figure 7.34] The center patches are given unique surface groups and assigned different colors to aid in future steps.

Before I was ready to convert this geometric shape into a sphere, I wanted to increase the geometry a bit, so I subdivided the mesh into 960 quads. With a denser mesh and more polygons to work with, I performed a little magic! I wanted to deform this mesh into the shape of a sphere, so I used a deformation tool that shrink-wraps any geometry into a sphere. The result, shown in **Figure 7.35**, was a perfect sphere with the topology that I mapped out earlier.

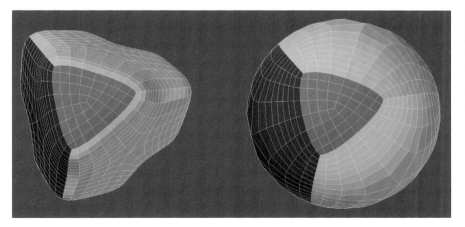

[Figure 7.35] The base mesh is subdivided in preparation of deformation, which will occur in the next step (left). The result of deforming the mesh into the shape of a sphere (right).

Without the initial preparation, I could have generated a ball object, but the underlying polygon flow would have been less than desirable.

The sizes of the tip panels were too small. I wanted to increase them so that they were in proportion to the center panels. I selected the polygons that made up the tip sections and expanded the selection so that four new polygon bands were part of each of the tip's selection. I changed the surface of the selected polygons so they all used the tip surface. **Figure 7.36** shows the result.

[Figure 7.36] The tip patches' surface groups are expanded to match the size of the real-world patches on the Jabulani ball.

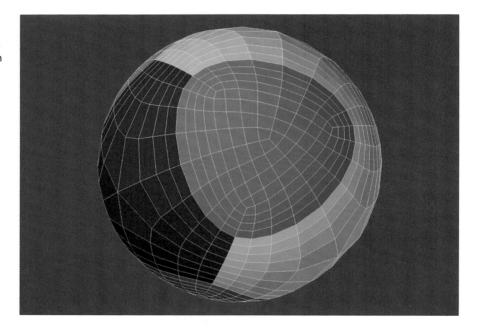

The object had a low polygon count, which would reveal faceting when viewed up close. That wasn't going to work. I wanted this soccer ball to be seen at much higher resolutions, so I subdivided it again (**Figure 7.37**).

I could see that I had accomplished my goal of creating the proper paneling of a Jabulani ball, but it was missing the seams that would allow the edges of the paneling to catch light. Adding this level of detail to a model will only enhance a mesh and add more realism to the final render.

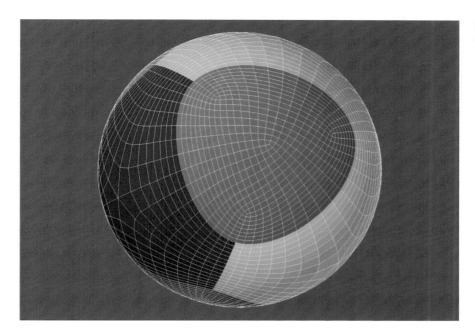

[Figure 7.37] The mesh is subdivided again.

To create the seams on the ball, I created a beveled edge around each patch, as shown on the yellow polygons in **Figure 7.38**. Because I planned ahead and created a different surface group for each patch, it was an easy task. I selected the polygons that made up one of the center patches and beveled it using a small shift and inset value.

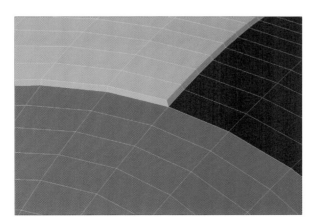

[Figure 7.38] The "yellow" patch is selected and beveled with a small shift and inset to start the creation of the seams in the ball.

I deselected the polygons and repeated this process until all eight patches (triangle centers and tips) had been beveled (**Figure 7.39**).

[Figure 7.39] Each patch is given a bevel to complete the seam work.

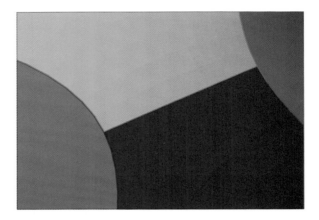

With the seams in place, I subdivided the mesh one more time to increase the poly-count and smooth out the seams' edges so they didn't appear unnatural and sharp.

I changed the surface attributes for all the panels that made up the object to solid white instead of creating a new surface group so that I could get a better look at the final mesh (**Figure 7.40**). Changing the color of the existing surfaces gives me the ability to go back at a later time and edit each patch independently by selecting polygons by surface.

[Figure 7.40] The mesh is subdivided again to smooth out the newly created seams and all of the surface group's colors are changed to white.

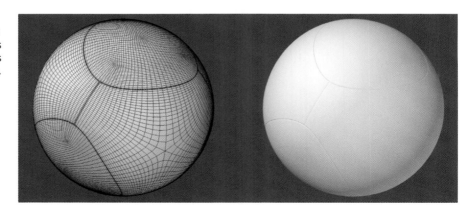

Goooal!!!

There you have it! With a bit of preplanning and taking a little extra time in the beginning, I not only successfully completed what I set out to create, but I set myself up with clean polygon flow and patches that are mathematically identical for the eight-panel design that makes up the 2010 World Cup Jabulani soccer ball.

Although I invested an entire work day developing this technique, using it allows me to generate this soccer ball in less than five minutes, whereas the spline patch modeling method took over an hour, and the topology wasn't as accurate as I would have liked it to be.

For every digital model you create, your goal should be to deliver a clean mesh with optimal topology. Sometimes revisiting an object you've already created and thinking outside the box can lead to new techniques that shave hours off of your future modeling sessions.

Polygonal Modeling Exercise #2

If you're looking for a similar challenge to this one, try modeling the 2006 Teamgeist soccer ball shown in **Figure 7.41**. It has its own set of challenges and is a fun project to tackle. Here's a hint to get you started: The first step involves another platonic solid. You've gotta love geometry!

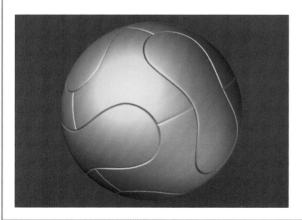

[Figure 7.41] Take the 2006 Teamgeist soccer ball challenge and re-create this ball in 3D.

CHAPTER EIGHT

Subdivision Surface Modeling

Once primarily used for organic objects, subdivision surfaces (SubDs) have since become widely used in all areas of modeling. They provide the smoothness of NURBS surfaces with the local detail and texturing capabilities of polygonal meshes.

Although subdivision surface modeling doesn't completely replace polygonal modeling, it does have numerous advantages. One of those advantages is the ability to work on a low-poly model with the effect propagated automatically to the subdivided mesh in real time. SubDs allows you to work with a simpler and lighter model for faster interaction rather than dealing with a heavy, denser, high-resolution version.

The biggest advantage of working with SubDs is the ability to change the level of subdivision for the mesh, both during the modeling process and at render time. Simply stated, subdivision surface modeling is multi-resolution modeling.

In this chapter, I'll show you the power of SubDs and share techniques that produce clean and efficient models using this modeling method.

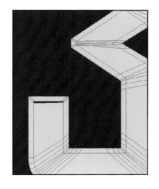  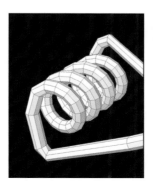 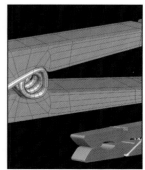

Modeling 3D Text with SubDs

Creating 3D text has always been a straightforward process. Digital modelers are quite often tasked with generating 3D text for everything from PowerPoint presentations to print graphics, feature film credits, and more. Modeling 3D text with SubDs involves a little more work but allows for resolution independence similar to vector files, making it worth the extra effort. Being able to build one mesh and change the amount of geometry created at render time allows you to avoid faceting on the curved shapes that make up many typefaces while maintaining a simple mesh that is easy to manipulate. It's also a snap to create realistic edges on a SubD mesh.

For the example in this chapter, I chose the Agency typeface because its letterforms are made up of both hard-edge and curved corners. This will allow me to share some techniques you can use for any typeface you choose on future projects.

Getting Started

I begin building SubD text the same way I would if I were going to construct it with the traditional polygonal method, using one of three methods. I could import an EPS or Illustrator file, build the letterforms from scratch (as I did in Chapter 7), or simply use the text tool found in most 3D software. For this example, I used the text tool in my 3D modeling software to create the number 3 and the letter D (**Figure 8.1**).

[Figure 8.1] These two letterforms are made up of n-gons that will need to be reworked into an all quad mesh.

This generated two n-gons that would work perfectly if the final model were going to be a polygonal mesh, but would collapse if I tried to apply SubDs at this point. There are many techniques used to generate SubD text, but I have found that adding support edges provides the cleanest mesh with the most flexibility.

Adding Support Edges

SubD text needs support edges to maintain the model's shape, so I started creating this support geometry by beveling both of the n-gons with a slight inset. **Figure 8.2** shows the result of the inset on the two letterforms.

[**Figure 8.2**] Creating a small inset produces a clean edge loop of quad polys.

By creating these insets, I added handy edge loops consisting of quad polygons that border the edges of each shape. These edge loops not only help support the shape, but allow for a more refined edge. As long as I maintained this clean flow of polygons, I avoided the potential creasing and pinching that are commonly seen in SubD text models by other artists.

At this point I selected both n-gons and deleted them. Although that's not a requirement for this technique to work, removing them gave me better visibility of the edge loops and allowed me to work faster. If I applied SubDs to the mesh at this point, the curved corners in each letterform would maintain their correct shape but the rigid corners would completely fall apart. **Figure 8.3** shows a comparison of the object with and without SubDs.

[Figure 8.3] The polygonal mesh (left) maintains the original shape, whereas the SubD mesh (right) loses its shape without proper support segments.

To maintain the shapes of each letterform, I needed to add additional support to the corners with sharp angles. To do this, I simply added hold segments to the sides of the edges that made up the corners. **Figure 8.4** shows a before and after view on two of the corners that required hold segments.

[Figure 8.4] This close-up of one of the ends of the 3 shows before the segments were added (left) and after (right).

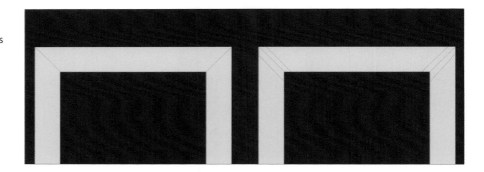

There were a total of 17 corners that I had to add segments to. With all of them in place, I applied SubDs to the mesh. **Figure 8.5** shows the two letterforms maintaining their shape with assistance from the newly created edges.

[Figure 8.5] With the support segments added in all of the required areas, the letterforms hold their shape when SubDs are applied to the mesh.

Patching in Polygons

With the letterforms holding their shapes, I needed to fill in the holes that were created when I deleted the n-gons. Although most SubD algorithms support n-gons, I like to avoid them and try and stick to an all quad mesh for cleaner results.

I switched back to a polygonal mesh and started with the D, creating individual four-point polygons that bridged the two inner edges that made up the letterform. This required me to add an additional segment for each curved corner of the D to keep the mesh all quads. **Figure 8.6** shows one of the curved corners patched and the entire letterform completed.

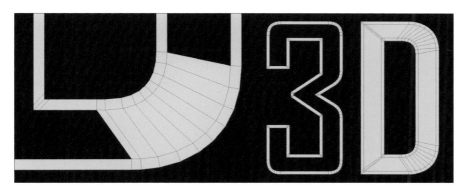

[Figure 8.6] To finish off the D letterform, the inner edges were bridged together, creating a series of quad polygons.

Moving on to the next shape, I started by adding additional segments to the edge loop so that I had the same number of edges on both sides of the gap in the 3. This generated an additional 33 polygons but would make bridging the gap much cleaner. As I did for the D, I patched in four-point polygons, filling the inner hole of the 3. I left the two ends of the letterform unfinished so that I could create a custom configuration. **Figure 8.7** shows the result.

[Figure 8.7] Additional segments were added to the edge loop of the 3 to allow for an equal number of edges on each side of the shape. This made it easier to generate an all quad mesh. Quad polygons were generated to fill in the 3 with the two ends being left undone for a custom configuration.

Instead of using the six points that made up each of the end caps and creating two quads, I opted for the four-poly configuration shown in **Figure 8.8**, which avoided the creation of tiny quad polys that might cause issues later. This created a cleaner result while still maintaining clean polygon flow.

[Figure 8.8] To fill the holes in the ends (left), a four-quad polygon configuration was used (right).

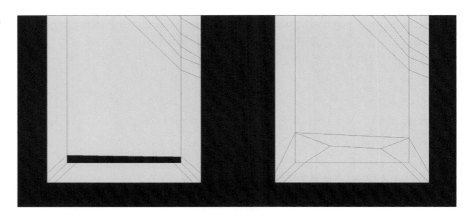

Adding Depth

With the two letterforms complete, I added depth by extruding them. I applied SubDs to the mesh to review the result shown in **Figure 8.9**. Although this could have been considered final, I wasn't happy with how soft the edges were and wanted to adjust them.

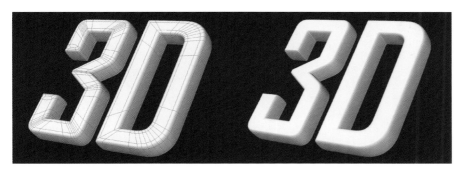

[Figure 8.9] The flat letter-forms were extruded to give them depth.

Knowing that SubDs smooth the mesh's surface based on the proximity of bordering geometry, I cut two segments into the sides of the letterforms. The closer I moved these new segments to the border, the sharper the letterform edges became. If I moved the segments farther apart, I had a larger area to smooth and produced a softer edge. I settled on a placement that gave me the edge that I was after (**Figure 8.10**).

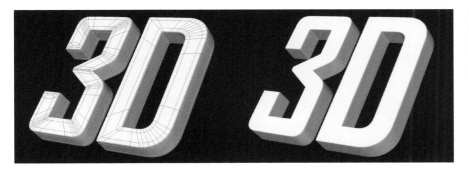

[Figure 8.10] Two new segments were cut into the sides of the letterforms and moved close to the outer edges to create a tighter edge.

Adding Detail

Because I worked clean poly-flow with edge loops into the letterforms, I was able to add details to the letterforms to take them to the next level. **Figure 8.11** shows two examples of what is possible with just a few simple bevels.

[Figure 8.11] These are two examples of how you can take advantage of the clean poly-flow that was created to enhance the shapes of the letterforms.

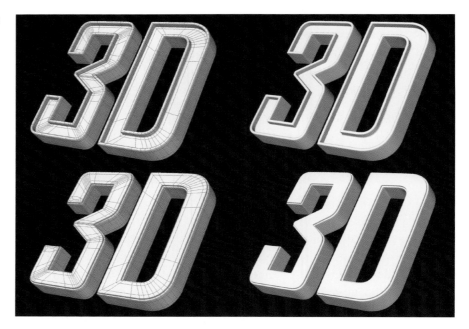

Creating SubD text involves only a few simple steps, and the payoff is well worth the time spent. The more letterforms you create with SubDs, the quicker you will become at delivering them to your clients.

Subdivision Surface Modeling Exercise #1

To start gaining speed with this technique, choose a font and generate the entire alphabet in SubD letters that you can pull from when the need arises. Challenge yourself by working with an array of fonts that include multiple curves, serifs, and any other details that require additional hold segments. Your time will be well spent, and the skills that you gain from the experience will aid you in other hard-surface models you're likely to build using SubDs.

Modeling a SubD Object

I continually tell students and artists who are new to digital modeling to get as much modeling time under their belts as possible and practice constantly. I often get the same response: "What should I model?"

The short answer is, "Anything!"

It really doesn't matter what you model. Every model you build will only strengthen your ability to build the next one. Remember the earlier quote from Renée Descartes: "Each problem that I solved became a rule which served afterwards to solve other problems."

For this next example of modeling with SubDs, I chose a standard wooden clothespin that I had lying around the house. Using the clothespin allows me to demonstrate the same technique we explored for creating the SubD letterforms but also introduces a new challenge.

Reference

I fired off a few photos of a clothespin so that I could display the images on my second monitor while I worked. I also had the actual clothespin close by so I could reference it if the images didn't supply enough information. **Figure 8.12** shows one of the reference photos I took.

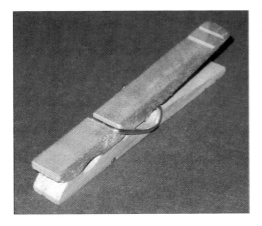

[Figure 8.12] This clothespin consists of three components: two wooden prongs and a metal spring.

Studying the clothespin, I knew that I could create the wooden prongs using the same technique that I used to create the SubD letterforms. I also decided that I only had to create one of the wooden parts and the other one could be duplicated to save time.

After giving some thought to the metal spring, I decided that I would have the most control if I rail extruded a simple flat disc along a single spline. The *rail extrude* operation allows a flat shape (polygon or group of polygons) to be extruded (extended) along a spline with the newly created geometry conforming to the shape of the spline. With my plan in place and references handy, I was ready to begin.

Getting Started

I started by creating one large n-gon for the wooden prong. Because I knew I would be taking advantage of SubDs, I used very few points to define the curved portions of the shape. **Figure 8.13** shows a comparison of the number of points I would use if this were going to be a polygonal mesh and what I created for this SubD mesh. Notice the lower point count on the version that will take advantage of SubDs.

[Figure 8.13] The prong on the top uses more points to define the curves and is what I would use for a polygonal mesh. The prong on the bottom uses fewer points to take advantage of SubDs smoothing algorithm.

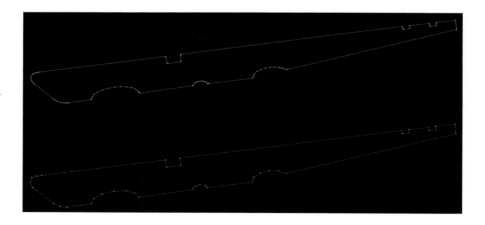

Beveling the polygon with a small inset created an edge loop of quad polys that bordered the silhouette of the wooden prong. I deleted the n-gon and applied SubDs to the mesh to see where I stood. **Figure 8.14** shows the results of these two steps.

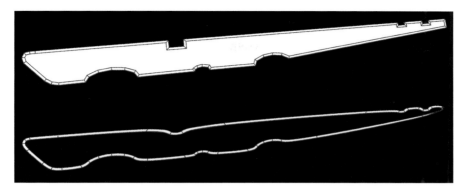

[Figure 8.14] The prong's n-gon was beveled with a small inset (top). Once beveled, the n-gon was deleted and SubDs were applied (bottom).

I added more segments throughout the edge loop to maintain the wooden prong's shape and to allow me to patch in the center using four-point polygons (**Figure 8.15**).

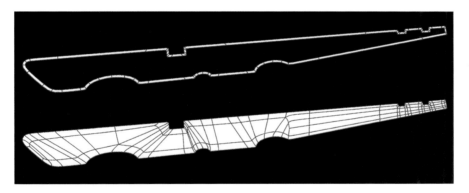

[Figure 8.15] Extra hold segments were added to maintain the shape of the wooden prong (top), and then the center hole was patched with quad polys (bottom).

I was happy with the silhouette of the wooden prong, so I gave it depth by extruding it. The result produced soft edges, so I added two segments running the length of the object, placing them close to the existing border edges to produce a tighter edge (**Figure 8.16**).

[Figure 8.16] The flat shape was extruded to give it depth (top), and extra hold segments were added to sharpen the edges (bottom).

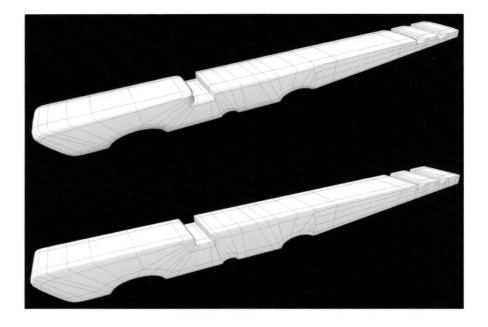

With the wooden prong completed, I mirrored it to create the other one and rotated it into place. **Figure 8.17** shows the two finished wooden prongs.

[Figure 8.17] The second wooden prong was created by mirroring the original one.

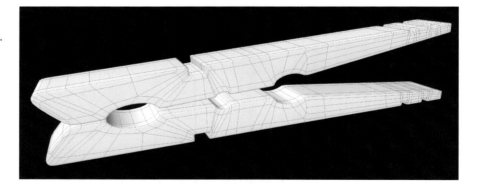

Creating the Metal Spring

Next, I needed to create a spline that I could use to generate the metal spring. I started by creating one piece of the coiled portion that I duplicated three times and then merged them into one spline. From that single spline, I added the two arms that extended out from the spring to produce the shape I needed. I merged the two arms to the coil to produce a single spline. **Figure 8.18** shows this process.

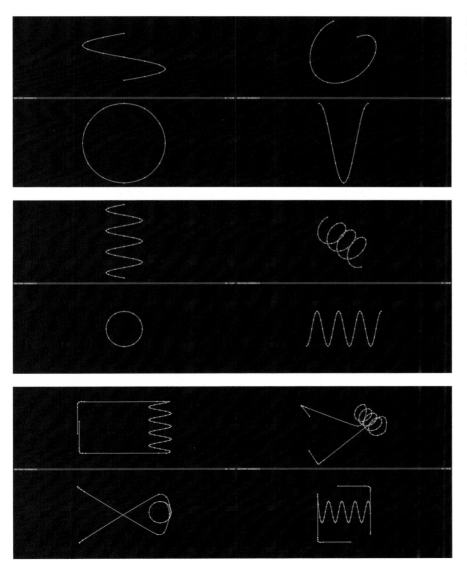

[Figure 8.18] Multiple splines were created and merged to produce a single spline in the shape of the metal spring.

I created a disc polygon that I could use to extrude along the spline. I only used eight points to define the shape of the disc to keep the polygon count low. Too often artists use too many sides and segments on discs, balls, and other shapes that could be created using fewer. Remember that SubDs will generate a smooth surface using a low-resolution polygonal cage.

I moved the flat eight-point disc to the head of the spline and rail extruded it to generate the metal spring (**Figure 8.19**). It's a good idea to keep the spline used for the rail extrusion for future use. I know a lot of artists who delete their splines after they've used them and then later find they need them again. Why set yourself up to do the same task twice?

[Figure 8.19] An eight-point disc was created to extrude along the spline. The disc was aligned with the spline (left) and then extruded along the spline to create the metal spring geometry (right).

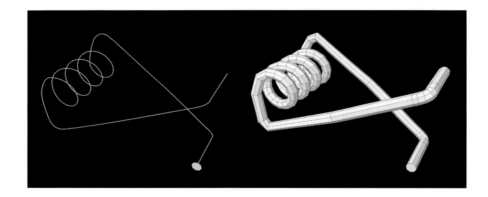

All that was left to complete the metal spring was to produce cleaner end caps to replace the n-gons. To do this, I beveled the two n-gons at the ends of the spring three times to produce a slightly rounded shape. I created a pole of triangle polygons out of the n-gons and then merged the triangles into four-quad polygons. **Figure 8.20** shows this process.

[Figure 8.20] The ends of the spring were beveled to round them off, and the n-gons were converted into triangles. Those newly created triangles were merged to create quad polys.

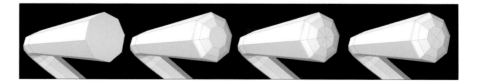

With the metal spring modeled, I applied SubDs to it and resurfaced all three components of the clothespin to get the final results shown in **Figure 8.21**.

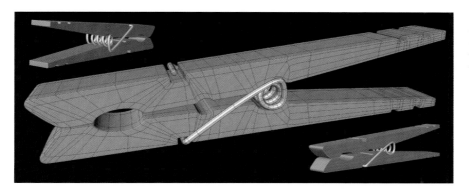

[Figure 8.21] The final clothespin consists of all quad polys and is ready for the next phase of production.

As you can see, the techniques used on the letterforms earlier in the chapter can be just as useful on other meshes. The same goes for the rail extrude technique. I've used rail extrude to create everything from rollercoaster tracks, hoses and wiring, and more. Once you have the spline, you can try extruding a variety of shapes to generate completely different results. Every time you pick up a new modeling technique, commit it to memory, and you'll soon have enough techniques in your toolkit to solve any modeling challenge.

Subdivision Surface Modeling Exercise #2

Select an everyday item, like a stapler, tape dispenser, hair brush, or nail clippers, and re-create it using SubDs. Take some photos that you can use as reference and have the actual item nearby. Remember to study your reference and formulate a plan before you ever launch your 3D software. Not only will this exercise give you more modeling experience, but it will also allow you to start building a library of 3D assets that may come in handy on future projects. You may also be surprised at how much these everyday objects sell for on a site like TurboSquid (www.turbosquid.com). The important thing is to keep modeling.

CHAPTER NINE

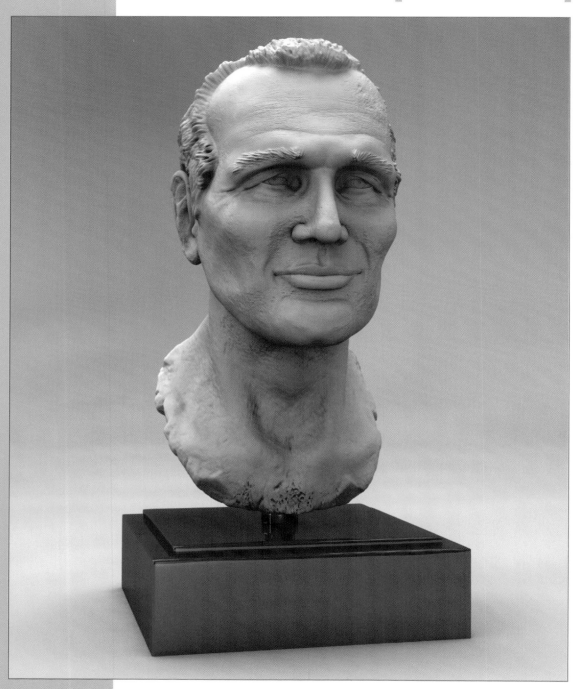

Modeling a Realistic Head

Chances are good that at some point in your digital modeling career you will be tasked with creating a 3D model of a realistic head. It might be used for a live-action television series in need of a CG stunt double, for an animated game cinematic, or any number of projects that require a photorealistic 3D human head.

The biggest challenge when creating a realistic head model is that just about everyone can spot a bad CG face from a mile away. This is because we see faces every day. Reference and observation, once again, are key to the success of re-creating a human head in 3D.

In this chapter, I'll walk you through creating a realistic head with these four main objectives in mind:

- Using subdivision surfaces

- Matching reference material

- Building a clean mesh that is ideal for animation

- Making extensive use of the edge extend (extrude) build out modeling method

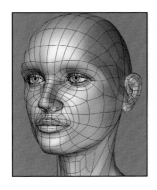  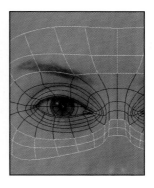 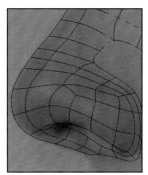

Choosing a Method: Edge Extend vs. Box Modeling

There really is no *one* technique that you have to use when creating any digital model. That said, the two most popular methods for creating a character head are box modeling and the edge extend build out method. With box modeling, I would start with a primitive object (box, ball, disc, and so on) and would work on the primary details first, like the overall head shape. I would then build in the finer secondary and tertiary details. Using the edge extend method, I would start with the tertiary details, like a fully detailed eye, and build out additional geometry from there. To create the realistic head used as the example for this chapter, I chose the edge extend method.

It's important that I take a minute to explain why I chose the edge extend method of modeling for this particular model, because I don't want you to get the wrong idea. I've read quite a few articles and forum threads, written by industry professionals, that would lead you to believe that the edge extend technique is the only option when building a realistic head, and that other methods, such as box modeling, are not accurate enough. Also, some would say that you can tell the difference between a head that has been created using the build out method and one that has been created using other methods. This couldn't be further from the truth.

I've used the box modeling method for creating more realistic heads in my career than any other technique. **Figure 9.1** shows a couple of head models created using the box modeling technique. I've even tried my hand at other methods of modeling a head, and regardless of the technique used, they all delivered similar results. There is really no way to tell how a model was created. The only attributes of the model that a discerning eye can recognize is whether or not it matches the reference and whether it's a clean mesh.

Why have I chosen the edge extend method? I tend to choose the edge extend method when I'm in a pinch and short on time. It's by far the fastest way I know to create a production-ready, realistic head. It is also the easiest method for someone new to modeling to learn.

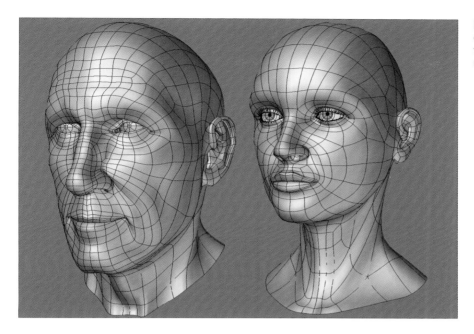

[**Figure 9.1**] The box modeling method was used to create these two head models.

For the walkthrough in this chapter, I wanted to use a young female model, because I find female models to be more challenging than male models. Most female faces are smooth, whereas most male faces are on the rougher side. With a male model, you're more likely to get away with a mesh with dents and dings because the features can add character to a male face, but on a female model that same texture can look unattractive and distracting.

My friend April Warren (www.aprilwarren.com), shown in **Figure 9.2**, is the subject for this chapter and is an ideal candidate for us to reference.

[**Figure 9.2**] Actress and digital artist April Warren will be our subject for this chapter.

Using Reference

April was kind enough to supply not only great front and side reference snapshots, but she went the extra mile and delivered a collection of photos showing a range of expressions (**Figure 9.3**). These shots are a great resource and demonstrate why good poly-flow is essential to a realistic head that will animate. These facial expressions are driven by motions or positions of the muscles of the face. When we create proper poly-flow in our 3D meshes, we can mimic the movement of these muscles. Keep this in mind when I walk through the process of building the areas of the face that you see undergoing the most change in these various expressions.

[Figure 9.3]
Facial expressions are an important channel of non-verbal communication and play a substantial role in character animation.

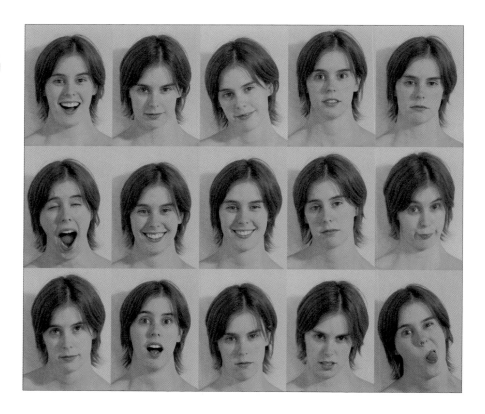

Preparing the Background Templates

After a good study of the reference images, the next step was to prepare the front and side images that were used as the background templates for modeling on top of. This preparation required using Photoshop to scale and rotate the two images in order to line up key areas like the corners of the eyes, tip of the nose, corners of the mouth, and chin (**Figure 9.4**).

It's common that the ears remain a little off due to camera lens distortion and the fact that ears sit closer to the camera in a side-view photo. As you can see in Figure 9.4, the bottom of April's ears line up, but the top of the ear in the side view is higher than the front. When possible, it's ideal to use a long lens to reduce this type of distortion, but because these photos were taken with a simple point-and-shoot camera, I just needed to compensate for the difference when I modeled the ears. To do this, I focused on the side-view reference when modeling the ear and overlooked the fact that it wouldn't match the front-view reference. Once the final mesh was created, I eyeballed the difference and chose an ear height that looked good.

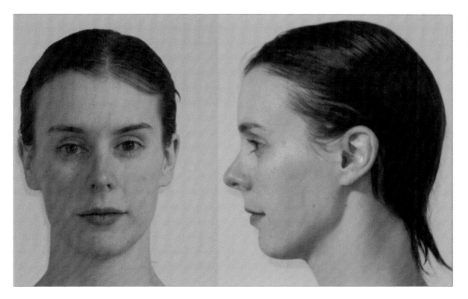

[Figure 9.4] Matching the front and side images is an important step before modeling begins.

Taking Advantage of Symmetry

Taking advantage of symmetry on a mesh like this means only having to model one half of the head, and can also make for more efficient UV mapping, morph target creation, rigging, and more. If you look at the front view of April in Figure 9.4, you can see a slight difference between the two sides of her face. Using Photoshop, I mirrored the (screen) right side of her face over to the (screen) left (**Figure 9.5**).

[Figure 9.5] Mirroring a person's face may look alien, but it can save valuable production time when modeling.

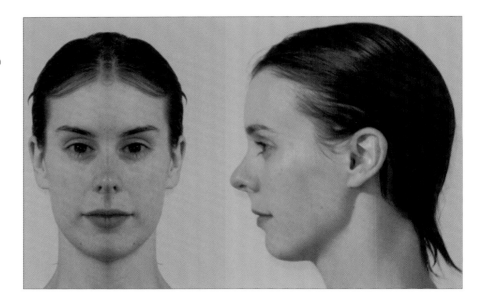

The new reference now looks a bit alien, and it's important to understand that no real-world human has a perfectly symmetrical face. CG human models with symmetrical faces can stand out as not being realistic and are, unfortunately, commonly seen throughout the industry. The trick is to create an asymmetrical model and use an asymmetrical morph during the rigging phase. This allows for all departments to take advantage of symmetry while not losing the asymmetrical qualities of a real-world person in the final render.

Modeling the Head's Components

With the reference prepped and a modeling method chosen, I was ready to start modeling. The six main components that I needed to tackle on the mesh were:

- Eyes
- Ears
- Nose
- Jawline
- Mouth
- Rest of the head

Using the edge extend technique, or any form of build out, allows you to start modeling any area of a model. But I find the eyes to be the best place to start when modeling a human face.

Eyes

If you don't match the eyes, it's nearly impossible to create a likeness of a particular person. If the eyes on a CG model are identical to the reference, other areas can be close enough and you can usually get away with it. I used this knowledge to my advantage when modeling a series of celebrity M&M's, like the Brooks and Dunn M&M's shown in **Figure 9.6**, because they required a likeness without having a nose, ears, or other key defining attributes that usually help capture a likeness.

[Figure 9.6] These celebrity M&M's relied on the eyes to capture the likeness.

Eyeballs

Many artists begin modeling a character's face without starting with an eyeball mesh, which I find to be less efficient than having an eyeball in place to conform the eyelids to. Although I used the edge extend technique for modeling the head, I cheated and built the eye out of a low-poly sphere primitive. Because I took advantage of subdivision surfaces (or SubDs, which we defined as a refinement algorithm that creates a smooth, curved surface from a coarse polygonal mesh), I limited the amount of sides and segments that made up the sphere to keep a low poly-count. **Figure 9.7** shows the back of the eyeball.

[Figure 9.7] Keeping the poly-count low on a character's eyeballs will help increase render times later during the production.

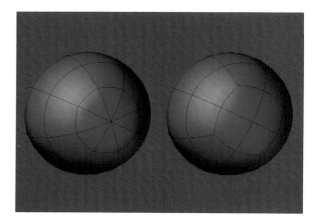

After I created the eyeball base mesh, I lined it up with the background images. For the front of the eyeball, I selected the eight triangles, flattened them, and performed five bevels to create the shape of the iris and pupil. When I was happy with the shape, I merged the eight triangles into four quads like I did on the backside. **Figure 9.8** shows the results of these steps.

One last element needed to be created for the eyeball mesh to be finished, and that was the cornea geometry. Using a slightly larger sphere, I went through the same steps as before, but this time I beveled the polygons on the front of the mesh outward to create a slight bulge for the cornea (**Figure 9.9**). When textured, this geometry will be made transparent with reflective and refractive properties, giving the appearance of a shiny, glasslike surface at render time. For the rest of this walkthrough, however, we will shelve this portion of the mesh because it's not required for the remaining steps.

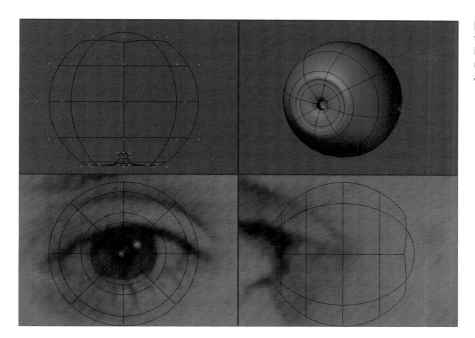

[Figure 9.8] Modeling the iris flat and the pupil indented will produce much more realistic renders than a perfectly round eye.

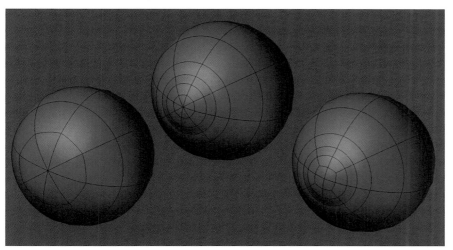

[Figure 9.9] The cornea geometry will be made transparent and reflective with a level of refraction to give the eyes a glasslike quality.

Eyelids

With the eyeball created, I moved forward by creating the eyelid area of the face. I started with a flat plane that I sliced into eight polygons. I wasn't picky about where I made the cuts because I knew I would eventually adjust the points, conforming to the shape of the opening of the eye. Using the reference images and the eyeball as guides, I moved the points to create an arched leaf shape (**Figure 9.10**).

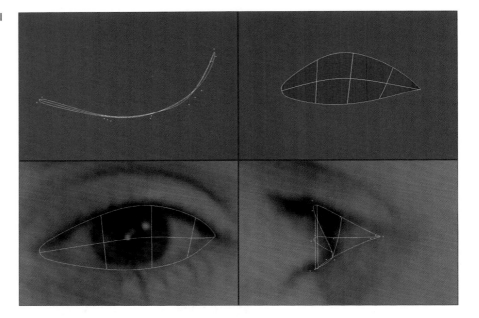

[Figure 9.10] Taking special care with point placement early on will save clean up time later in the modeling process.

Before I started edge extending, I cheated again by not edge extending and instead beveled the geometry four times to create the inner ridge of the eyelid as well as something that I refer to as the eye-sack (**Figure 9.11**). The eye-sack is just extra geometry behind the eyeball that can come in handy later in the modeling process, as you will see. It is also necessary if you plan on creating a 3D print of the mesh, because you can't have open edges on a mesh when printing.

It was finally time to start the edge extending. I selected the open edges around the eye and extended them three times, creating the eyelids (**Figure 9.12**). It's important to create enough edge loops to be able to properly close the eyelids during animation but not so many that it causes unwanted creases. Also, it's tempting to continue extending the edges, but it's important to reshape the newly created geometry first, because it will save time in the long run.

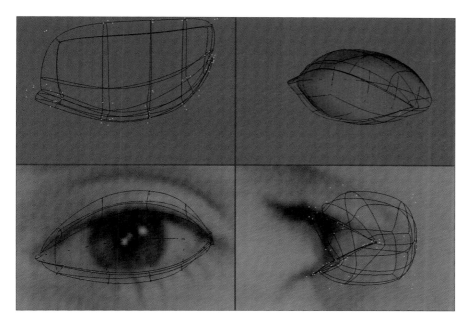

[Figure 9.11] Beveling allows you to quickly create the inner portions of the eyelids.

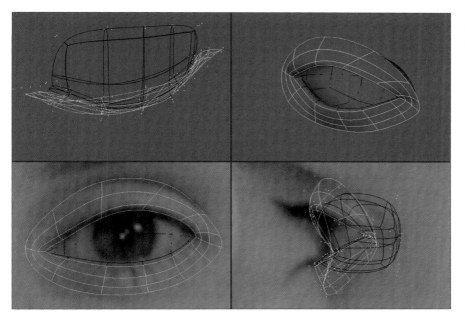

[Figure 9.12] Using the rule of three, I made sure I had enough segments to allow the eyelids to close properly.

A close look at the reference material shows the lacrimal caruncle—the small mass located at the inner corner of the eye. I wanted this mesh to be realistic, so I needed to re-create this mass of skin. I even add the lacrimal caruncles to most of my cartoon character models as well and have found that most people spot the detail and comment on it favorably.

I selected the inner corner polygons and beveled them to generate localized detail. I wanted to also take advantage of the extra polygons along the edge, so I deleted the existing corner polygons shown in purple in **Figure 9.13**, and reshaped the newly created geometry.

Eye socket

I extended the open edges of the eyelids two times to create the eye socket area of the face. When I was happy with my point placement, I mirrored the entire mesh across the X axis. The results are shown in **Figure 9.14**.

[Figure 9.13] Adding the lacrimal caruncle gives a higher level of realism to a model's eyes.

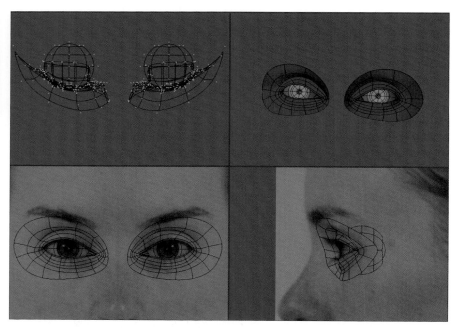

[Figure 9.14] Mirroring and working with symmetry allows you to create character meshes in half the time.

Eye mask

Connecting the inner edges of the eye sockets with four rows of quads allowed me to construct the root of the nose. I then extended all of the open edge twice to create what I refer to as the eye mask, or Zorro mask (**Figure 9.15**). At this point, I took a few minutes to make sure I was happy with the eye region of the face. It's always important to go back over the mesh from time to time to ensure that you're still on target.

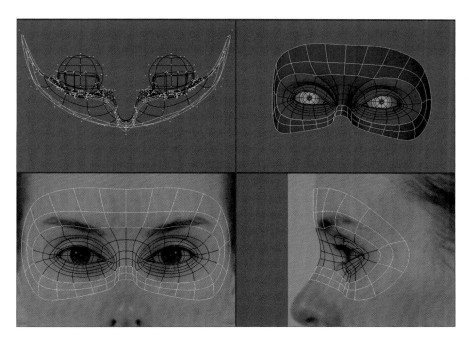

[**Figure 9.15**] Always take time to go back over your mesh when you've completed the eye mask region and make sure you've captured the reference's likeness.

Nose

For the nose region, I started by extending the bridge of the nose several times, making note of where I would need extra rows for future use. I then extended geometry around the wings of the nose. I bridged the wings to the bridge with three rows and then closed the hole that was generated by creating the necessary quads. The results are shown in **Figure 9.16**.

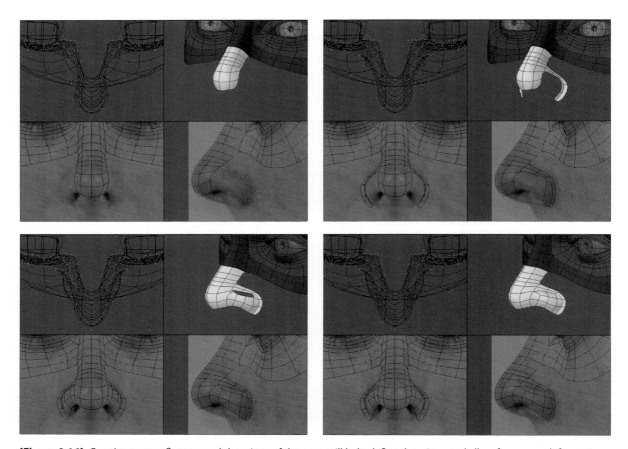

[Figure 9.16] Creating proper flow around the wings of the nose will help define the wings and allow for proper deformation.

I then extended three rows of polygons off the tip of the nose to create the septum, and extended the edges around the nostrils and wings of the nose. I extended the end edges of the nostrils one time and then connected them to the end row around the wings with a single polygon, which gave me the results shown in **Figure 9.17**.

Extending the inner nostril edges again allowed me to then create new polygons to close off the inside of the nose, as shown in **Figure 9.18**.

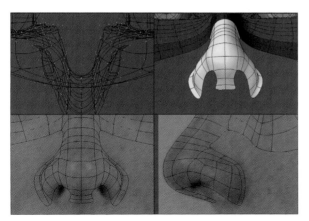

[Figure 9.17] Having a row of polys flow around the wings and into the nostril gives a natural look to the mesh that holds up well during animation.

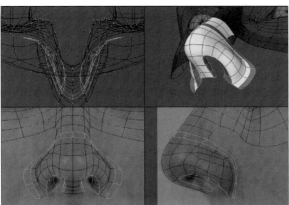

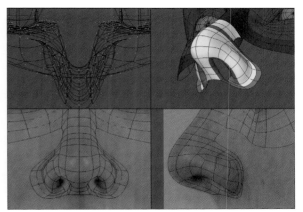

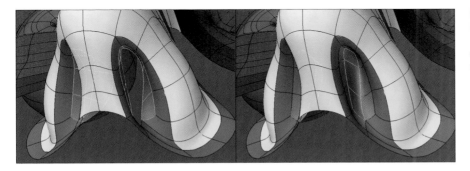

[Figure 9.18] Although most camera angles won't reveal the inner nostril, it's always a good idea to close off the geometry.

Laugh Line

Before moving on to the mouth, I like to make sure I get a solid laugh line in place. A proper laugh line edge loop should border the mouth, run around the wings of the nose, and cross over the bridge of the nose. This region of the mesh is often overlooked by modelers, leading to undesirable results when a character makes extreme expressions with his or her mouth. A strong laugh line is key to successful deformations, so it's always a good idea to get it in place early on. **Figure 9.19** shows the progression of extending the laugh line geometry.

[Figure 9.19] The laugh line poly flow plays a substantial role in good deformations through a wide range of a character's facial expressions.

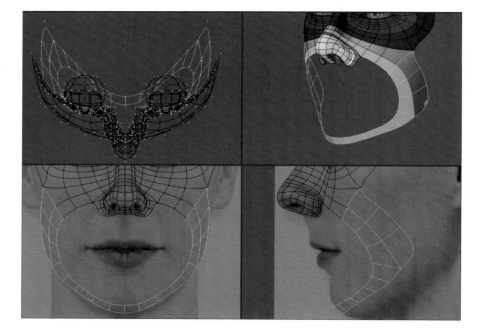

Mouth

Many modelers will continue to extend off the nose to create the mouth, but I've found that it's much more efficient to build the mouth separately in the same fashion as I built the eyes. I started with a flat plane, sliced it into 12 polygons, and pushed points to shape the geometry to the reference images. The result of this process is shown in **Figure 9.20**.

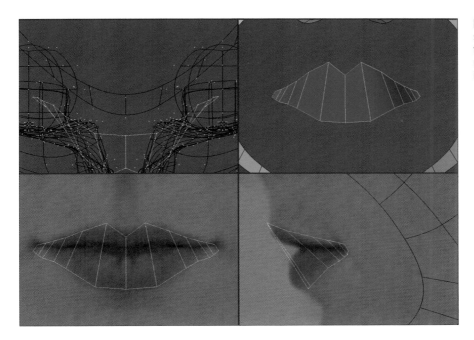

[Figure 9.20] Using a separate piece of geometry for the mouth produces results quicker than extending from the nose region.

I beveled the mouth polys six times to create the lips and the inside of the mouth. Each time I beveled, I adjusted the points to conform to the reference. It's important to not be in a rush when adding new geometry and to take the time to refine the mesh as you go. **Figure 9.21** shows the result of these six bevels with refinement.

With the lips in place, I selected the open edges that made up the mouth and extended them three times. These edge loops are important because they will allow for smooth deformations to take place around the mouth.

I connected the six polygons located in the top center to the nose region of the face, extended the remaining open edges of the mouth twice, and connected the new geometry to the bordering polygons to create a seamless mesh. The results are shown in **Figure 9.22**.

[Figure 9.21] Similar to the eye-sack technique, beveling the mouth geometry to create the lips is a trick I've used for years and saves production time.

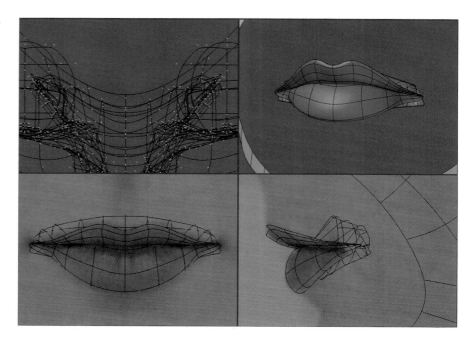

[Figure 9.22] The edge loops around the mouth allow for clean deformations in that region when animated.

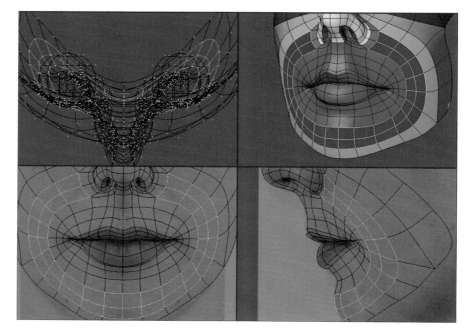

Jawline

When a character opens his or her mouth, it requires the entire jaw to hinge open. I've found that creating a row of polygons that follows along the jawline, although not 100 percent necessary, can be a safe bet for good deformations. So, I extended jawline polygons off of the laugh line and then extended the row up to the ear.

With the jawline in place, I completed the area by extending polygons and connecting them to their neighboring polys. **Figure 9.23** shows the results.

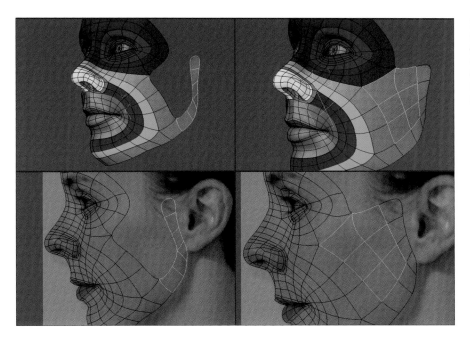

[Figure 9.23] Creating poly flow along the jaw can help define the jawline. Extending polygons and connecting them to their neighboring polys finishes off that region of the face.

Before moving on to the ear, I wanted to finish off the face mask, also referred to as the *death mask* region of the face, by adding a forehead. I simply extended off the eye mask edges and connected to the jawline. Note that the polygon shown in blue in **Figure 9.24** was used to reduce the forehead geometry from flowing into the jaw area. Although I only saved one row of polygons, every polygon counts at render time, so avoid any unneeded geometry whenever possible.

[Figure 9.24] Terminating rows of geometry where it is not needed allows for localized detail and a cleaner mesh.

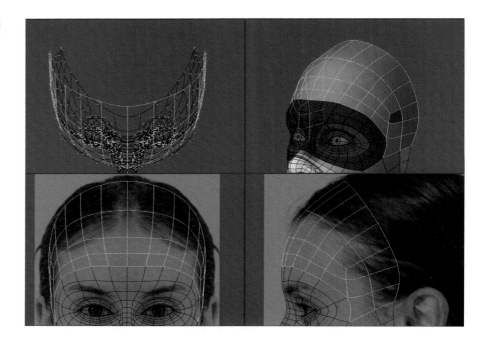

Ears

Many artists struggle with modeling ears, but I think it has nothing to do with the difficulty and everything to do with psyching themselves out before they begin. If it helps, don't think of the shape as an ear but simply as an organic form that has specific shapes. I always start modeling an ear the same way when using the edge extend method and used the same technique on this mesh. I started by mapping out the outer rim of the ear (the helix), as shown in **Figure 9.25**).

With the helix in place, I spent a few minutes patching in the inner ear based on the reference. Polygon flow is far from important when dealing with the inner ear, but sticking to an all-quad mesh is always desirable. **Figure 9.26** shows the inner ear base mesh completed.

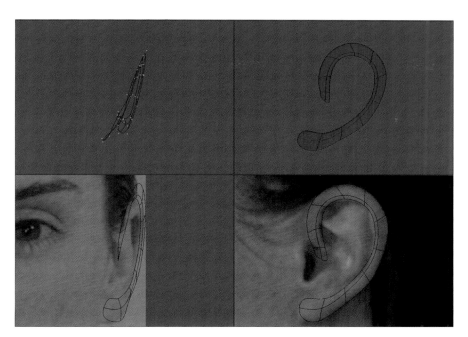

[Figure 9.25] Starting with the helix allows you to define the borders of the ear.

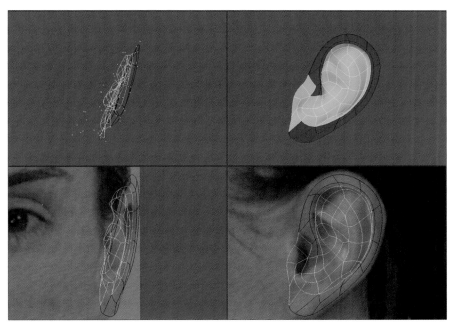

[Figure 9.26] Poly flow is not important when creating the inner polygons of the ear because it doesn't undergo the same level of deformation as the face.

Next up was creating the external auditory canal. I selected the geometry shown in green in **Figure 9.27**, beveled it twice, and adjusted the mesh to create the canal.

[Figure 9.27] Depth in the auditory canal will add realism to your ear.

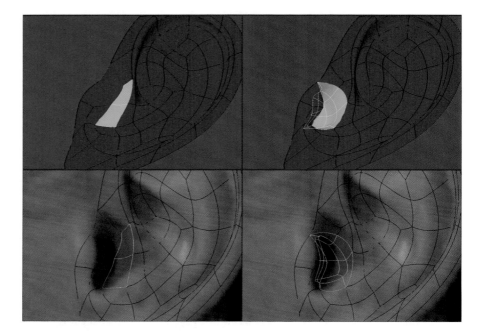

To finish off the ear, I extended the outer edges of the ear three times, wrapping the new geometry around to the back of the ear. Extending the edges off the ear and connecting them to the face mask allowed me to create a seamless integration of the components, as shown in **Figure 9.28**.

Finishing Off the Head

With the eyes, nose, mouth, and ears completed, I had light work ahead of me. Starting with the open edges on the forehead, I extended 11 times, connecting the newly created geometry to its bordering polygons with each extension until I reached the base of the neck. The result is shown in **Figure 9.29**.

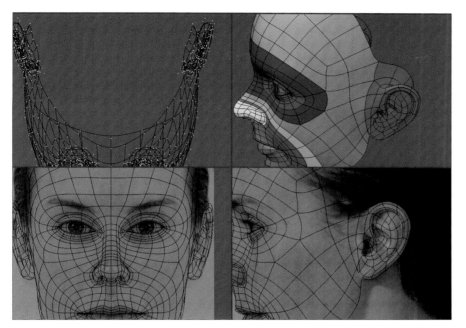

[Figure 9.28] Creating the back side of the ear is a snap by simply extending the outer rim of the ear. With the ear completed and connected to the rest of the face, the most detailed regions of the head are now complete.

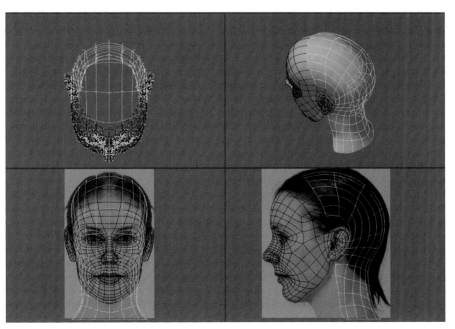

[Figure 9.29] Keep the poly-count low for the back of the head because there is little to no detail needed.

I continued the process off of the jawline to create the throat area and finish off the neck (**Figure 9.30**).

[Figure 9.30] Give yourself enough segments in the throat area to allow for subtle deformations when a character is talking or swallowing.

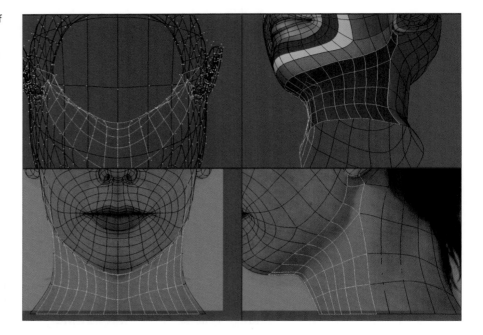

With all of the head's geometry in place, I went ahead and resurfaced the mesh to get a better look at what I had created. The final result is shown in **Figure 9.31**.

Using this edge extend method of modeling a head, you'll spend only 10 percent of your time creating new geometry and 90 percent pushing and pulling points into their proper place. This technique is quite straightforward and allows you to move quickly. Getting proper flow in your geometry is as simple as placing the polygons where you want them, and at its core, that is what makes this technique so favorable to modeling from background images.

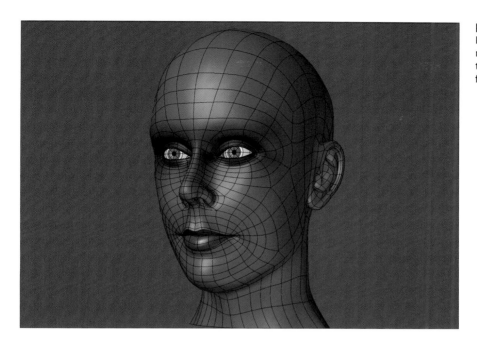

[Figure 9.31] In short order I've created an all-quad mesh with clean poly flow that will hold up during facial animation.

Head Modeling Exercise

Now that you've seen the process of creating a realistic head model using the edge extend method, take reference photos of any willing person and create a CG double of that person. Not only will it be a good learning experience, but you will create a mesh that might come in handy on future projects when a generic character head is needed.

Remember to be mindful of poly-count and polygon flow, and constantly reference your photos to stay on mark. After you have created two or three head models, the process will become second nature.

CHAPTER TEN

Modeling a Stylized Character

Whether I'm working from another artist's concept or pulling from my own imagination, I love building 3D characters. Without a doubt, digital character modeling is what attracted me to the animation industry, and it's what has kept me satisfied as an artist, creatively and professionally, to this day. I've literally created hundreds of 3D character models, ranging from realistic to cartoon, but I have a passion for creating stylized characters. I like the idea of creating something that the world has never seen before—something that nobody could simply take a picture of.

Although it's good practice to have clean geometry in every mesh that you create, it's extremely important when building a character model. Creating a digital character model is one thing; creating a character that is easy to rig, texture, and animate, and renders properly is a different matter altogether. Every aspect of your model needs to have good topology with a manageable poly-count to make your mesh production ready. Simply put, character models need to consist of squeaky-clean geometry.

 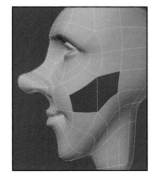 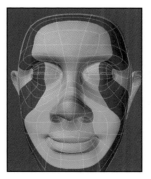 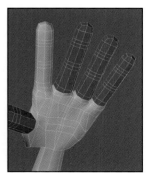

In this chapter, I show you one of the techniques I use to quickly create a complete, stylized, biped character model. I take you through the process of building clean geometry and show you how to find the form and detail of a character, starting from a simple box primitive. Although I demonstrate this technique on a cartoon-style character, it can be applied to any number of styles, including realistic. This technique is also not limited to character modeling, so feel free to explore the possibilities once you have an understanding of this method.

Box Modeling a Character Mesh

Box modeling is my favorite modeling method, and I find that it's my go-to solution when building characters. Most times, I can box model a character faster than creating a 2D drawing of the same subject, making this method ideal not only for quickly developing character concepts, but also for producing finished meshes ready for production.

When I worked on Pixar's animated short *Partly Cloudy*, I used the box modeling method to create an array of cute animals and props in a variety of shapes and details. **Figure 10.1** shows a few of the characters you might recognize from the film.

When employing the box modeling technique, I find that I only use a handful of tools. Doing this allows me to focus on the creative aspects of modeling more than the technical aspects, while still delivering a clean mesh ready for production. For this modeling example, I didn't work with reference material; instead, I chose to build a biped male character from my imagination while keeping the following goals in mind:

- Create an all-quad mesh with localized detail.

- Use subdivision surfaces.

- Build a clean mesh with good topology that is ideal for animation.

- Make extensive use of the box modeling method.

[Figure 10.1] Working from a 2D artist's concepts, I box modeled these characters for Pixar's *Partly Cloudy*.

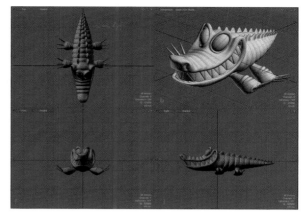

All images ©Disney/Pixar

Getting Started

When starting a character model without reference, I prefer to start with the head. I find that the head drives the overall design of a character, and once I capture the look I'm after, the rest of the mesh can be child's play. I also like to take advantage of symmetry on my character models, because it means I only have to model half the character and the software handles the other side.

Although you can start with any primitive as a base mesh when box modeling, I usually use a box. It's extremely low poly and gives me an all-quad mesh to start with. To start the head, I created a simple box primitive and subdivided it to gain access to more polygons and to round off the base shape (**Figure 10.2**). Don't make the same mistake many modelers do and subdivide the mesh multiple times at this early stage. Keep the mesh as light as possible for as long as possible. The lighter the mesh, the easier it is to define the shape and make broad changes throughout your model. I like to dictate where every polygon is being created, and subdividing the mesh multiple times would produce unnecessary geometry in many areas.

[Figure 10.2] Subdividing a box gives a rounder shape and a few more polygons to work with to construct the head mesh.

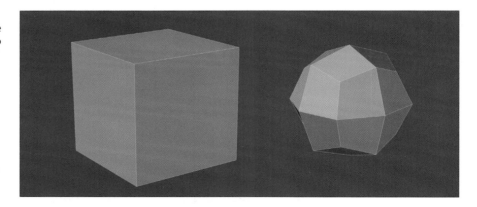

With that said, I did need more geometry to define the shape of this character's head. I started by extending two of the quads on the lower portion of the base mesh to create the mouth and chin area. With this simple step, I could already see a basic head shape taking form. **Figure 10.3** shows the results of the new geometry created.

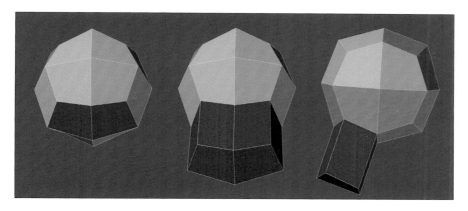

[Figure 10.3] Extending two polygons from the bottom of the base mesh created the mouth and chin area of the head (left to right).

I still needed more geometry to work with, so I added a segment through the mouth area and edge beveled the segment that ran through where I envisioned adding the eyes. I added another segment through the newly created eye row of polygons that would act as a center line for where the eyes would be placed. I then edge beveled the segment running down the center of the head to produce a new row of polygons that could act as the bridge of the nose, give me more geometry for the mouth, and help shape the forehead and the back of the head. **Figure 10.4** shows the results of these steps.

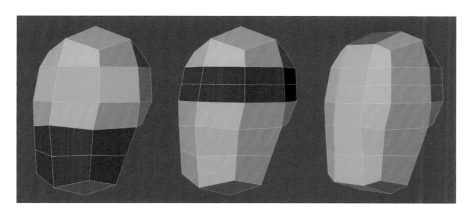

[Figure 10.4] I started laying the framework for the face by adding new segments to the base mesh. I cut through the areas in pink and edge beveled the segments to generate the areas in green (left to right).

At this point, I wanted to keep any new polygon creation localized and not add any unneeded geometry to the back of the head. I turned my focus to the eye area and added a new segment running through the border of the face.

I reshaped the eye area and then defined that region of the face by extending the geometry twice. This gave me the area I like to call the *eye mask*. **Figure 10.5** shows this process.

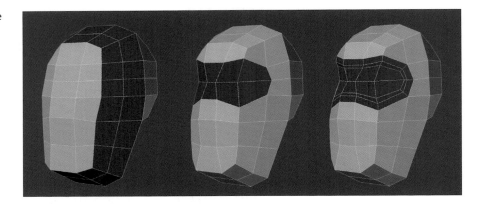

I avoided adding any more detail to the eyes and moved on to the nose. I used a technique that I developed years ago that is the quickest way I know to create the base nose shape. I simply selected an upside-down T configuration in the polys and extended them to produce the entire nose structure in one step. Unlike the other areas of the nose, I wanted the top portion (the root) to flow smoothly into the forehead. To do this, I reconfigured the geometry by spinning one edge on each side of the forehead and then tweaked points. Every 3D application has at least one tool that can perform this action, but each may call it something different. Some common names are SpinQuads, Flip Edge, Spin Edge, and Rotate Edge. **Figure 10.6** shows these four steps.

It's never too early to have topology in mind when creating a mesh, so the next area I concentrated on was the character's laugh line. A lot of artists forget to include a row of polygons that borders the mouth and nose, and also crosses over the bridge of the nose. This geometry mimics the underlying muscles in the face, allowing for clean deformations when the character speaks and makes expressions. All that was required for me to create this necessary feature was to spin one edge to redirect the polygon flow, thus producing a clean edge loop (**Figure 10.7**).

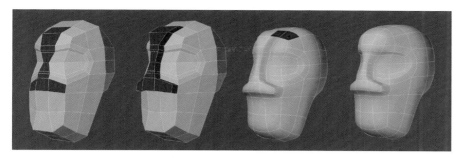

[**Figure 10.6**] The entire base shape of the nose was produced by simply extruding the shape out of the base mesh and spending a few seconds tweaking the newly created geometry (left to right).

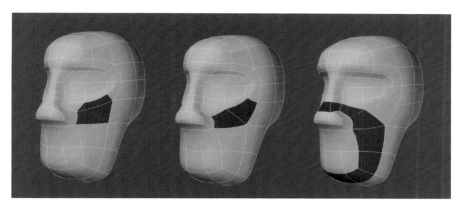

[**Figure 10.7**] Reconfiguring the polygon flow to produce a clean edge loop for the laugh line was as simple as spinning one edge (left to right).

Hopefully, you are starting to see the power of spinning edges to rapidly produce clean polygon flow. It truly is my secret weapon when box modeling, and once you've mastered the process, you'll gain full control over the topology of your mesh.

I wanted to flesh out the character's face more, so I extended the base of the nose to give it more shape (**Figure 10.8**).

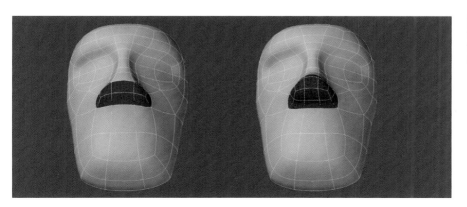

[**Figure 10.8**] Extending the nose geometry allowed for a rounder shape (left to right).

The template for the face was almost complete. The only thing left to create was the mouth. I selected the six polygons located just inside the laugh line, extended them, and tweaked the points to produce a rough mouth shape. **Figure** 10.9 shows the process.

With all the facial elements prepped to be detailed, I added a neck by extending a group of polygons on the bottom of the head twice and reshaping them (**Figure** 10.10).

[Figure 10.9] The rough shape of the mouth was created by extending and tweaking the geometry (left to right).

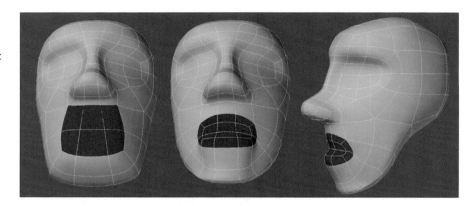

[Figure 10.10] Adding the neck allowed me to get a better idea of what I was going to do with the character's jawline (left to right).

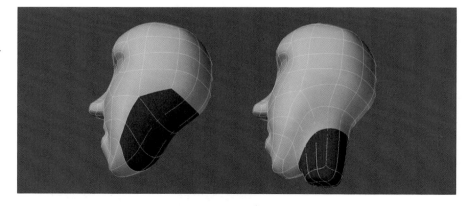

Detailing the Face

Next, I refocused my attention on the character's eyes and extended the eye socket geometry a few times to form basic eyelids (**Figure 10.11**). I wasn't concerned with how many segments were needed. I was more interested in the size and shape of the eyes.

With the basic shape of the eyes in place, I decided to finish off the nose. I extended the nostrils, added an additional segment through the nose, and reconfigured the geometry to get the shape I was after. **Figure 10.12** shows the result. As with every area I detailed, I kept any addition to poly-count localized to that area. Doing so keeps the mesh light while still gaining needed polygons to get the shapes you're looking for.

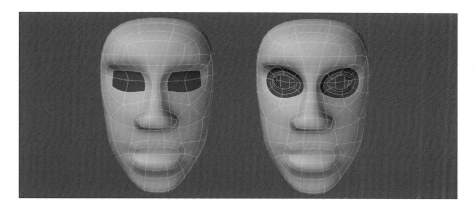

[**Figure 10.11**] Extending the geometry that made up the eye sockets a few times allowed me to form the character's eyelids (left to right).

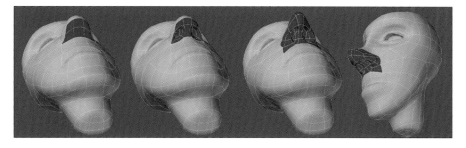

[**Figure 10.12**] Additional geometry needed for the nose was added locally instead of throughout the entire mesh (left to right).

Creating the mouth involved the same process used on the eyes. I simply extended the mouth geometry a few times and adjusted the points until I was satisfied with the shape of the lips (**Figure 10.13**).

[Figure 10.13] The mouth was created using the same process that produced the eyes (left to right).

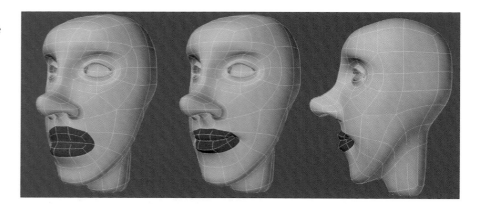

With the eyes, nose, and mouth looking good, I spent a couple of minutes reshaping the brow and forehead. No new geometry was created at this time— I was simply pushing points around to define the shape I was after. I find that I spend 90 percent of my time pushing points and only 10 percent creating new points to push. It's important to adjust the geometry as you build. This adjustment allows you to make changes more quickly, defining the character as you build instead of at the end of the modeling process. **Figure 10.14** shows the transformation of the forehead and brow area.

[Figure 10.14] Tweaking the points' placements on the brow and forehead gave me the shape I was after and made for a more interesting look for the character (left to right).

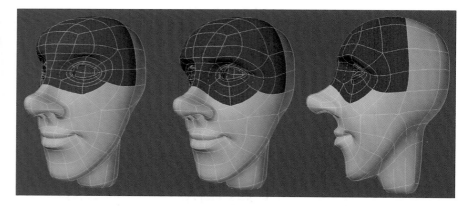

Before moving on to the ear, I wanted to do a little house cleaning on the side of the face. I knew it would be easier to tackle before the ear was in place, so I started by changing the polygon flow with a single spin edge. This created undesirable topology where the base of the ear would sit, so I chased the config-uration past the ear area and to the back of the head. *Chasing* refers to spinning edges to move a particular polygon configuration from one area to another. You don't remove the layout, you simply give it a new home. **Figure 10.15** shows this process.

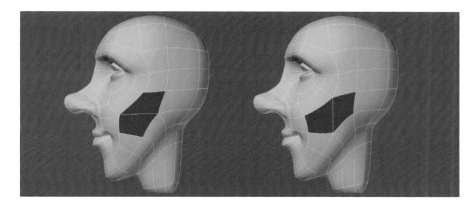

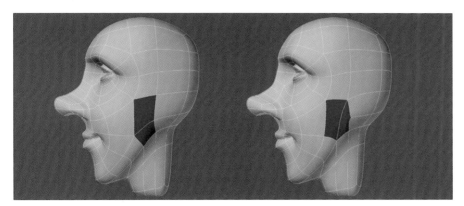

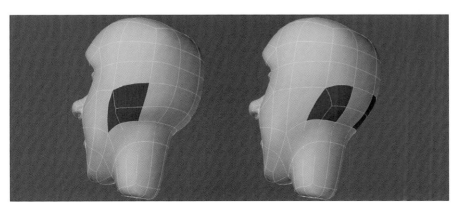

[Figure 10.15]
Reconfiguring the side of the head's topology produces much cleaner polygon flow and creates a nice edge loop from the chin to the top of the head (left to right).

While I was in cleanup mode, I reconfigured the neck geometry to produce cleaner topology. This required spinning a few edges (**Figure 10.16**).

At this point I realized that I had forgotten an important detail on the eye geometry. Although I liked the shape of the eyes, I didn't create enough segments to produce clean deformations when animated. One of the easiest ways to check for this is to model the eyelids closed. The last thing you want to do is deliver a mesh missing key segments to the rigging department that limits its ability to make your model shine during animation. That's a situation where everyone loses, and it's easily avoidable. **Figure 10.17** shows the newly created segments and the character with his eyelids closed.

[Figure 10.16] Spinning a few of the edges in the neck produced a cleaner mesh with better topology (left to right).

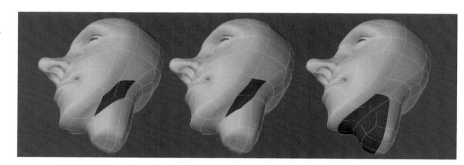

[Figure 10.17] Adding two new segments around the eyes allows for clean deformations when the eyes are opened and closed (left to right).

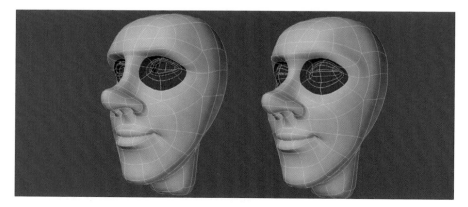

When it comes to box modeling, one of my favorite areas of a character's head is the ear. I have a prime spot picked out for where I want the ear to be. I want the top of the ear to be in line with the corner of the eye and the bottom to line up just under the character's nose. I only need two polygons to create an ear that can have any level of detail, from cartoon to realistic, but this character looked like he needed a stylized ear to go with the rest of his cartoony features.

I started off the ear by extending the two polygons a few times to create the basic shape and to give me more geometry to work with. You can see this process in **Figure 10.18**.

I wanted a more defined shape to the ear, so I extended a patch of polygons at the top of the ear and spent some time reconfiguring the geometry by spinning edges and pushing points until I was happy with the results. **Figure 10.19** shows the progression of the ear being refined.

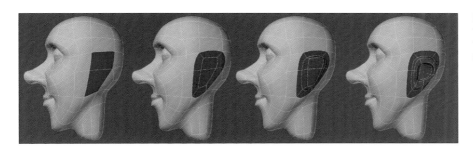

[Figure 10.18] Extending the two polygons a few times creates the basic shape of the ear (left to right).

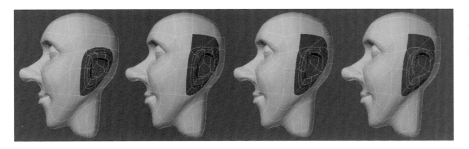

[Figure 10.19] Extending the patch of polygons at the top of the ear allowed for the refining of the shape of the ear (left to right).

I thought the design of the ear was fitting for the character, but I wanted to give you an idea of how the same two polygons could produce a more detailed ear using the same process I just covered. **Figure 10.20** shows the result of a few more minutes of extending, spinning edges, and pushing points.

[Figure 10.20] Any level of detail can be added to the ear by extending patches of geometry, spinning edges, and pushing points.

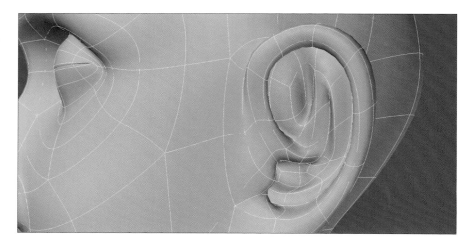

With the ear polished (and a backup ear with more detail saved), I wanted to add a few more segments to the head and neck before moving on to the body. I started by adding a segment to the neck and refining the shape. I thought it was too thick for the character design, so I made the circumference smaller (**Figure 10.21**).

[Figure 10.21] Adding a new segment through the neck allowed me to create a skinnier neck that was more fitting for this character design.

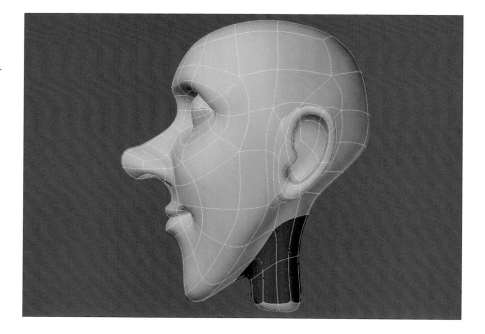

I finished off the head by adding two new segments to the face. The first segment was added to the chin, cheeks, eyelids, and forehead through one edge loop. I wanted to give myself more control points to work with when deforming the character for facial expressions during animation.

The second segment was added to the laugh line to ensure that I had the rule of three in place. The basic idea of the *rule of three* is to have a hold segment on either side of the segment through which the deformation will take place. In the case of the laugh line, the center segment creates the crease in the face, whereas the outer segments hold the cheeks and mouth in place. **Figure 10.22** shows the new segments that were added to the face.

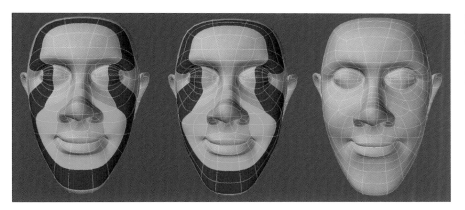

[Figure 10.22] Two new segments added to the face allow for more control points to aid in facial deformations during animation (left to right).

Building the Body

This character was in need of a tall, lanky body to match his thin goofy face. I selected the polygons that made up the base of the neck and extended them several times to give myself enough segments to shape the body. Once I roughed out the shape of the chest, midsection, and pelvic area, I selected the polygons that made up the shoulder and hips, merged them into n-gons, and converted them to polygonal mode (non-SubDs). **Figure 10.23** shows the result of this process.

[Figure 10.23] Creating the body out of the neck is a quick task. It's important to use the time you save to tweak the newly created geometry to get the shape of the body right before moving on to the next step (left to right).

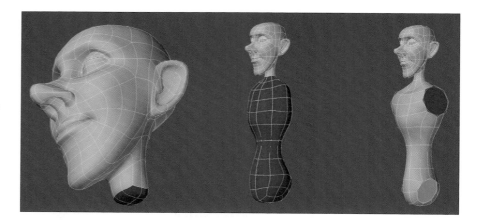

Converting the shoulder and hip geometry to polygonal n-gons allows me to focus on the shape of the torso. This conversion also ensures that the point placement of the hips and shoulders are evenly distributed into a circular shape before creating the arms and legs.

The next step was to create the arms. I extended the n-gon at the shoulder several times, refining the shape with each extension. I made it a point to add the rule of three at the shoulder and elbow to ensure that proper deformations would occur during animation. **Figure 10.24** shows the results.

[Figure 10.24] When creating arms on a character, it's important to include the rule of three for the shoulders and elbows to produce proper deformations during animation.

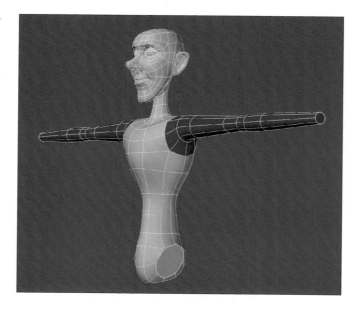

I used the same process to create the legs for the character, making sure that I added the rule of three at the hips and the knees. I also used my trusty underwear rule. The *underwear rule* is a good way to check to see if your character's pelvic area will hold up during animation. Basically, if you can select polygons that are in the shape of a swimsuit or underwear, you're probably in good shape. Make sure there is a gap of polygons separating each leg and that there is geometry that separates the hip from the belly. I've seen too many character models that don't have this topology, and it usually ends in disaster when rigging and animating. **Figure 10.25** shows the results of creating the leg geometry, as well as the underwear rule in action.

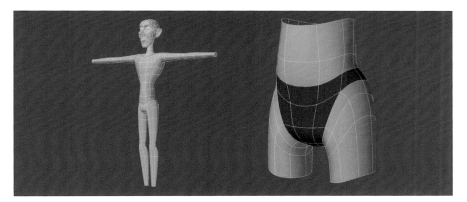

[Figure 10.25] Always remember the rule of three for the hips and knees, and check to see if you have proper flow for the pelvic area.

With all four limbs of the character created, I extended the feet out of the end of the legs and reshaped them to look like they were wearing socks. I made sure that I included the rule of three at the ankle and the base of the toes. Most artists remember to add the segments at the ankles but miss the hold segments for the toes, causing the foot to deform in an unrealistic way when animated. It's important to put just as much care and thought into something as simple as a foot as you would the character's face. **Figure 10.26** shows the feet being created.

[Figure 10.26] The ankle and base of the toes require the rule of three for solid-looking deformations (left to right).

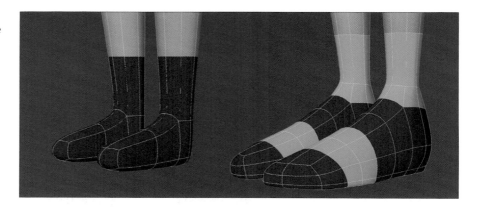

Give 'em a Hand

Before growing the hand out of the wrist, I needed to convert the n-gons that I created earlier back into four-point polygons. Having n-gons on a mesh that will deform during animation is a disaster waiting to happen. N-gons, like triangles, tend to produce pinching and render errors on the surface of the mesh when manipulated during animation. You should always strive for your mesh to consist of all-quad polys if deformation will take place. **Figure 10.27** shows the process of converting the n-gons into triangles and then merging them into four quad polys.

[Figure 10.27] Converting the n-gons to quads allows for the hand to be extended with the proper polygon configuration (top to bottom).

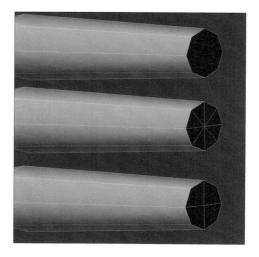

To create the base shape of the palm and top of the hand, I extended the wrist geometry once and then extended the sides of the palm out to add some width and enough geometry to create four fingers. **Figure 10.28** shows these steps.

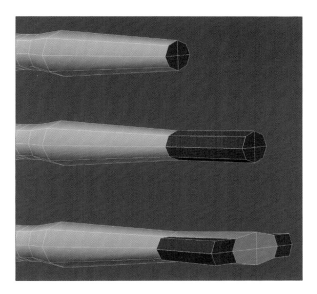

[**Figure 10.28**] Extending the wrist geometry allows for easy creation of the palm and top of the hand (top to bottom).

I needed more geometry to work with to produce the nice, round cartoon fingers I wanted for the character. To do this, I added segments to the ends of the hand. I created four n-gons on the top and four on the bottom of the hand. This was only a temporary measure that I would need to address at some point to get the model back to its all-quad topology. These new segments are shown in **Figure 10.29**.

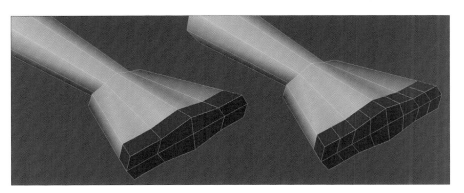

[**Figure 10.29**] Adding additional segments allows for rounder fingers to be created from the hand (left to right).

Using the same technique that I used on the shoulders and hips, I created the base for the four fingers (**Figure 10.30**).

[Figure 10.30] Taking the time to reshape the base of the fingers makes light work of actually growing the fingers later (left to right).

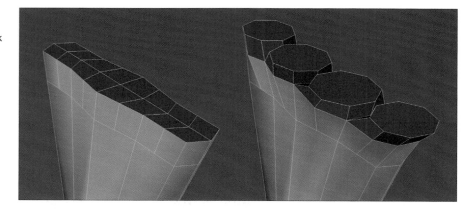

Before adding the base of the thumb, I needed two more segments running through the hand, so I added them and reshaped the hand to make it less boxy. **Figure 10.31** shows the results.

[Figure 10.31] Additional segments were added to the palm in preparation for the base of the thumb and to produce a less boxy hand shape (left to right).

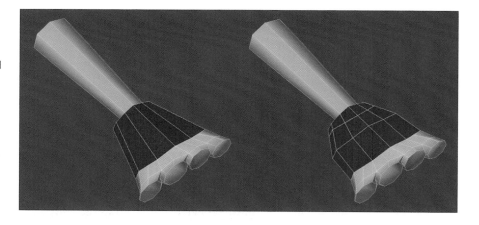

The base of the thumb was created, and the hand geometry was adjusted. My goal was to create what looked like a hand that had its fingers cut off. **Figure 10.32** shows the resulting mesh.

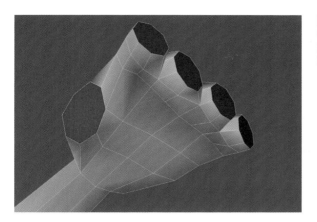

[Figure 10.32] The base of the thumb was added to prepare for creating all five phalanges.

Before growing the fingers and thumb out of the hand, I wanted to clean up the n-gons I created earlier. I started by converting each n-gon into a quad and triangle combination on both the top and palm of the hand. **Figure 10.33** shows the result of the conversion on the palm of the hand.

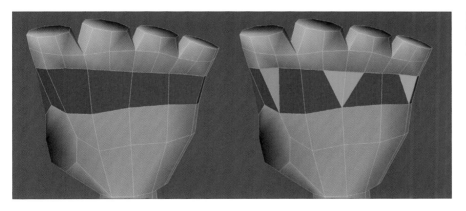

[Figure 10.33] To remove the n-gons created earlier, a quad-triangle combination was used (left to right).

I also wanted to add a gap between each finger to allow them to deform better when spread open during animation. To do this, I created an edge bevel down the top and palm of the hand. **Figure 10.34** shows the result of the edge bevels on the palm of the hand.

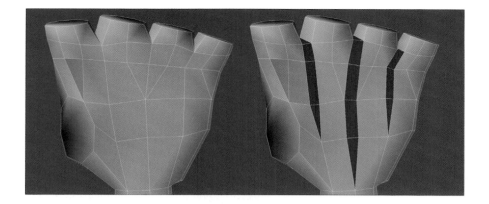

I prefer my meshes to be made up of all quads, because they deform better
and transfer between different software packages much easier. At this point,
the hand was unacceptable in this regard, so I created new edges that converted all of the triangles into quads. **Figure 10.35** shows the conversion.
The topology was far from ideal, but I planned to address the issues once I had
the entire hand in place. At this point, I knew I was halfway there with the
mesh being made up of all quads.

[Figure 10.35] Adding
edges to the mesh allows
for all of the triangles to
be converted to quads (left
to right).

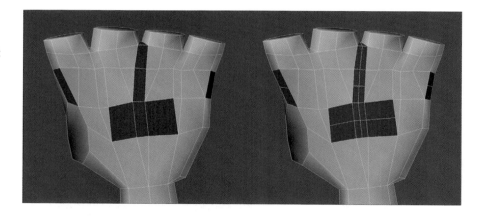

I was ready to add fingers to the hand, so I started with the index finger.
Because I prepped the base of the fingers early by making them round, all
that was left to do was extend several times and convert the tip from an
n-gon to quads, using the same technique I showed for the wrist earlier. I made
sure to include the rule of three for each joint on the finger before moving

on to the other fingers. **Figure 10.36** shows the progression of all the fingers being created.

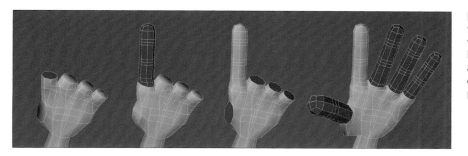

[Figure 10.36] Growing the fingers out of the hand was an easy task because I prepped the geometry at the base of the fingers earlier during the modeling process (left to right).

With all the geometry created for the hands, it was time for a bit of cleanup on the palm and top of the hand. The first issue that needed to be addressed was the shape. The thumb was a little too close to the index finger, and the palm was too short. Both issues were easy to address by simply moving the thumb towards the body of the character and pulling all four fingers away from the body. I also added a third segment to the wrist to apply the rule of three.

I then turned my focus on the topology of the mesh. Spinning several of the edges and pushing points, I reconfigured the geometry to create better polygon flow, thus allowing for better deformations when animated. **Figure 10.37** shows where the hands started and what they looked like after they had been reconfigured. By using this topology, I was able to transition from 28 polygons on the edge loop located at the knuckles down to 8 polygons at the wrist. This should be a shining example of how you can add localized details on any model without adding unnecessary geometry elsewhere on the mesh.

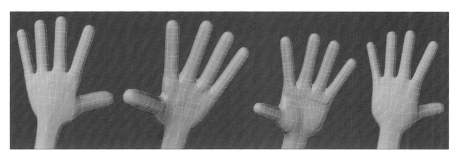

[Figure 10.37] Taking the time to reconfigure the hand's topology pays off when the character is rigged and animated. The original mesh is on the left, and the final topology of the hand is on the right.

The great thing about modeling hands is that you have reference "handy" at all times. Be sure to create multiple shapes with your hands when referencing them to see how they deform in the various poses. This will give you an idea of where you should place edge loops for deformation.

Final Character Review

With the hands completed, I had a full character modeled, and took some time to review the mesh. I always like taking a break from the mesh at this point so that I can come back with a fresh set of eyes and look for anything I may have missed. Some particulars that I look for include:

- If I'm working from reference material, does the mesh match the reference?
- Did I include the rule of three in all the right areas?
- Is 100 percent of the mesh created out of four-point polygons?
- Does the mesh have proper polygon density?
- Is the mesh in the proper pose for rigging? (T-pose or relaxed pose)
- Is the mesh facing in the correct direction with its feet planted at zero on the Y axis?
- Is the mesh the proper scale?
- Does the overall mesh have clean topology?

After my review of the mesh, I was satisfied with the look and structure that I had created. The model consisted of 2,200 quads. Half of those polygons were used on the hands, and less than a quarter on the head. You can check out the final mesh in **Figure 10.38**.

Depending on the production requirements, you may find that the base mesh needs to have a higher density. You can accomplish that by simply subdividing the geometry as many times as required to hit your target density. **Figure 10.39** shows the character after being subdivided once. Be sure to save a version of the object before subdividing it so you can always go back and make broad changes quickly on the lower-resolution mesh.

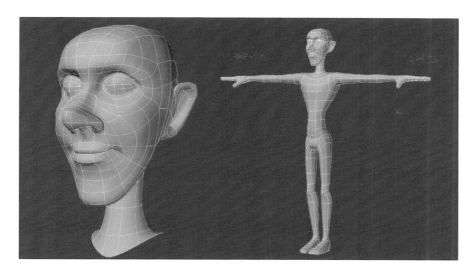

[Figure 10.38] The final mesh is ready for some clothes, hair, and other accessories to add to the character's personality.

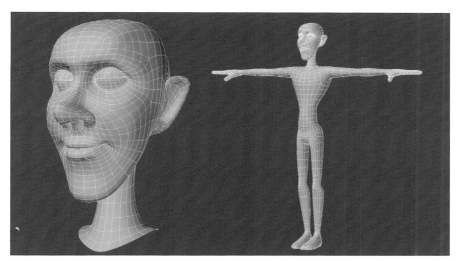

[Figure 10.39] Subdividing the geometry creates a denser mesh, which is sometimes required for production.

Character Modeling Exercise

With box modeling fresh on your mind, create a stylized character using the techniques described and shown in this chapter. Keep in mind all of the details I covered to ensure that you create a clean mesh with proper polygon flow. Once you have the base figure created, begin adding details like hair, clothes, shoes, and so on. Continue enhancing your box modeling skills by starting some of these elements with other primitives, such as a ball or a disc.

CHAPTER ELEVEN

Product Modeling for Print Graphics

Product modeling has always been big business in the visualization market of the industry. Within the last ten years, product modeling has exploded into the world of print graphics with CG renders of digital models replacing the majority of product imagery. Working with digital artists gives an art director the ability to produce imagery that would be extremely difficult or impossible to achieve with traditional photography and in some cases can be more cost-effective.

Almost all product photographs must be retouched to eliminate a variety of problems: Reflections of studio equipment, such as cameras and lights; seams and other subtle manufacturing imperfections; and unwanted shadows are just a small sample of the undesirable elements that come with using the traditional method of presenting a product. Because cameras and lights in CGI can provide illumination without physically appearing in reflections, 3D-generated images are extremely clean and typically require little, if any, post processing. This makes digital modeling the ideal solution for generating picture-perfect product imagery. The same 3D assets can be used to produce animated sequences for product displays and promotional materials, thus providing greater flexibility and cost-effectiveness.

 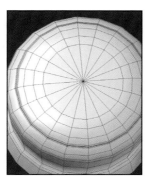  

In this chapter, using the spline patch modeling method I walk you through the process of creating a digital model of a product with a clean mesh that is ideal for high-resolution imagery.

Building a Better Product

Although I've digitally reproduced many products for clients over the years, ranging from vehicles, industrial equipment, computer hardware, and more, the majority of my digital product modeling has fallen into the consumer packaging market for print graphics. This includes boxes, blister packs, cans, bags, bottles, and more. Bottles tend to be the most interesting to model. Over time, they have grown in complexity, making them an ideal challenge for even the seasoned digital modeler.

Even though some digital models created for other markets in the industry, such as feature film, can hold up to the extremely high resolutions of product print graphics, most models can't. Here are a few details that separate product print models from the rest:

- Unlike other markets, you usually want to avoid dirt, grime, scratches, dents, and other wear that usually help sell a digital model as being realistic. I like to add a little waviness to the paneling of a car to help add realism, for example.

  For product shots, in most cases you're trying to achieve a hyper-realism with flawless qualities. CG artists are used to adding in the details that photo-retouchers get paid handsomely to remove. Without all those details to sell a model as real, the challenge then becomes to fine-tune surfacing and lighting, and to create an environment for the object to reflect and refract.

- Avoid adding details like manufacturing seam lines, embossed product codes, and any other imperfections in the surface of the product. **Figure 11.1** shows examples of details you'd want to avoid modeling for a product shot.

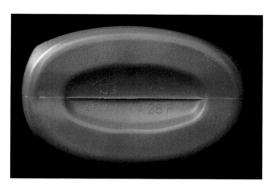

[Figure 11.1] Although details like manufacturing seams would add realism to the model, they are best avoided when creating a product shot for print.

- Subdivision surfaces (SubDs) have become a requirement of sorts to ensure that no faceting will appear at render time. Building meshes with SubDs allows you to work with a manageable polygon count while modeling, and affords you the ability to render with incredibly high poly-counts and resolution independence.

- Tertiary model details like micro-bevels become required for product shots, because any edges without them will be obvious and will make the mesh appear as CG.

- Your goal should always be to create a clean mesh for every project—when modeling for print, that goal becomes imperative. You have to model as if every area will be seen under a microscope. Any pinching, creasing, or other imperfections in the model's surface caused by bad polygon flow or the use of triangles, n-gons, or poorly distributed geometry will stick out like a sore thumb when viewed at extremely high resolutions.

You're not re-creating reality when you produce a model for product shots; you're creating an ideal version of the object that can fool the viewer into thinking it's real. Simply put: perception is, indeed, reality.

Think about it this way: How many times have you ordered a meal at a restaurant based solely on the photo in the menu, only to be disappointed when it is delivered to your table? The difference between the photograph and the meal you were served is that all the tricks in the book were probably used to make the photograph look good. This could include using white glue instead of milk, motor oil instead of syrup, and spray deodorant on fruit to give it a frosty veneer—and let's not forget what the power of Photoshop affords us.

Although you could create hundreds of bottles with just a primitive and a few simple steps, for this modeling walkthrough, I chose a stylish plastic bottle design that consists of several compound and reverse curves similar to what you'd find on most modern vehicles.

Compound curves normally consist of two curves joined together and curving in the same direction, whereas *reverse* curves consist of two curves joined together but curving in the opposite direction. Simply put, this bottle has a complex surface with a lot of curves that flow into each other seamlessly.

Reference: CAD Geometry, Photos, and Blueprints

The three common reference types you will usually receive from a client when tasked with the creation of a product model are CAD geometry, photos, and blueprints. CAD geometry is rarely suitable for rendering directly, because its polygon density is usually notoriously high, but it can serve as a perfect template from which to build a new, clean model. I have found it rare that a client supplies CAD data, but it's always a good idea to ask if it can be made available to you.

Photographs are the most common reference but are rarely ideal because they often have lens distortions that change the overall shape of the product. **Figure 11.2** shows an example of this type of distortion. This can lead to the digital model not being 100 percent accurate, and although the average person won't catch the discrepancy, the client definitely will.

Blueprints are my weapon of choice for product modeling when available. They give you a clean template to build from and are usually more accurate than photos. If photos are supplied, consider using them as a template to create your own blueprint, which would allow you to make adjustments to the line art to account for lens distortion. This could prevent some headaches during the modeling stage.

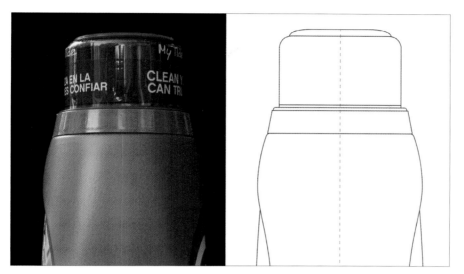

[Figure 11.2] The distortion in the photo of the bottle (left) can cause issues when trying to accurately re-create an object. Using blueprints (right) is more ideal.

For this walkthrough, I used the blueprint shown in **Figure 11.3** as a template to create the bottle. I prepped the reference by creating individual images of the different views so they could be loaded into my 3D software and used in the background to work on top of.

[Figure 11.3] This line art of the bottle was used as a blueprint to model on top of.

Studying the blueprints, I began formulating a plan of attack. There were some areas that I wasn't sure how I would tackle, so I did what any smart artist would do: I contacted my friend Lewis (www.lewis.tomsoft.hr) and had a quick Skype chat. Sometimes discussing a problem with a fellow modeler can be the quickest way to develop a solution. Why go it alone if you can enlist a second problem solver? As the old saying goes, *two heads are better than one.*

After bouncing ideas back and forth, we came to the conclusion that spline patching the basic shape of the mesh was the ideal method for generating the complex, curved surface of the bottle. Spline patching would require me to generate multiple curves, convert those curves to patches of polygons, and refine the mesh with any needed details.

Getting Started: Creating Splines

With the reference prepped and a plan in place, I started by creating individual splines that matched the reference blueprints. At this point, I wasn't concerned with how I was going to break the surface area into polygon patches; I was more interested in capturing the overall shape of the bottle based on the blueprint. Because the bottle is symmetrical in shape, I had to generate splines for only half the object. **Figure 11.4** shows the splines created based on the blueprints.

With the base shape of the bottle outlined, I started adding more splines to create the framework that allowed me to break the surface of the bottle into multiple patch zones. I tried to create each of these zones using four splines so that the polygons that were generated when the splines were patched would consist of all-quad polys. I ended up having to resort to using three splines for a few of the zones, which I knew would generate three-point polygons. I didn't let that slow me down, because I knew I could sort out those areas when the time came. **Figure 11.5** shows the bottle being broken into multiple zones with the creation of additional splines.

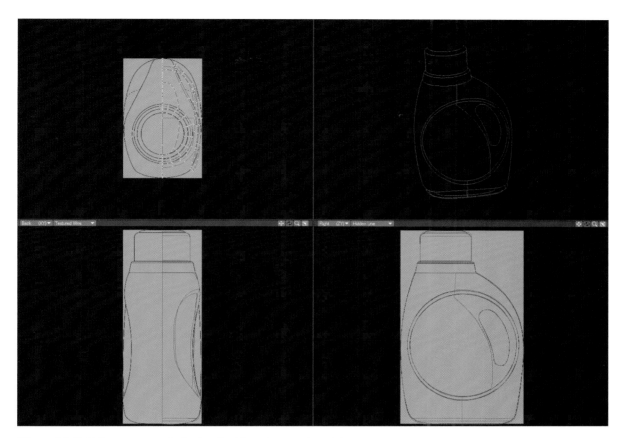

[**Figure 11.4**] Splines were created using the blueprints as a template.

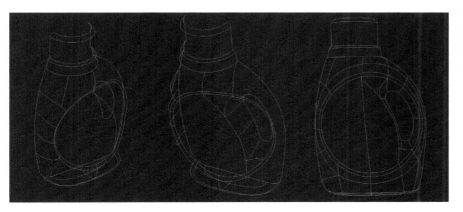

[**Figure 11.5**] Additional splines were created to break the bottle into multiple zones for the next step of patching polygons.

Spline Patching

When I was happy with the spline cage, I began creating polygon patches. Although I could attempt to patch all of the zones in one go, I opted to patch one at a time to keep a close watch on the polygon flow as well as the shapes being generated. I kept the amount of polygons generated to a low number, knowing that the final mesh would take advantage of subdivision surfaces. **Figure 11.6** shows several patches being created.

[Figure 11.6] Patches of polygons were created one zone at a time to ensure that proper polygon flow and a clean mesh were being generated.

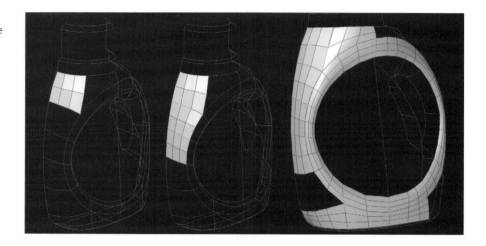

I ran into a zone in the lower-left corner of the bottle that produced undesirable results. I've found that I can spend more time trying to create new splines than if I just patch by hand, so I opted for the latter. Fortunately, this was an easy area to create. I simply bridged the edges from the top to the edges on the bottom, creating three quad polygons. I then cut two new segments into these polys and closed the remaining hole with two quads. These steps are shown in **Figure 11.7**.

With the left side of the bottle complete, I turned to the right side and continued to create patches of polygons using the splines (**Figure 11.8**).

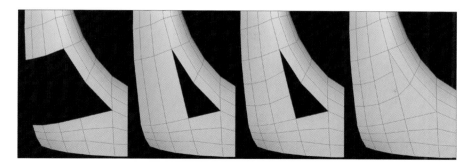

[Figure 11.7] Manually patching this portion of the bottle allowed for a cleaner topology.

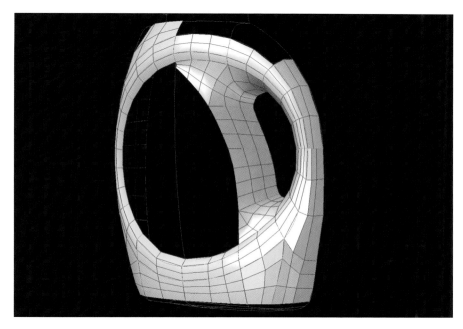

[Figure 11.8] The bottle really started taking shape once the majority of the zones on the right side of the bottle were patched.

I ran into an issue on the lower-right side of the bottle that I wanted to address before moving forward. The lower portion of the bottle required more rows of polygons than the upper part of the handle. Instead of adding a row, I decided to terminate the extra in the upper part to keep the poly-count as low as possible. This created a three-point polygon that I would address at a later time. While I reworked this area, I also did a little housecleaning on the mesh (**Figure 11.9**).

[Figure 11.9] The topology of the mesh on the left was not ideal. With a little reconfiguring of the geometry, I was satisfied with the mesh on the right.

Just when I thought I was in the clear, the top of the bottle gave me a similar issue, so I reworked it as well. **Figure 11.10** shows a before and after of this portion of the bottle's mesh.

[Figure 11.10] Reconfiguring this portion of the mesh produced a cleaner topology and a smoother surface.

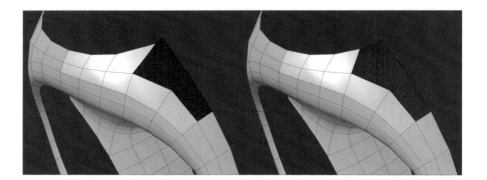

Before I started patching the bottle cap, I went ahead and extended the edges of the mouth portion of the bottle (**Figure 11.11**) to help generate the seam that exists between the base and the cap.

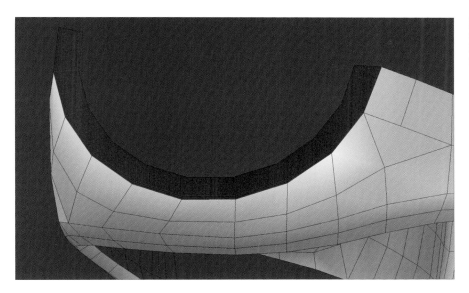

[**Figure 11.11**] Using the edge extend method made light work of the mouth of the bottle.

The cap proved to be the easiest portion, although I'm sure that comes as no surprise. After patching the cap, I created the full cap by mirroring the newly created geometry and then temporarily closed off the top with an n-gon. With the top closed, I beveled the geometry multiple times to achieve the rounded shape that matched the reference. These steps are shown in **Figure 11.12**.

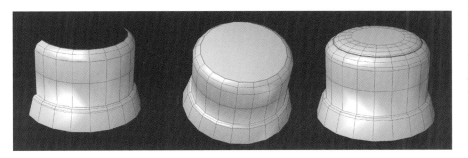

[**Figure 11.12**] After patching half of the cap (left), I mirrored the geometry and closed the top off with an n-gon (middle). Beveling the top multiple times gave me the shape I was after (right).

To clean up the top portion of the cap, I collapsed the n-gon and merged the newly created three-point-polygons to create an all-quad configuration. **Figure 11.13** shows the results of these steps.

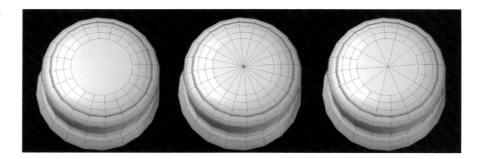

Because the cap was so close to being finished, I went ahead and added the tertiary details to the lower portion by generating several edge bevels to refine the shape. **Figure 11.14** shows the completed cap.

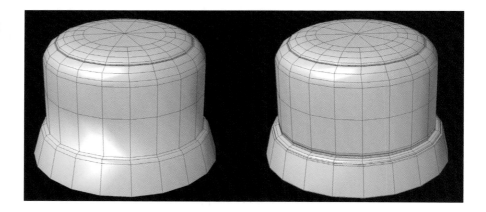

I knew the middle of the bottle was going to be tricky, so I moved to the bottom and patched the outer rim of the base. Because it seemed to work well for the cap, I decided it would be faster to bevel in the rest of the bottom, so I mirrored the entire bottle and then capped of the base with an n-gon. **Figure 11.15** shows the results of these steps.

I created multiple bevels using the blueprint as a guide and then cut in the required edges to convert the n-gon to an all-quad configuration. This process is shown in **Figure 11.16**.

After several failed attempts to generate clean, polygon flow by spline patching to the remaining middle portion of the bottle, I opted to manually create the polygons using the build out method. Because I had the bordering polygons in place and a spline cage and blueprints as a guide, this was surprisingly easy to accomplish. **Figure 11.17** shows the middle of the bottle being created at multiple stages.

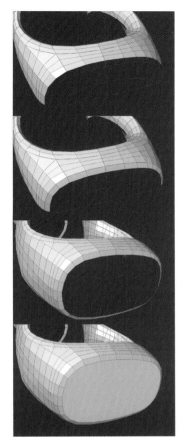

[Figure 11.15] The border of the bottle's base (top) was patched, the entire mesh was mirrored (middle), and the hole was capped with an n-gon (bottom).

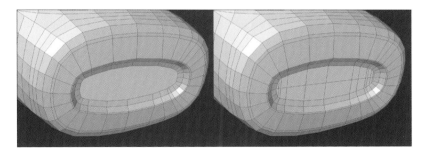

[Figure 11.16] The n-gon was beveled several times (left) and then converted to an all-quad configuration (right).

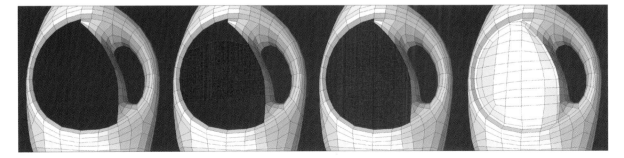

[Figure 11.17] The center of the bottle was created using the build out method to create an ideal topology.

Final Details

With all the elements created, and the spline patching portion of the modeling out of the way, I applied subdivision surfaces to the mesh. I was pretty happy with the results but added an edge bevel around the circular center to tighten up the edge. Often, additional segments need to be created to compensate for the smoothing that occurs when polygonal meshes are converted to SubDs. **Figure 11.18** shows the results with the additional segment.

The mesh looked complete so I mirrored the geometry to create the full bottle. I took some time to survey the topology and discovered six three-point polygons. I always try my best to avoid triangles when working with SubD meshes, and because there was an even number of triangles, I knew it would be an easy fix. I selected all six triangles and merged them into three quads (**Figure 11.19**).

I took another couple passes over the mesh. Once I was satisfied that I didn't miss anything, I created a few surface groups and changed their attributes to add color and specularity to get a final look at the completed model. **Figure 11.20** shows the completed mesh.

Although there were a few areas that proved to be quicker using other modeling methods, spline patch modeling was the clear choice for creating the complex curves that made up the design of the bottle. Exploring alternate modeling methods gives you the ability to use the right technique at the right time. You can never have too many tricks in your modeling toolkit.

Product Modeling Exercise

Product modeling can be big business for a digital modeler. Choose a bottle or package design that has some challenging areas and re-create it using a modeling method that is either new to you or that you aren't very comfortable with. Challenging yourself can be the quickest way to increase your problem-solving skills as well as your modeling speed. As always, be sure to create a clean mesh and stay true to your reference.

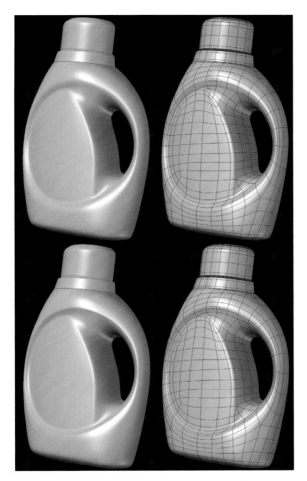

[Figure 11.18] The circular edge in the center of the bottle was too soft when SubDs were applied (top), so an edge bevel was added to tighten the edge (bottom).

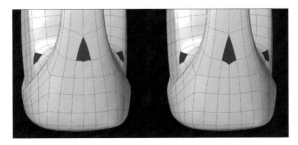

[Figure 11.19] The six triangles in the mesh (left) were merged to create three quad-polys (right).

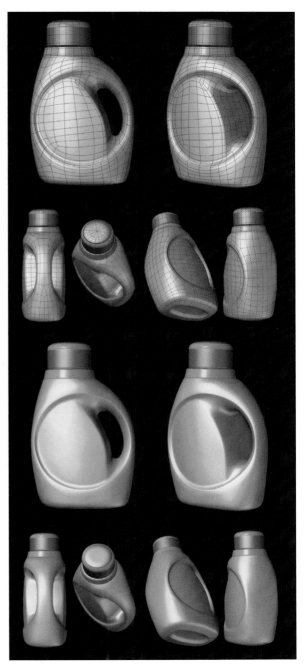

[Figure 11.20] The completed bottle has good polygon flow and is a light model made up of a low poly count, making it ideal for production.

CHAPTER TWELVE

Digital Sculpting

Artists throughout the 3D industry have introduced digital sculpting to their modeling workflow. In a nutshell, *digital sculpting* is the art of manipulating a mesh with digital brushes using software instead of physical clay. This method of modeling has enhanced production pipelines for feature films, broadcast media, the gaming industry, and more. I've used digital sculpting in my print graphics work to easily achieve levels of detail in my 3D models that would have been difficult or impossible to do using any other method.

Although digital sculpting has changed the playing field for the production portion of a pipeline, it has also been adopted in the pre-production phase. Traditionally, concept artists working in the visual design department worked in clay to create maquettes (small scale models). Because of the advancements and accessibility of today's digital sculpting packages, many concept artists now choose digital sculpting over making physical maquettes, allowing them to work faster, have more creative freedom, and explore more options.

   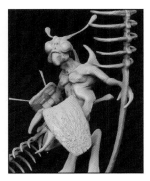

In Chapter 2 of this book, a few of my industry buddies share their experience and advice to help create a clearer picture of a digital modeler's contribution is in a production pipeline. In this chapter, I've asked my good friend Glen Southern (southerngfx.co.uk) to share some of the techniques he employs when using the digital sculpting method of modeling. Glen has been sculpting most of his adult life in one form or another but has been digitally sculpting almost exclusively for the last ten years. He was one of the earliest adopters of digital sculpting and continues to be a leader in this new method of modeling.

In this chapter, Glen covers modeling a creature maquette, starting with a primitive sphere. While explaining the fundamental process of digital sculpting, Glen shares some of the sculpting techniques he's developed over his many years of experience. So, without further ado, I hand the reigns over to him for the rest of this chapter.

Digital Sculpting with Glen Southern

Instead of using clay to create dimensional sculptures, I now sculpt using a Wacom graphics tablet (www.wacom.com) and a computer. I use ZBrush for digital sculpts, which was developed in the late 1990s by Pixologic and has become the industry standard tool for digital sculpting. Even though other packages allow you to achieve the same results (such as Mudbox, 3D-Coat, Silo, and Modo), I have chosen to stay with ZBrush for most of my career. Sculpting is very different from other digital modeling methods, which may seem strange when you discover that the underlying algorithms—SubDs—are exactly the same.

One major difference is that digital sculptors don't often think in terms of topology and polygon flow. The sculpting is done on top of a primitive shape (a sphere, for example) or onto an imported mesh from another 3D package. Either way, the process is the same, but the artist doesn't often get to see or really care about the underlying polygons. The idea is that once your highly detailed sculpture is made, it is possible to go back and, using a technique called *retopology*, re-create the surface of the mesh with better polygon flow. When using a sculpting package, I start off by pulling or pushing a simple 3D mesh into whatever shape I'm after. Once I create a rough *armature* (the basic structure from which the sculpture is built), I can add the detail stage by stage using a wide range of brushes (**Figure 12.1**).

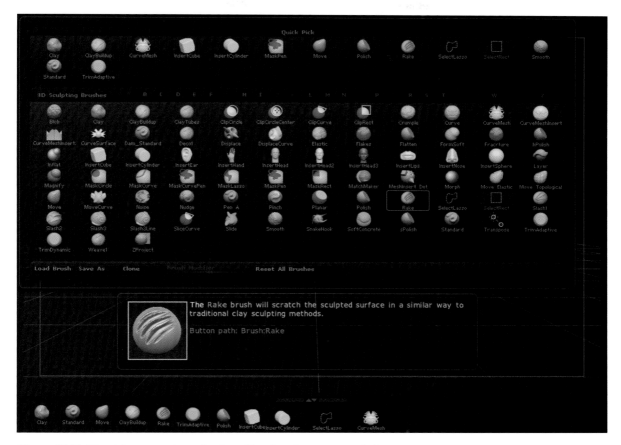

[Figure 12.1] ZBrush has a massive collection of brushes that can overwhelm a new user. It is possible to configure the interface and put the tools you need right at your fingertips.

I can further enhance these sculpting brushes with *alphas* (grayscale images). When a grayscale image is used as an alpha, the details in the image control the shape of the brush. Alphas allow for an endless number of custom brushes that make light work of details that would be extremely time-consuming otherwise. **Figure 12.2** shows my library of alphas.

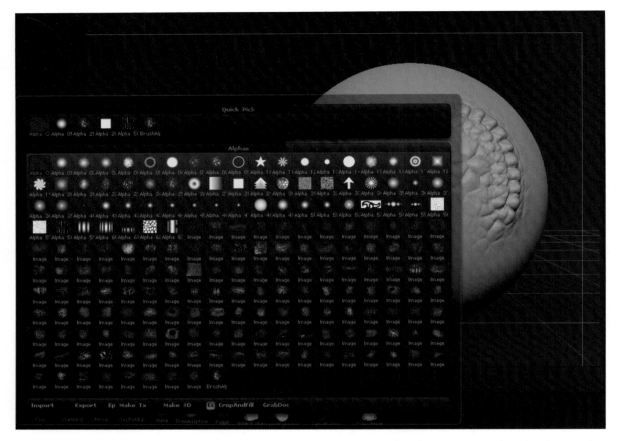

[Figure 12.2] Brushes can be even more powerful when they are combined with grayscale alpha textures. ZBrush has quite a few alphas built in, but they become even more useful when you create your own.

Creating a Digital Creature Maquette

Instead of working from a 2D concept sketch, I used a digital model as the "sketch" of this creature maquette. In the same amount of time that it would take to create a 2D concept sketch, I produced a 3D sketch. The speed in which a digital sculpt can be created is one of the many reasons digital sculpting has gained popularity in the industry so quickly.

In earlier versions of ZBrush, a polygon mesh that was stretched too far would become an issue, because the sphere is actually made up of subdivided polygon quads or triangles. If a portion of the mesh was pushed or pulled too far, it would become blocky and pixelated, as shown in **Figure 12.3**. Now, using a new technique called Dynamesh, the model is re-meshed on the fly, which means that if the polygons are getting stretched out of shape, the software redistributes them evenly across the entire model. Dynamesh was introduced in ZBrush 4, Release 2 and has changed the way a lot of modelers work. I used Dynamesh a great deal for this project, so as you read and come across portions where I re-mesh or Dynamesh an object, it simply means I was redistributing the polygons at that point.

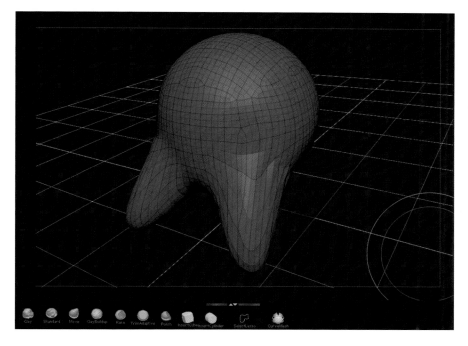

[Figure 12.3] Pulling and pushing polygons on a sphere leads to stretched polygons. That is where the power of Dynamesh comes into its own by redistributing the polygons evenly throughout the mesh.

For this sculpt, I started with a primitive sphere. I find that I usually start with a simple object such as a sphere, which allows me to head in any direction I want without being constrained by the shapes of a more complex mesh. I also took advantage of the Symmetry option and enabled it across the X axis. Symmetry is a great feature for a character modeler because most living things are more or less symmetrical. This is not only a major time-saving feature, but as you create your model, you can adjust the proportions by seeing both sides at the same time.

The early stages of sculpting are all about creating the basic anatomy before moving on to looking at proportions and form. This means that the first thing you should do is pull out chunks of geometry to be used for the legs, arms, and head.

Sculpting Legs

Using a basic Move brush, I pulled down a thigh and a lower leg, and then used the Inflate brush to build up some volume around the knee area (**Figure 12.4**). If at any time an area of the mesh looked too raised or messy, I used the Smooth brush to smooth out the area immediately under the brush. Most of the core sculpting of this creature was done using these three brushes.

[Figure 12.4] The body is created out of a sphere. By using simple brushes like Move, Inflate, and Smooth, it is possible to make almost anything.

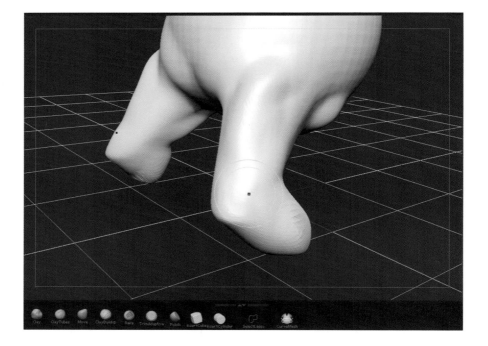

It's extremely important that all sculptors obtain an excellent grasp of anatomy. When I'm modeling a fictional subject, such as an alien or creature like this one, I still think in terms of real-world anatomy and muscle structure. I based the legs of this creature on a goat's legs that end in a sort of split hoof.

To keep the figure accurate, I worked out where all the major bones would be and then created the shapes in the model to match that concept.

I can't stress enough the importance of gathering good reference material for any of your projects. If you choose to model from memory, you often end up doing the same thing over and over with very similar results. Try to collect a reference library to use for future projects. A good library of images is a great place to get inspiration and always a good place to start a project.

Once the legs and feet were pulled into place, I went over the area with a combination of the Smooth and Inflate brushes, making sure that the creature was roughly in proportion with enough volume in the necessary areas (**Figure 12.5**).

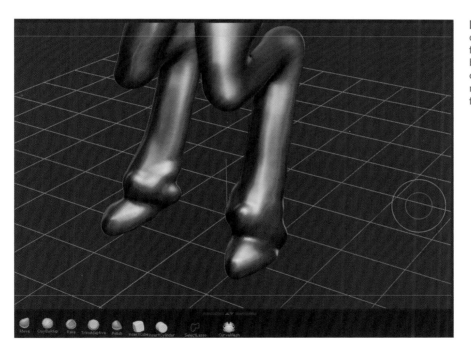

[**Figure 12.5**] Once I had created the basic anatomy for the leg, I used the Move brush to get the proportions correct—always turning the model to make sure it works from all angles.

One method that I use to allow me to focus on the object's overall form and not be distracted by the details is to make the model completely black (**Figure 12.6**). I then spin it around a few times to view it from multiple angles. If you use a black material, you will be limited to the silhouette of the object, which can sometimes help you spot potential issues, such as flat areas that need more volume or odd-looking muscle groups. I suggest doing this several times during the sculpting process to make sure you're producing a solid overall form.

[Figure 12.6] A great way to see if the image is reading well is to make it 100 percent black and rotate it. This helps you see the silhouette and check for flat areas.

Sculpting Arms

Although I mentioned the need for sculptors to understand anatomy (and you may think that this next bit of modeling might contradict that statement), I decided to give this creature four arms. I still wanted to make the creature believable, even though the anatomy is nonstandard, so I referred to real-world references. I used the same tools that were used on the legs and pulled out geometry to create the top shoulder.

I reworked the area with the Smooth and Inflate brushes and then pulled out more geometry for the arms. I continued repeating these steps down through the bicep, elbow, and onto the forearm. At first, I just created a basic shape for the limb (essentially a long cylinder) and then adjusted the shape to fit the concept I was after. I could have continued on to the hands/claws at this stage, but to stay focused on the overall shape, I decided to move to the second set of arms. I used the same technique to create the second pair of arms as I did for the first set. The results of this process are shown in **Figure 12.7**.

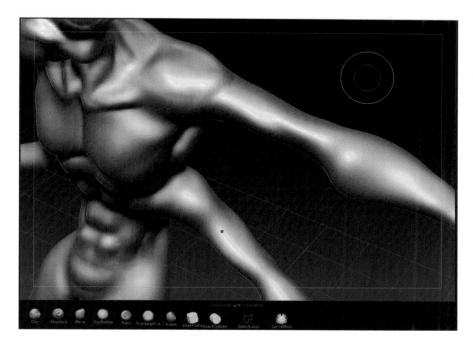

[Figure 12.7] The four arms were created by pulling geometry out of the shoulder area and refining the shapes.

Sculpting the Head

Once I was happy with the arms and legs, it was time to sculpt the head detail. I pulled out the neck, gave it some muscle definition, and started to build up volume where the head would be. Using the Inflate brush, I then built up the eyes, nasal area, and chin.

Keep in mind that if the resolution of the mesh is not sufficient to give you high-resolution detail, you can always adjust the density of the Dynamesh setting, which controls how many polygons will be created. However, I am always careful not to add too much sculpted detail in the early stages and rather focus on good proportions and shape to avoid getting stuck into detailing any one area. Once you get into the fine detail of an area, it becomes difficult to make global changes. I use a very similar approach when creating a traditional 2D sketch.

At this stage, I defined the eyes and eyelids, the nasal area, and the lips. I used very little detail but added a good suggestion of where the feature was going to be placed. **Figure 12.8** shows the results.

[Figure 12.8] At this stage in the sculpting process, it's important to keep facial details at a minimum. This allows for broad changes to be made quickly.

One very powerful tool in the digital sculptor's arsenal is the ability to mask off an area of the model. With an area masked, any brushwork will only affect the nonmasked area. I created the horns/antennae on this creature by masking off the entire body and most of the head, only leaving the bumps where the horns would be placed. I then inflated that area to give me some geometry to work with. I used the Move tool to pull out the horns 45 degrees from the back of the head.

Once I had the basic shape for the stump of the horns, I cleared the masking and re-meshed the creature again. I switched the mask back on and then switched from Draw mode to Rotate mode. Draw mode is where you will spend most of your time in ZBrush, and the Rotate, Scale, and Move modes are used to adjust things once they are built. This allowed me to use a very power feature called Transpose. With Transpose activated, you can reposition, rotate, or scale parts of your model. In this case, I wanted to angle the horns to suit my concept, so I used rotate. Using Transpose with masking makes the process even more useful, because you can limit which areas of the mesh are affected. **Figure 12.9** shows the mask and Transpose tool activated.

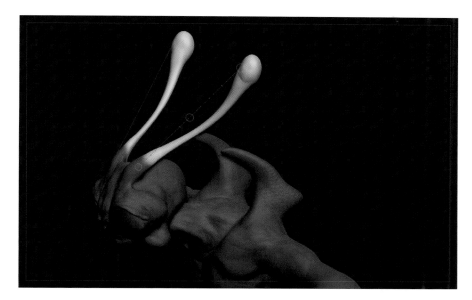

[Figure 12.9] Using a mask allows you to limit which areas of the mesh are affected. You can switch to Rotate, Scale, and Move modes and use the Transpose tool to pose portions of the model.

When I was happy with the horns' placement, length, and angle, I simply switched back to Draw mode and finished off the horns with the Smooth and Inflate brushes.

In the images I've shown so far, you can see that I used several different materials on the surface of the mesh. Each material has different settings for surface attributes, such as diffuse colors, specularity, reflection, bump, and so on. It's a good idea to change the materials regularly to check your progress. Using different materials with different properties allows you to see how light falls on your model. If you use the same material throughout the modeling process, you may find that at the end, when you change to a different material, the overall look is wrong.

To complete the initial body sculpting, I added two claws to each of the four arms using the same techniques I used on the rest of the mesh (**Figure 12.10**). It's important to point out that to get to this stage of the model, I still only used three of the brushes that ZBrush has available. Although it is good to be aware of what tools and options are available to you in an application, don't feel like you have to use every one of them. All artists find a favorite set of brushes that suits their style, but it takes time to work out what each one does and how to use each brush effectively.

[Figure 12.10] To finish the first pass, I added small claws on the end of the arms.

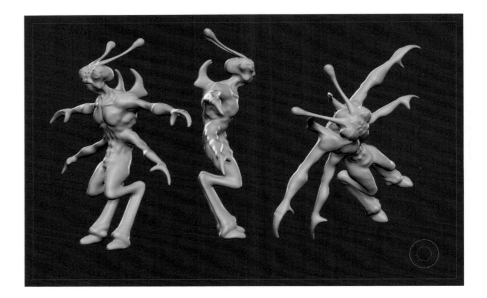

Second Pass over the Sculpt

When I had the overall shape of the body finished, I started the second pass. This involved going back to each area of the mesh and adding tertiary details and features. I started by detailing the face. Using the Inflate brush with a very low *focal shift* (which adjusts how fast the brush's effect "falls off" as it approaches the edge of the brush) gave me a nice, hard-edged stroke and allowed for good creases around the eyelids and lips. In this model, the eye-balls are part of the mesh and are fairly large. For speed sculpting, having the eyes attached makes things easy. For more detailed projects or models, such as the head and shoulders, it may be worth making the eyes separately. As digital sculpts increase in complexity and poly-count, they can slow down your computer. One way to cope with this is to hide portions of the mesh **(Figure 12.11)**.

[Figure 12.11] To help your computer cope with high-resolution models, you can hide parts of the mesh while you work on other areas.

It's very important to keep rotating the mesh as you model to ensure that the shape stays accurate. It is easy to do a lot of work in a particular view, only to realize that it doesn't work well in a side profile. I constantly spin the mesh and look at it from all angles, including from above and below. I worked down the entire body, adding the muscle detail stage by stage. The abdomen was based on a human torso, so I added muscles that you would expect to see there. I focused on areas like the elbows, shoulder blades, knees, and ankles. By simply adding volume with the Inflate brush, I quickly defined all of the major muscle groups. **Figure 12.12** shows the results.

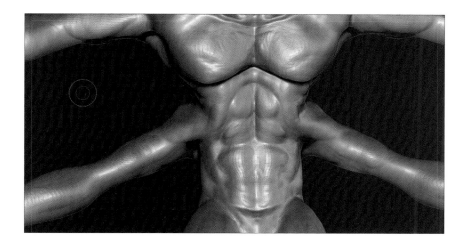

[Figure 12.12] Using reference images of a human abdomen, I added tertiary details to the creature.

Detailing

The next stage of the sculpting process was to add surface detail. I changed my stroke type to Drag Rectangle and then chose a set of alpha textures that matched the look I needed. The Drag Rectangle option allows you to drag out alpha images and apply them dynamically to the surface of your mesh.

I made some custom alphas for my brushes using images of elephant skin, some wrinkles from an older person, and other images that provided the details I was after. **Figure 12.13** shows a few of these textures.

[Figure 12.13] These simple grayscale images transformed the standard brushes into detailed powerhouses when used as alphas.

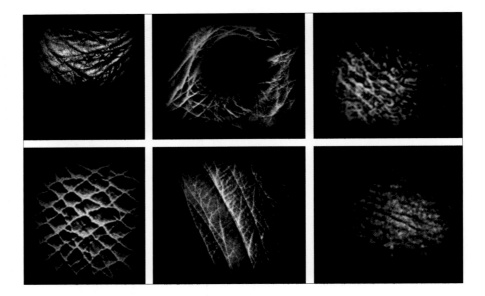

I tried to build up the surface detail by overlapping the alphas wherever possible. My goal was to create believable skin details that would bring this fictional creature to life. **Figure 12.14** shows the results of these details applied to the mesh.

Although having Symmetry activated helps to speed up modeling, there comes a time when it needs to be switched off. In nature nothing is perfectly symmetrical. In fact, creatures can look odd if you don't break the symmetry in your model. I switched off Symmetry and then started to adjust the pose a little. The best way to do this is to mask off parts of the model and then use the Transpose tool in Rotate mode. I did this to the arms and adjusted the transpose pivot point (the point in 3D space around which all rotations, scaling, and transformations are centered) to allow me to get the best angles. I moved the arms down at the shoulders by a few degrees and then bent them slightly at the elbow. I moved each arm separately and in a slightly different way (**Figure 12.15**).

[**Figure 12.14**] With a set of decent alpha textures, you can transform the look of the model in minutes.

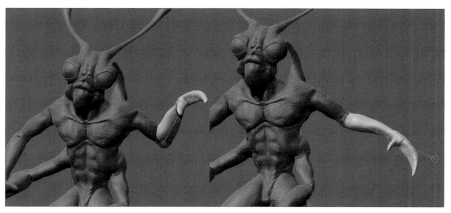

[**Figure 12.15**] Posing a figure in ZBrush is done with the Transpose tool and using masks. I masked off the arm and used the Transpose Rotate tool to reposition it.

I turned one of the legs outwards to change the stance a little and gave a small rotation to the foot. I made sure I was happy with the creature's pose from various angles and applied a different material to the surface to look for any imperfections in the mesh (**Figure 12.16**).

[Figure 12.16] It's important to continue to view the model from all angles and with different materials, even at this stage of the sculpting process.

To finish the model, I made some accessories from primitive shapes in the same way I created the main body. I also created a basic stand for the creature to be displayed on. I added these items as subtools (separate meshes), which allows me to add new parts to an existing character project but keep these new items as objects separate from the main mesh. Using subtools for these additional elements allows any changes to easily be made in the future. **Figure 12.17** shows the final creature maquette, posed and ready to be showcased.

Digital Sculpting Exercise

Now that you've seen the process, you can have a go at creating a 3D creature sketch. Find some reference material of a creature you would like to model (or sketch your own if possible). Start the project with a primitive sphere and concentrate on making the overall shape before going onto the detailing. Spend the time looking at the reference material carefully and try to match the anatomy as accurately as possible. Switch to a black material to see the model in silhouette and remember to keep changing the material to see how the sculpting is progressing.

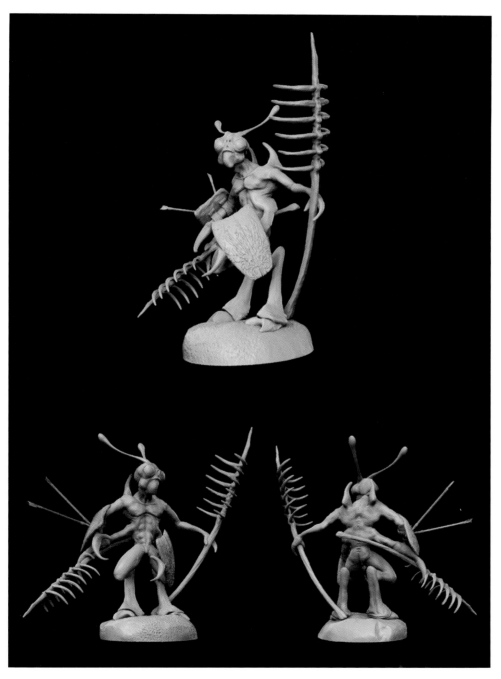

[**Figure 12.17**] The creature was finished by adding some accessories. Once you place the figure on a stand, you may need to adjust the feet using Transpose to suit the scene.

CHAPTER THIRTEEN

Game Modeling

Real-time 3D gaming has shown amazing growth over the years. Because of this, the opportunities for digital artists have grown as well. There has never been a better time than right now to be an artist working in gaming.

The 3D models being created for the latest console and computer games (commonly referred to as *next generation* or *next-gen* models) allow for an amazing amount of detail that, in many cases, match the details of the digital models seen in feature films. Hardware and software continues to evolve, allowing the amount of polygons used in game assets to increase at an amazing rate. A character model used in a top console game 15 years ago may have been limited to 500 polygons; today it can reach 30,000 polygons and up.

Games require everything from characters and creatures to vehicles, weapons, and environmental models, which allows digital modelers a plethora of opportunities to create varied subject matter.

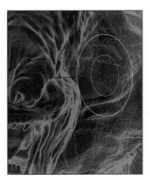

My friend Glen Southern (www.southerngfx.co.uk) is currently creating digital models for a real-time 3D game being developed with the Unity 3 game development tool (http://unity3d.com). I asked him to share his process. In this chapter, Glen walks you through the creation of a next-gen game model. The process involved creating a high-resolution digital sculpt, performing retopology to generate a lower-resolution mesh, and creating multiple image maps.

Next-Gen Game Modeling with Glen Southern

The game I'm currently working on calls for a variety of creature models, including a quadruped beast called a Hellhound, which I'll use for this walkthrough. This creature required a fairly high level of surface detail while maintaining a low-polygon count for real-time playback in the game engine.

There are several ways to create all of the intricate details seen in next-gen game models, but I find that creating a high-poly digital sculpt, like the one created in Chapter 12, to be the quickest solution. The purpose of the high-poly model is to provide the details used in a normal map for the low-poly game assets. *Normal mapping* is a technique used to apply details to a low-resolution mesh, based on the surface of a high-resolution mesh. Simply put, a normal map adds surface detail without adding polygons.

When creating the high-resolution digital sculpt for a next-gen game model, remember that you're not creating the final mesh. There is no reason to spend time worrying about topology or polygon count, since a new mesh will be created. You're free to be as messy with the mesh as you'd like, as long as the surface displays the details you're wanting.

Creating the Creature Sculpt

I chose to use ZBrush (www.pixologic.com) to make the high-polygon sculpt of the Hellhound creature. However, several options are available for sculpting high-resolution meshes, such as Mudbox (www.autodesk.com/mudbox), 3D-Coat (http://3d-coat.com), Sculptris (www.pixologic.com/sculptris), and others. Starting with a basic sphere, I began to shape the creature with a variety of brushes by pulling the mesh into the form I needed.

Although this creature doesn't exist in the real world, I wanted it to have features from a dog and a gorilla, so I collected several images that I used as reference. I pulled out two basic stumps at the front of the mesh that would become the creature's front legs, using the gorilla images as reference. I then pulled two additional stumps towards the rear of the mesh for legs based off the dog reference I gathered. I also pulled out a lump for the head and made the chest area larger to complete the base shape I was after (**Figure 13.1**).

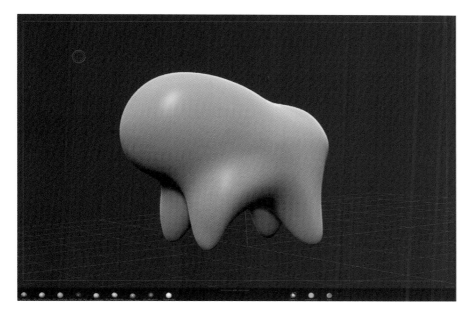

[Figure 13.1] Starting with a basic primitive sphere, I pulled out the legs and arms of the creature.

Once I had the basic, blocky shape to work from, I went back and reshaped the limbs using the Smooth and Move brushes. I made sure to reference the gorilla and dog images I gathered to ensure I was creating realistic shapes. I positioned the thigh, stifle (knee), hock (ankle), and hind foot of the back leg and posed it to match the dog reference images. I modified the front limbs to be jointed like a gorilla's arms with hands tucked under, as seen in **Figure 13.2**.

[Figure 13.2] I continued to refine the basic anatomy in roughly the correct proportions using a gorilla and dog as reference.

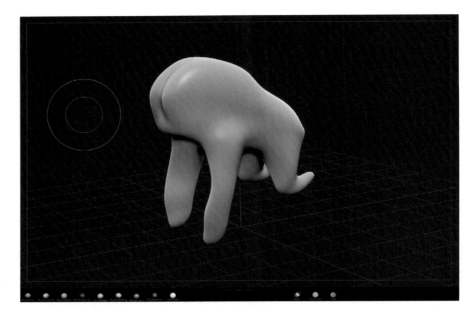

It's important to get the basic anatomy and idea of the overall form of the creature at this stage in the process before sculpting in any of the fine details. Sculpting tertiary details at this early stage doesn't allow for broad changes to be made easily. It's tempting to want to start creating those details, but don't let temptation lead you down the road of inefficiency.

The next step in bringing this creature to life was to start adding mass to the basic shape using a Clay Buildup brush. This brush allowed me to quickly add volume in the shape of muscle mass. Working my way around the entire mesh with the Clay Buildup brush, I added bulky muscle groups that helped to define the overall shape of the creature. I used a Smooth brush in areas that had too much volume and then reworked the area with a lower intensity setting until I was satisfied with the shapes I had created. I repeated this process, adding more muscles, rotating the mesh to make sure it was getting closer to my reference.

I then indented the front of the face in preparation for sculpting a mouth, tongue, and teeth later in the process. I also prepared the front portion of the mesh, making a space to pull out the horns. The results of the steps can be seen in **Figure 13.3**.

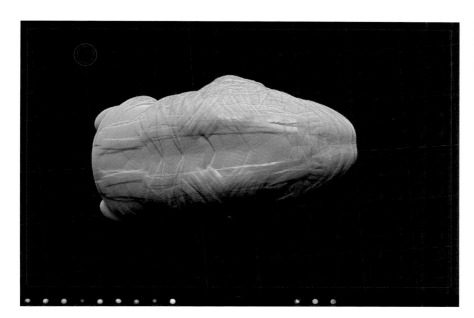

[Figure 13.3] I added muscle groups using a Clay Buildup brush on a low intensity setting.

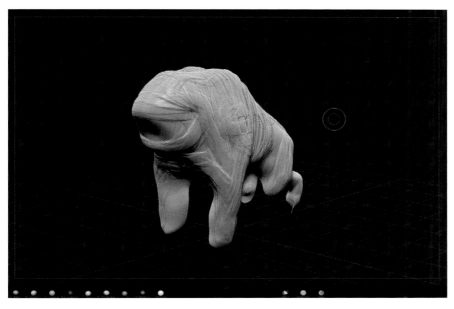

I used a feature that is unique to ZBrush called Dynamesh throughout the sculpting process. Dynamesh redistributes polygons evenly across the entire model. This option allows you to add an endless amount of detail to your digital sculpture without over-stretching polygons.

Using Dynamesh and the Clay Polish brush, I continued refining the surface of the creature without losing the overall shape. This smoothed out the roughness created by the Clay Buildup brush, but didn't lose any of the muscle mass. I pulled out a set of horns from the back of the head and re-meshed using Dynamesh several times until the polygons were evenly distributed. I put my focus on the Hellhound's horns and made sure they had a good amount of volume by building up their mass with a variety of brushes (Clay Buildup, Standard, Inflates, Rake, and Trim Adaptive). With the horns in place, the base mesh was complete and ready for tertiary details. (**Figure 13.4**)

[Figure 13.4] Horns were added to the creature by pulling out new geometry from the head.

The last sculpting pass for this creature allowed me to really bring it to life. I wanted the surface to follow the lines of the creature's muscles but have a striated, scratched look. I brushed scratch marks into the surface using the Rake brush and sculpted details to get the appearance of muscle. The more detail I put into the surface at this stage, the better-looking the final creature would be, so I took just as long doing this final pass as I did on the preliminary modeling. I continued to finesse the surface of the creature until I was satisfied with the entire mesh. The final results of the high-resolution sculpture can be seen in **Figure 13.5**.

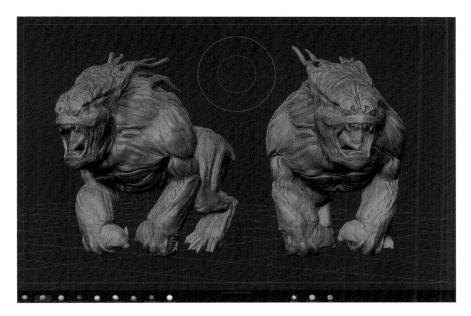

[Figure 13.5] The Rake brush helped to get a striated look and made the muscles stand out.

Performing Retopology to Create the Game Model

When a 3D model has been sculpted in a program such as ZBrush or Mudbox using millions of polygons, or the model simply has poor topology, it might be useful for still images but won't perform well when animated or used in a real-time game environment. Creating a new mesh with cleaner topology is not only important for controlling how the mesh deforms, but can greatly reduce the poly-count of the model. The process of creating this new mesh is called *retopology*.

Each 3D application has its unique workflow and way of performing retopology. No matter what program you use, when you break it down to the most basic level, retopology, in its essence, is the process of creating new topology for a model. The new mesh is created by using the surface of the existing mesh as a template to build on. The high-resolution data can then be projected back onto the low poly mesh using a normal map, thus saving precious processing power for real-time games.

When creating a low-poly model for games, remember that less is more. Use as few polygons as possible while still capturing the shape needed to sell the mesh. Make sure you have enough geometry in the low-poly mesh to produce a good silhouette. Always check with your team to find out what the budget of the game assets are before building anything. You wouldn't want to create a mesh with a poly-count that the game engine couldn't support. For the Hellhound creature mesh I needed to keep the poly-count to around 6,000 three-point polygons in order for it to work properly in the Unity game engine.

I used ZBrush to create a low-poly mesh for the Hellhound creature. The first step was to load a ZSphere in a new document. A ZSphere is a tool unique to ZBrush that allows for the creation of new geometry (**Figure 13.6**). In other applications you can simply start creating new geometry without the need of a ZSphere, but it is required when creating new geometry in ZBrush. For this project, you can think of it as simply a placeholder for the geometry to be created.

With the ZSphere placed into a new document window, I opened the Adaptive Skin, Topology, and Rigging panels from the Tool menu to allow for quick access to the tools I use during retopology. In the Rigging panel, I loaded the high-poly Hellhound creature. I find it easier working with the high-poly object when I can see through the mesh, so having transparency activated from the main window sidebar helps. See **Figure 13.7**.

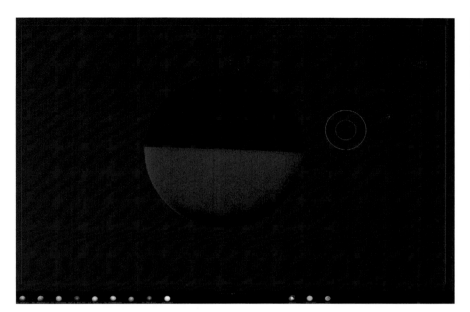

[**Figure 13.6**] The first step in creating a game version of the creature in ZBrush was to load a ZSphere to act as the base for the retopology mesh.

[**Figure 13.7**] The high-poly creature was loaded, and the transparency option was activated for better visibility.

I scaled down the ZSphere until it fit completely inside the creature (**Figure 13.8**). This is where the transparency display option really helps, because you can easily see right through the mesh. When performing retopology in ZBrush, it's important that the ZSphere sits completely inside the mesh in order for the rest of the process to work correctly. If the ZSphere protrudes out through the high-polygon mesh, there may be errors in the retopology mesh later in the process.

[Figure 13.8] I scaled down the ZSphere and ensured it was fully inside the body of the creature.

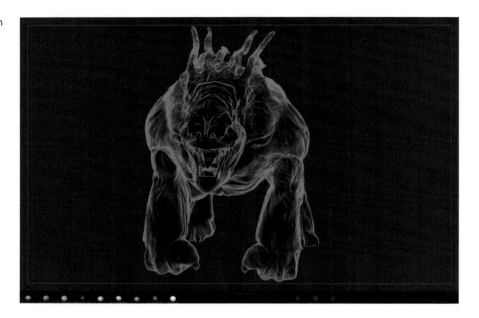

I activated the symmetry option across the X axis, which allowed me to perform retopology on both sides of the mesh at the same time. This is a massive time-saver for symmetrical meshes.

In the Topology panel, I selected the Edit Topology option and closed down the Rigging panel because it was no longer needed. I then began to lay down the first rows of new geometry. Because I had symmetry enabled, I worked down the left-hand side of the mesh, and the right side was created simultaneously. This process is similar to the edge extend build out method used in Chapter 9 to create the April head model.

I clicked along the center line and connected vertices until I had a few polygon faces strung together (**Figure 13.9**). Although all game engines require triangle (three-point) polygons, I kept the mesh as close to 100 percent quads (four-point polygons) as possible to keep my mesh more efficient while I worked, knowing that the game engine would convert all the polygons to triangles.

[Figure 13.9] Working down the center of the mesh, I began creating new geometry.

I kept the principles of good topology in mind with every new piece of geometry I added. I placed a complete ring of polygons inside the nasal cavity, building off of those rings to create the muzzle portion of the face (**Figure 13.10**). Whereever possible, I tried to flow the polygons around the muscles to ensure proper deformation would take place when the creature was animated.

Areas of the creature's anatomy that would need to be animated, such as the eyes, needed more polygons to allow for greater detail in the game engine. I focused on the creature's face and worked down around the eyes, over the cheeks, and down to the chin. The results of these steps can be seen in **Figure 13.11**.

[Figure 13.10] Edge loops were created around the creature's nasal cavity.

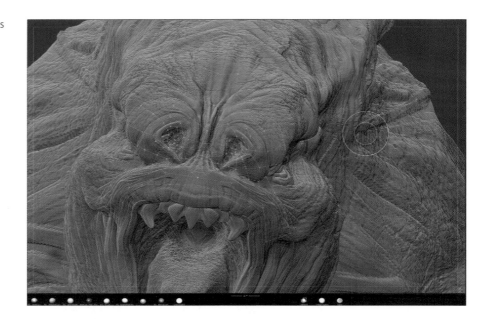

[Figure 13.11] Adding more polygons to areas that undergo deformation during animation ensures cleaner results in-game.

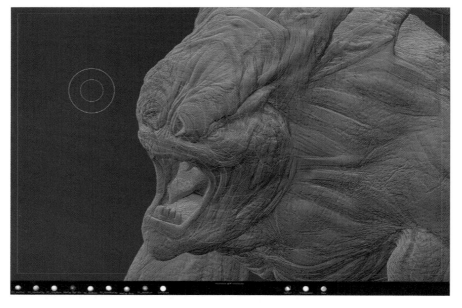

On a regular basis I took breaks from creating new geometry and checked to see how the low-poly mesh was looking. It's important to take these breaks to ensure that you're heading in the right direction before you get too far along. To view the low-poly mesh, I pressed the A key on the keyboard and could see an approximation of the geometry I had created (**Figure 13.12**). I could see the overall clean shape and was happy with the direction I was going in.

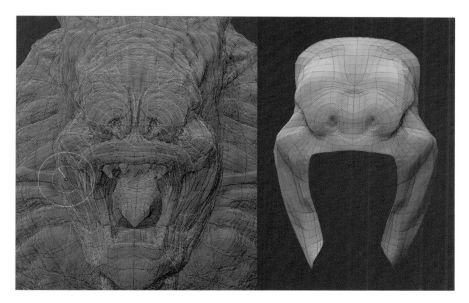

[**Figure 13.12**] Reviewing your work on a regular basis is an important step that shouldn't be overlooked. It's better to catch any issues early on than once all the geometry is created.

I was happy with the new low-poly portion of the mesh I created, but I find it helpful to preview how the new mesh will look with the high-resolution details projected onto them. I used the Project buttons in the Project panel and also increased the Presubdiv slider to add more detail. In ZBrush, the Presubdiv slider allows you to subdivide a new mesh before details are projected onto it. The higher the value is set, the more details can be captured by the new mesh.

With these settings in place, I could see the low-poly mesh with all the high-resolution data projected onto it by pressing A (**Figure 13.13**). This gave me a good idea of what I could expect the final low-poly object to look like with a normal map.

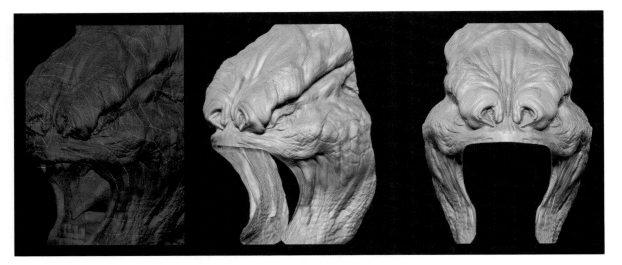

[Figure 13.13] The Project options allow you to review the high-poly details applied to the surface of the low-poly mesh.

I repeated the retopology process across the creature's entire body. The teeth and horns were more detailed than the rest of the body, so they took longer than the large flat areas. I continued using the A key to check the mesh to see and how the projection was working out. Once the horns and mouth areas were completed, I continued working down the back and onto the legs using the same process I described earlier. Once I finished creating geometry for the entire body, I went back over the entire mesh and reduced any unneeded polygons to keep the model as low-poly as possible, while keeping details in the areas that needed it, such as the mouth, horns, and so on.

Once I was happy with the new low-poly mesh, I exported it from ZBrush as an .OBJ file ready for UV unwrapping. The results of the final mesh can be seen in **Figure 13.14**.

[Figure 13.14] The final low-poly creature model ready for UV unwrapping.

Creating UVs for the Low-Poly Model

To generate the image maps that the Hellhound required for use in the game, I needed to create a UV map for the mesh. UV mapping sets up a relationship between the two dimensions of an image, U and V, with the three dimensions of an object surface, X, Y, and Z.

Although you can create UVs in any 3D software, I used Headus UV Layout (www.uvlayout.com), a standalone application dedicated to the creation of UVs, which is very straightforward and produces efficient UV maps quickly. I loaded the low-poly Hellhound model into UV Layout and sectioned off the individual parts of the mesh, such as the arms, legs, horns, and so on. Adding seams and splitting the parts off into sections allows the parts to be unwrapped and flattened without too much stretching occurring when image maps are applied to the surface of the mesh.

The green edges in **Figure 13.15** show the borders of each section where the mesh will be split and unwrapped (laid out on the UV map).

[Figure 13.15] The low-poly model was sectioned off into individual parts before unwrapping.

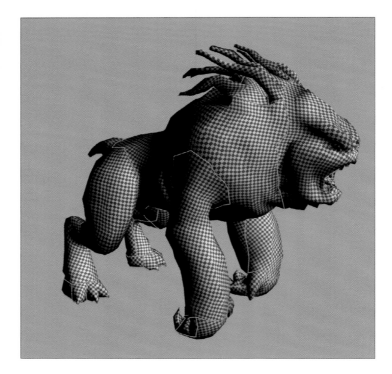

With the edges of each section selected, I unwrapped the mesh and flattened them out on the UV grid. I then positioned each polygon island to optimize the UV real-estate and exported the model to a new OBJ file to be reloaded into ZBrush. **Figure 13.16** shows the final UV layout of the creature mesh.

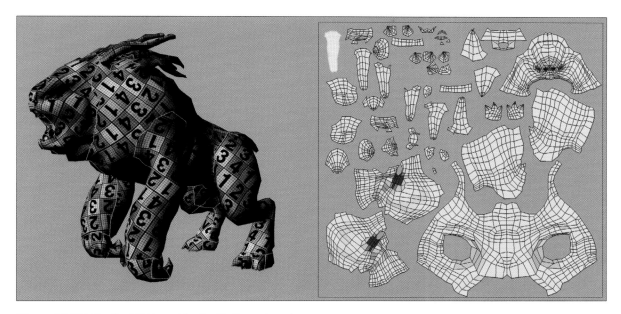

[Figure 13.16] The final UV layout for the Hellhound mesh.

Generating Maps for the Low-Poly Model

I reloaded the low-poly model with the newly created UV map into ZBrush and set it to the lowest SubD level of my creature. Some maps (normal maps and displacement maps) can only be created from the lowest SubD level. This model then had a low-poly base with UV coordinates and six levels of high-frequency detail to use in map creation. The higher detail allows for a higher quality map at extraction time.

Color Map

The first map I wanted to create was a *color texture* map. A color texture map adds surface details to a mesh and is similar to applying colored wallpaper to a white wall. I grabbed some lava textures from my resource collection and painted a fairly basic black and red texture on the surface of the creature. ZBrush is very powerful for texture creation as you can paint the texture live in 3D right onto the mesh using a feature called Polypainting. I converted my basic texture to Polypaint and then used a range of alphas to make the creature's skin interesting. I used alphas that were made from skin textures, which add a great deal of realistic surface detail. **Figure 13.17** shows the resulting image map.

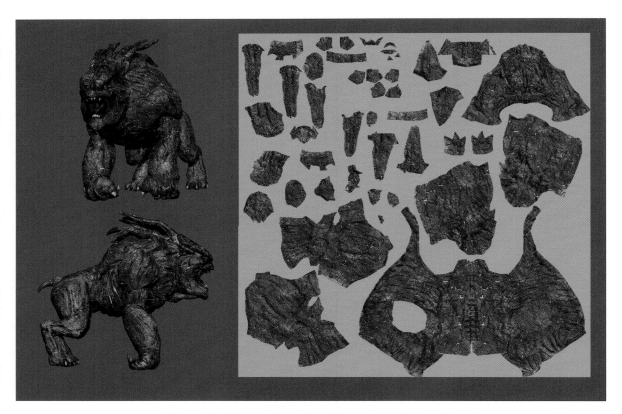

[Figure 13.17] Using Polypaint in ZBrush, a detailed lava-like color map was created.

Bump Map

When I was happy with my color map, I converted it into an *alpha map* (gray-scale image) and saved it out to be used in the Bump channel (**Figure 13.18**). The Bump channel simulates raised and recessed areas on the surface of a mesh without generating additional geometry.

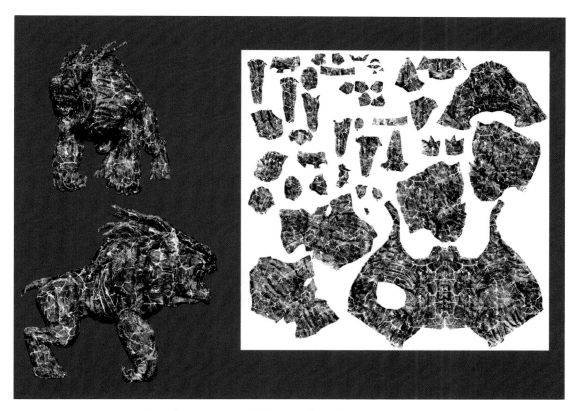

[Figure 13.18] Converting the color map into an alpha map allowed me to save out the image to be used in the Bump channel.

Normal Map

The final map I needed to create before the model was ready for Unity was a normal map. A normal map's RGB (Red, Green, and Blue) values correspond to the X, Y, and Z coordinates of the surface normals of a 3D object. Simply put, normal mapping allows you to create a high-poly model made up of millions of polygons and bake the high-resolution detail down to an image that stores the surface data of the model.

To create a normal map for the Hellhound, I lowered the subdivision levels of the mesh to the lowest setting and then adjusted the settings in the Normal Map panel, using the Adaptive mode which produces a higher quality map. Once the image was generated, I cloned and exported it. Cloning the map copies it to the texture panel making it ready for export. At that stage the texture needs to be flipped vertically prior to saving it. ZBrush inverts all its maps, and other programs won't read them correctly unless you invert vertically. **Figure 13.19** shows the normal map that was generated.

[Figure 13.19] This normal map stores the surface detail of the high-poly model.

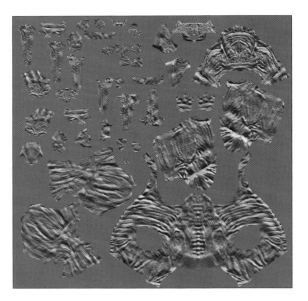

With all the maps exported, the Hellhound creature was ready for some action in the Unity. Using the low-poly model and the three maps (color, bump, and normal) that were generated in ZBrush, I loaded the assets into

Unity to see the model as it would be seen in-game (**Figure 13.20**). Happy with the results, I passed the final model onto the rigging artist who placed bones and controls into the mesh that allowed the animators to add motion to this beast.

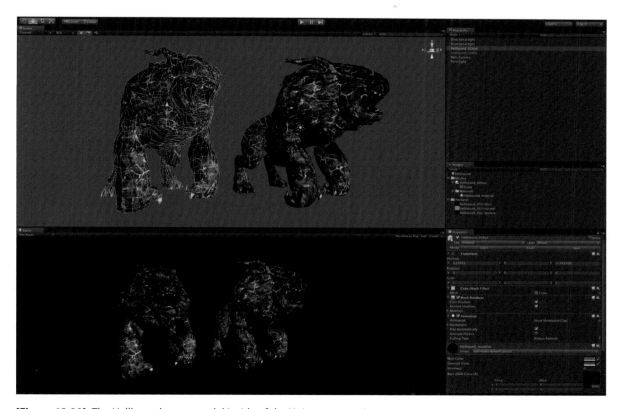

[**Figure 13.20**] The Hellhound game model inside of the Unity game environment.

Game Asset Modeling Exercise

Now that you've seen the production of the Hellhound Creature model, create a weapon that could be used to take on this massive beast. Start with a concept sketch and build a high-resolution mesh that could be used to generate a normal map. Create a low-poly model ideal for real-time rendering. A common poly-count for weapons in current games falls into the range of 1,500 to 2,000 polys.

CHAPTER FOURTEEN

3D Printing of Digital Models

When I started my career as a professional artist, my first introduction to working in 3D was to create what was then referred to as *3D illustration*. Basically, I created physical clay sculptures, built small props, took photographs of them, and then used those photos to create illustrations. These sculptures began to take up a lot of space, and before long I had an entire room devoted to storing them. Soon after, I discovered computer graphics and eventually 3D modeling and animation. No longer did I have to find an unused shoebox to store my newest character. Instead, I could simply save it to a disk. But there was only one thing missing: being able to hold my creation in my hand and place it on a shelf for others to see.

With the advent of *3D printing*—the process by which a digital model in a computer can be turned into a physical object in the real world—artists can now have the best of both worlds: the freedom of working on a computer with all its abundant bonuses and the ability to hold their creation in their hands.

In this chapter, I cover how to prepare a model for 3D printing to ensure a smooth process and share my experience of bringing a toy to market.

3D Printing Overview

3D printing is a form of rapid prototyping that uses the method of *additive manufacturing*, the process of joining materials to make physical objects from 3D model data. The physical model is created by building up multiple layers on top of each other, one layer at a time, as opposed to traditional machining, which uses *subtractive* manufacturing—starting with a solid shape and removing portions until the desired shape is formed.

To visualize how 3D printing works, consider an apple. If you were to slice the apple into wafer-thin layers, save each layer, and then restack them in order, you would re-create the shape of the original object. 3D printing accomplishes this by stacking very thin layers on top of each other from the data of a digital mesh. As this technology has advanced, the thickness of each layer has decreased, allowing for a smoother surface to be generated.

Several options are available for how these layers are created for printing a physical object. Some methods for 3D printing involve printers that lay liquid materials and harden them one layer at a time; others melt materials to produce the layers. The most common method of 3D printing is the ink jet printing system.

Ink jet printing consists of several stages, and I'll step through each one to paint a better picture of this process. Of course, the first step is to generate a 3D model that you want to print. **Figure 14.1** shows an award I designed and built in 3D that I took through the printing process.

The 3D printer shown in **Figure 14.2** has a spreader that scrapes a thin layer of powder from the feed chamber over the build chamber and prints the shape of the layer on the powder using a binding agent (think superglue).

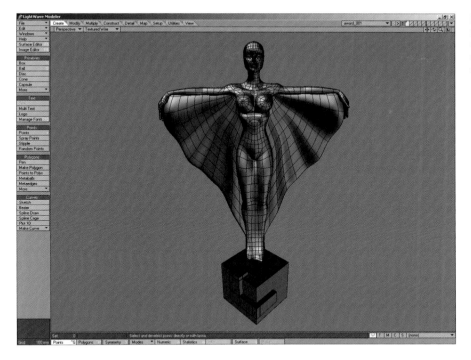

[**Figure 14.1**] Every 3D printing job starts with a digital model that can be created in your software of choice.

[**Figure 14.2**] The ink jet 3D printer used for this job uses two chambers: the feed chamber (left) and the build chamber (right).

The software that drives the printer slices the 3D mesh into thin layers. One of these layers is shown in black in **Figure 14.3**. The feed chamber piston then pushes powder up by one layer thickness, and the feed layer drops down by one layer thickness.

[Figure 14.3] The area shown in black represents the current layer being printed. Each model is made up of many thin layers to produce the entire object.

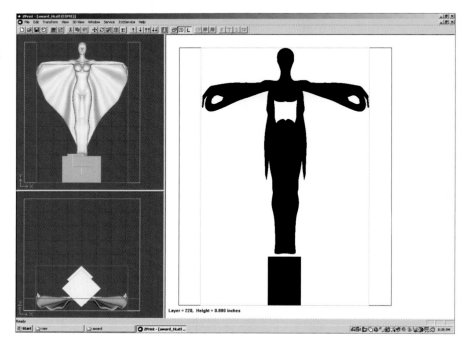

Figure 14.4 shows a layer in the build chamber with the binding agent applied; the binder holds the layer together. This step is repeated until all layers have been generated, and the entire model is built.

At the completion of the printing process, the part is buried in powder. This allows nearly any geometry to be printed because the surrounding powder provides support. The part is then extracted from the printer carefully by using a powerful vacuum to remove loose powder (**Figure 14.5**). At this time, the model is at its most fragile and can easily be damaged. Service bureaus often lose hours of printing time by destroying the print at this stage.

[Figure 14.4] The binding agent and powder are applied one layer at a time, fusing the two together.

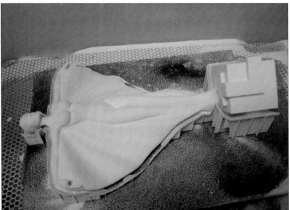

[Figure 14.5] The excess powder is removed from the chamber using a vacuum (left), and once the object is outside of the chamber, any additional powder is removed from it using compressed air (right).

Even after the vacuum has removed most of the excess material, the part is still covered in powder when it is extracted from the build chamber. At this point, it is then transferred to the cleaning station where the loose powder is carefully blown away using compressed air. The structure that outlines the cleaned part is generated by the printing software and is sometimes printed with the part for additional support.

When the part is free of the loose powder and the technician is happy with the result, it can be infused with the binding agent again to strengthen the 3D print (**Figure 14.6**).

When the process is complete, the part is ready for any additional sealing and finishing. **Figure 14.7** shows the finished 3D print of the award. Although I've had my 3D meshes printed in a variety of materials, including resin and plastic, powder prints are the most affordable. These powder prints can be finished off in a variety of ways by adding wax, polymers, and even metal. I suggest that you use some sort of sealant to protect your model before painting. I've found that clear coat acrylic spray works great. Once sealed, you can use spray paint, brush-on acrylic, or leave it as it is.

[**Figure 14.6**] A binding agent is applied over the entire 3D print to add stability.

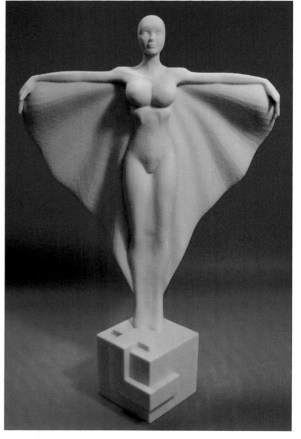

[**Figure 14.7**] The final 3D print was a perfect prototype for the award to get it in front of people before producing a mold and generating copies.

If budget is of no concern, resin is ideal for almost any prototype, mainly because it's more durable than powder. Metal printing is probably the best route for mechanical prototyping, but be prepared to empty your wallet.

3D printers have been around for several years, but until recently the process was far too expensive for an average artist to have a model printed. I compare it to the days of color printing when a single A4 color printout could cost up to $30 at a local service bureau. Now you can own a color printer for about the same price as the gas you'd use driving to the local service bureau.

Although 3D printing technology hasn't yet reached the point where you want to buy a 3D printer for your office—an entry-level prototyping unit such as Z Corporation's ZPrinter 150 (hwww.zcorp.com) currently costs $14,000—it can be very affordable to have your models printed by a third-party service bureau. Each model might cost as little as $40.

There are a growing number of 3D printing service bureaus, and I'd suggest trying several until you discover the one that fits your needs. For years I used a service bureau called 3D Art to Part, but it no longer offers those services. Some popular printing firms include

- **ShapeWays:** www.shapeways.com

- **NextFab:** www.nextfabstudio.com

- **Kraftwurx:** www.kraftwurx.com

- **Sculpteo:** www.sculpteo.com

- **Quick Forge:** www.quickforge.co.uk

- **Ponoko:** www.ponoko.com

If you're a student, you may be lucky enough to attend one of the hundreds of schools that have 3D printers on campus. You could even use an open source 3D printer, such as MakerBot (www.makerbot.com), if you have the basic technical skills required.

3D Printing Applications

So why would you want to print your models? Endless applications for 3D printing are found in a variety of markets, including aerospace, automotive, dental, fashion, jewelry, military, medical, and many others. Prototyping for product development is currently the biggest use of 3D printing technology. It allows designers and engineers to test ideas for 3D products cheaply before committing to expensive tooling and manufacturing processes. For example, industrial designers might want to prototype their designs to look for possible flaws that are hard or impossible to see on the computer screen.

Surgeons are printing body parts for reference before complicated surgeries. 3D printers are also used to create bone grafts for patients. Research is even underway by biotechnology firms and academia for 3D printing of organs and body parts from layers of living cells that are deposited onto a gel medium and slowly built up to form 3D structures.

I've used 3D character prints as physical maquettes to convince clients of a character design by allowing clients to actually hold their company mascot in their hands. **Figure 14.8** shows an example of a turtle character model I had 3D printed for use as a maquette to help pitch an animated TV series.

[Figure 14.8] 3D prints of digital models can be a great way to generate physical maquettes.

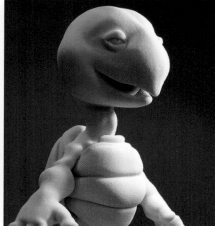

And what 3D artists don't want to add the characters they've designed to the toy collection that's proudly displayed around their computer? With the success of small-run vinyl toys, 3D printing offers artists the ability to create physical representations of their own designs and bring them to market.

We've used 3D printing at Applehead Factory to prototype a variety of products, especially after our initial success with 3D printing the Tofu the Vegan Zombie figure before having it manufactured in China. 3D printing has allowed us to work through design elements and also get our products out to focus groups for testing before committing to the heavy expense of manufacturing the final products. We are currently developing the bobble-top figure shown in **Figure 14.9** and using 3D prints to determine the best way to break it into individual parts for manufacturing and to test the market for price points.

Preparing a Digital Model for 3D Printing

How do you go about creating the 3D file that will be turned into a physical model? Is it the same process that you'd go through when creating a character for animation? Well, not quite.

[Figure 14.9] 3D printing of digital models before going to final production can be instrumental during the design phase of a product.

Using Closed Meshes

To start, you need to be working with closed meshes. A *closed mesh* is any shape that contains a volume. Any open edges on a 3D model will cause issues when trying to print it. Think of your model as a watertight mesh. If you could fill it with water, leaving no places where the liquid could leak out, you've done it right.

One common problem is with characters whose eye sockets are open when the eyeballs are modeled and inserted into the sockets separately. If such a figure were filled with water, the water would run out of the sockets. A quick solution is to cap off the sockets behind the eyeballs, like I did in Chapter 9 on the April head mesh. **Figure 14.10** shows the eye socket with and without the needed cap polygons. Although this would be wasted geometry for animation, it is a must for 3D printing. A complex model with many openings can create problems, but it's straightforward to fix.

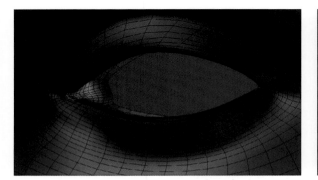 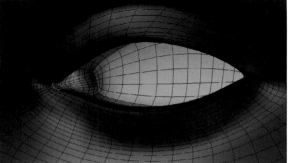

[**Figure 14.10**] Open edges on meshes cause printing issues, like the one here in the eye socket (left). Simply capping them off will solve the problem (right).

Avoiding Texture or Displacement Maps

You don't want to use texture or displacement maps because the 3D printing process won't use them. Any surface detail must be modeled into the mesh and be represented by polygons. This principle applies to surface modifiers or smoothing modifiers. Make sure that the object is a polygon mesh with any smoothing or subdivision applied previously.

It's important that your model be something that can function in the real world. Although you can get away with a top-heavy model within your 3D package by "cheating" on the animation, if you want to print such a character, it would just fall over. The base has to be large enough to support the weight of the model.

Also, although your 3D model and the base don't have to be a seamless contiguous mesh and can be made of separate objects, they must be intersecting meshes. Intersecting separate meshes, like the ninja's tunic and straps shown in **Figure 14.11**, are seen as a seamless mesh by a 3D printer.

[Figure 14.11] Separate meshes can be combined during the printing process by simply having them intersect each other on your model.

Getting the Right File Format

You need to save the file in a format that the printing bureau can handle. Many service bureaus need models in the Stereo Lithography (STL) file format. If you need to save as an STL file and your 3D application doesn't export to it, you can use a program like PolyTrans (www.okino.com) or Deep Exploration (www.righthemisphere.com) to convert it. With that said, most service bureaus that I've worked with accept a variety of file formats and will do the conversion for you.

Guidelines for 3D Printing

Over the past nine years I've printed close to 100 models and have devised a simple list of guidelines I like to follow. By keeping these in mind, I prevent myself and the technicians doing the printing from running into issues. Follow these guidelines for a smooth printing process:

- **Avoid protrusions:** Avoid things that stick out of your model, such as swords, fins, or long, thin spikes. These can become warped during the build process and can be broken when they are removed from the machine or during shipping. Shorter, tapered projections like horns or fingers are OK.

- **Add thickness:** Try to keep part thickness greater than 0.07 inches (1 mm), about the thickness of a U.S. quarter. The ninja character's sash belt in Figure 14.11 shows a perfect example of where I adjusted thickness of the mesh for better 3D printing results.

  Always find out the suggested part thickness from the printing company because each printer will have its own limitations.

  Although many of my characters have large heads with thin necks, large hands with thin wrists, and large feet with thin ankles, these are not ideal for 3D printing. You want to thicken those areas for printing to ensure that they are strong enough to support the weight of the areas they are connected to.

- **Make larger prints for finer detail.** Although I've seen some amazing detail come from a 3D print, small features or fine surface detail usually won't show up, so you shouldn't expect things like modeled eyelashes or fine wrinkles to be reproduced. **Figure 14.12** shows two different prints of the same 3D model. The larger print has more refined creases and tighter edges than the smaller one. In general, the smaller the model, the less detail will show up.

- **Check your polygons.** Make sure all the polygons of your mesh point in the proper outward direction, or the printer might view flipped polygons as holes in your model.

  Remember that all your meshes must be watertight. This means your mesh mustn't have any holes caused by missing polygons.

[**Figure 14.12**] The smaller the model, the less detail you will see.

- **Consider how the model will stand up.** If you expect your model to stand by itself, you'll have to model it with the proper weight distribution or it will simply fall over. Alternatively, you can glue it to some sort of support base, but note the next point.

  Bases cost money. It's cheaper to model your character to support itself rather than print a separate base. In some cases, the base can almost double the cost. If you decide to include a base in the printing process, consider a small size to cut costs.

- **Use separate parts:** Because each 3D printer has a limit to the object size it can print, consider printing your model in parts to maximize the size of each part. Printing the wings of a dragon separately allows for a larger print of the model and only requires basic assembly of the parts after they have been printed.

[Figure 14.13] This 3D print breaks all of the guidelines and should be used as an example of what not to do.

Let the service bureau know if you're producing a model that will generate unconnected parts so it won't think they're an error. If you do want separate parts, make sure you separate the meshes by at least 20 mm to avoid individual parts fusing together during the printing process.

- **Ask questions.** If in doubt, ask. If you aren't sure about a particular portion of your model, ask the service bureau. It should be able to spot any potential problems right away.

Figure 14.13 was the first 3D print I produced back in 2002, and I could have benefited from the preceding guidelines. The neck, hair, and fingers were much too thin and frail, the base was just as expensive to produce as the character, and the figure ended up breaking in several spots. With just a few adjustments to the 3D model and a little bit of preplanning, I could have saved myself time and money.

From 3D Printing to Manufactured Toy

Most artists I know working in the industry have a collection of toys that would make any kid green with envy. My collection reached a point two years ago where I had to start limiting my purchases or I was going to need a second home just to house them. Throw a grandkid into the mix who guilts me into giving away portions of my collection and 3D printing my own designs instead of buying other artists' creations, and I think my collection stays manageable.

Once I started 3D printing my digital models, it became more and more obvious to me that I needed to take it to the next level and actually produce a toy. It's important to understand that although 3D printing can produce quality physical models, it's only the first step in having a digital model go through the entire process of manufacturing a toy and bringing it to market. Producing a few 3D prints can be affordable, but once you're ready for mass production, toy manufacturing in China becomes the only real option.

My first experience creating an actual toy was a few years ago when I started developing the Tofu the Vegan Zombie character (www.tofutheveganzombie. com). As with many of my 3D models, Tofu started as an idea that I just couldn't shake. He went through several designs in my sketchbook until I was happy with the look and several more redesigns as a 3D mesh. **Figure 14.14** shows Tofu during the final modeling phase of his creation. The same 3D model used for creating the prototypes was also used in the animated short *Zombie Dearest* (www.tofutheveganzombie.com/movie).

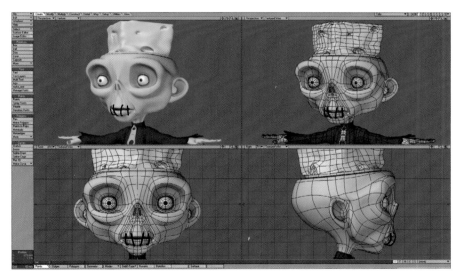

[Figure 14.14] The Tofu the Vegan Zombie toy started life as a digital model created in LightWave 3D.

Until you can actually hold the character in your hand, it's hard to determine what will work. When I was satisfied with the 3D model, I started creating poses and expressions with the character, and began generating 3D prints in various scales to get a feel for how large I would want the toy to be. **Figure 14.15** shows two early prototypes created during this phase of production.

In total, I created approximately eight 3D prints before settling on a size of seven inches and the pose shown in the CG render in **Figure 14.16**. I was able to use the CG render to start promoting the toy and raising awareness online while I worked out the challenging task of preparing the figure for production.

 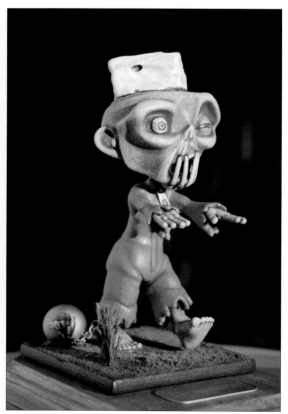

[Figure 14.15] Tofu went through several prototypes using a variety of materials. Resin was used for the figure on the left, whereas powder was used for the version on the right.

[Figure 14.16] The digital model was finalized and CG renders were used to market the toy while production continued.

Although there are guidelines you have to follow when 3D printing, it's important to know that even stricter rules apply when preparing a toy for manufacturing. A 3D ink jet printer can produce parts that wouldn't be possible for toy production. I worked closely with my two business partners at Applehead Factory and toy industry veteran Steve Varner, who's been running Varner Studios (www.varnerstudios.com) for over 30 years, to ensure that Tofu wouldn't have any issues when sent to China for manufacturing. Some guidelines that are key to successful toy production include

- **Making sure all your parts are moldable.** 3D ink jet printing allows for overhangs because the printed object doesn't have to be removed from a mold. To allow for removal of a part from a mold, the mold features must not overhang one another in the direction that the mold opens.

- **Ensuring that all the transitions from part to part work properly with the joints.** As a result, they will smoothly articulate against one another. Keeping these areas round is the trick to allowing them to fit together in the full range of movement.

- **Leaving the cutting of joints to the experts.** My first attempt ended in disaster. Varner's experience made light work of the task, and the results of the Tofu figure cuts worked out perfect for articulating the toy (**Figure 14.17**).

- **Working seam lines into the design of the toy.** Unlike 3D printing, a toy will have visible seams when two parts are brought together after being created from the molding process. The trick is to minimize their visibility by working them into the design. Tofu's jumpsuit was ideal for hiding seams along the natural seams of the clothing. These seams weren't in the original design of the toy but were added to help hide the seam lines, and in turn, it added nice tertiary details to the character.

- **Using the same guidelines for 3D printing when developing a toy.** For example, avoid skinny limbs and long spikes, keep thickness of the parts in mind, and so forth.

[Figure 14.17] The digital model was cut into parts for articulation (left), and the result is shown in the printed parts (right).

Once you've created the digital mesh following these guidelines, you can print out the final prototypes. A Chinese toy manufacturer will require that you send two, but I suggest making four because the manufacturer won't return the two, and you'll want prototypes to use to promote the toy at shows while it's being manufactured. **Figure 14.18** shows the final prototypes that were sent to China and one of the prototypes that stayed behind to be used at Toy Fair in New York.

Knowing the technical aspects is important when bringing a toy to market, but before you take the plunge and produce 5,000 copies of your favorite digital model, consider the following: Make sure you're committed to the process and that you're prepared for the amount of time you'll need to invest. The Tofu toy took just over a year to bring to market after the final design was selected, and I've spent the years since marketing and selling it.

Even more important is the financial commitment involved. The molds alone can range from $6,000 to $16,000, and that doesn't even get you one toy. The more toys you produce, the lower the cost per unit, so it's a catch-22. Do you produce fewer units and charge more per unit, or do you produce more units to bring the price down but have to sell more?

[Figure 14.18] Final prototypes were generated and sent to China (top) and used at Toy Fair and other shows (bottom).

My suggestion is to take it slow. Start by producing some 3D prints of your work and see if that satisfies your desire to make a toy. If you're committed to the idea, then make sure your toy is unique, has an audience, has the proper price point, and has a plan in place for distribution. Before producing my first toy, I had no idea there were so many costs involved. After all the units are created, you have to have them shipped from China, stored in a warehouse, and so forth. The initial cash flow of making a toy is out, out, out, out. You need to know that something is coming back, and the only way to do that is to research the market before you dive in.

Also know that you don't have to go it alone. Find places like Applehead Factory and Varner Studios that have experience bringing products to market and work with them. I can't imagine how difficult the process would have been if I had tried to do it on my own.

Since creating the Tofu figure, I've been fortunate to get work on toys for Pokemon, Polly Pocket, Littlest Pet Shop, several limited-run collectible toys, and more. As with anything else, the more digital models you take through the printing and prototyping process, the easier it becomes. It's good to know that most of the toy industry is moving away from traditional sculpting, which opens the doors for digital modelers to build a career in this market. For someone who loves modeling and has a passion for toys, I can't think of a better fit than modeling toys for a living.

CHAPTER FIFTEEN

Getting a Job in Digital Modeling

With 40,000 new graduates coming out of art schools across the nation each year, combined with thousands of jobs going to studios overseas, it is now more important than ever to find out the career options available to you and learn how to apply your digital modeling skills to land your dream job.

In this chapter, I walk you through the markets that make up the CG industry and share tips on how to showcase your skills and understanding of your CG toolset to open as many job opportunities as possible.

Overview of the Industry and Markets

How strong is this industry? When will artists stop finding good jobs? Both are very good questions. The short answer is that this industry is booming like never before, and there are plenty of jobs to be had for well-trained, professional digital artists.

When most people think about this industry, they think of feature films, television, and games, but these entertainment markets make up only a small portion of the industry as a whole. This leaves a variety of unexplored options that most artists are unaware of. To give you a better idea of the opportunities currently available, let's take a look at some of the most popular markets that make up this growing industry.

Film

A movie is an important art form that tells a visual story. Although artists have always been involved in the production of films for things like storyboards, set and prop design, costume design, and so on, their importance has increased dramatically over the years. *Avatar*, for example, required the skills of literally thousands of digital artists.

Based on worldwide gross revenue, 96 of the top 100 films of all time could not have been made without digital artists. That leaves only four films, and three of those were later updated and re-released with computer animation. That means 99 percent of the top 100 films relied on computer animation. (You are probably wondering who the lone gunman is. It's *Home Alone*, and it truly stands "alone" in this category.)

With only a few exceptions, every CG film made thus far has been a financial success. Films are the driving force of the 3D industry, and advancements in this market directly influence every other market. What you see being done in a film today will trickle down to television and games tomorrow, and the other markets after that.

There is nothing quite like being in a theater filled with people reacting to work that you helped create. Seeing your name in the credits also produces a unique feeling that lasts a lifetime.

Films can be broken down into three submarkets: feature, indie, and shorts.

Features

A feature is made initially for distribution in theaters and has a running time of at least 40 minutes. The budgets behind these productions can reach into hundreds of millions of dollars and can take several years from concept to completion.

It's not as difficult to break into this market as many would lead you to believe. All it takes is a strong reel that matches the quality of the work coming out of the studios that are currently working on features. I've placed quite a few recent grads in the industry whose first gig was a feature.

My friend Erik Gamache at Digital Domain (www.digitaldomain.com) has worked on features such as *Transformers: Revenge of the Fallen*, *The A-Team*, *I, Robot*, and others. The crew at Digital Domain was responsible for all of the robots and environments in the feature film *Real Steel*. **Figure 15.1** is a photo of Erik (center) and some of the crew at Digital Domain taking a break from their current production to enjoy the *Real Steel* premiere. They got to walk down the red carpet in Hollywood and see their work on the big screen. After the premiere, they spent time at the after party rubbing elbows with the likes of Hugh Jackman, Anthony Mackie, and Kevin Durand.

[Figure 15.1] Some of the Digital Domain production crew enjoy an evening at the movies for the *Real Steel* premiere. From left to right: Dan Brimer, Paul George Palop, Maribeth Glass, Erik Gamache, Justin van der Lek, Geoffrey Baumann, Meagan Rotman, and Swen Gillberg.

Indies

Indie films are usually made by independent production companies that are outside of the major film studio system. In most cases the financial and time budgets are much lower than those of a feature. They also usually get a limited release in theaters. Although these films have distribution and budget challenges, they also typically have the freedom to present unique story lines or work in styles that the major studios would see as too high of an investment risk.

This market has seen a massive increase in growth over the years, which has opened up thousands of opportunities for digital artists. One perk of an indie film over a studio feature is that artists can find these types of productions happening in their own backyard—not just in Los Angeles, New York, and Vancouver.

Iron Sky (www.ironsky.net), a science fiction comedy produced by Blind Spot Pictures and Energia Productions, was on the forefront of a new wave of indie movies. The filmmakers were in direct contact with the audience even before the movie was out, using the power of online communities in both creating the movie and in funding it.

Iron Sky required a great deal of digital modeling for an extensive array of virtual sets and spaceships. **Figure 15.2** shows a small sample of the massive amount of digital modeling required to create *Iron Sky*.

If you want to get experience working on a movie, there's bound to be an indie film being produced in your area that you could work on. Although you may be paid less than working on a feature (or not at all), the experience and the shots you will have for your demo reel could end up paying for themselves in short order.

[Figure 15.2] Virtual sets had to be modeled, textured, lit, and composited to marry them with the live action footage in *Iron Sky* (top). The Valkyrie ship (bottom) was one of the many spaceship models used in the film.

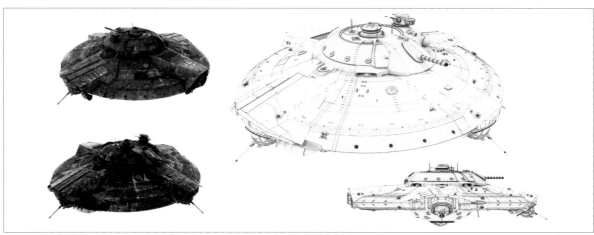

Shorts

A short film is any film with a shorter running time than a feature. Most shorts are in the five- to ten-minute range and are a first step for new filmmakers. Ten years ago there were very few shorts being shown outside of film festivals. Now, thousands of new shorts arrive online daily.

Short films are a great calling card for artists, directors, and even studios. Some studios use shorts to explore new technology, software, and even a new production pipeline (the path and schedule that a production follows). Pixar uses its shorts to train artists and directors for advancement in their careers. **Figure 15.3** shows Pixar's story artist Peter Sohn's first animated short, *Partly Cloudy*, which gave him an opportunity to direct and gave me my first Pixar credit as a character modeler.

Probably the coolest thing about shorts is that they allow anyone to tell a story, not just people with deep pockets or those with a connection to investors. You can produce a short with little or no money, but you'll need lots of time and persistence. With a decent computer, software, and the right skill set, you can create your own film from the comfort of your home studio. Hundreds of individual artists have already proven this is possible.

Don't let the word *short* fool you! Although these films are short, they must go through the same production pipeline as their big brothers and involve a lot of blood, sweat, and tears to produce. But their relatively manageable length makes them a perfect testing ground for new artists. I like to think of shorts as boot camp for features.

I've been involved in several animated shorts. Each time I work on one, I take away valuable experience that is equal to any larger production I've worked on.

[**Figure 15.3**] Pixar's animated short, *Partly Cloudy*, was shown in theaters before the feature *Up*.

© Disney/Pixar

Television

The television market is currently on fire. You can't turn on the television without being bombarded by the work of digital artists in every commercial and in a majority of the top-rated series. According to the A.C. Nielsen Company, the average American watches more than four hours of TV each day (or 28 hours per week, or 2 months of nonstop TV watching per year), so there is a large audience for this type of work. Television crews are much smaller than feature film crews and work with smaller budgets, yet they are asked to produce results similar to their film counterparts—every week. Although made-for-TV movies and other programs do use CG in their production, let's focus on television's two main kinds of programming: series and commercials.

Series

Whether a television series is fully animated, such as Nickelodeon's *Jimmy Neutron* or *Bubble Guppies*, or has digital elements married with live action, like *Falling Skies*, *CSI*, and *Terra Nova*, digital artists are behind the scenes helping to deliver this popular format for storytelling. The digital artists working on the popular children's series *CBeebies' Waybuloo* (www.waybuloo.com) blend stylized CG characters into live action (**Figure 15.4**).

CG elements appear in many shows without the viewer even being aware that there is any visual effects trickery. These hidden effects include digital set extension, CG vehicles like cars and planes added to shots, CG stunt doubles (one of my personal favorites), explosions, and more. AMC's *Breaking Bad* is one of my favorite shows of all time, and I'm always pleasantly surprised when my friend Bruce Branit, founder of Branit I FX, points out shots with digital effects that his studio created, because even I hadn't noticed.

All these elements are being created by digital artists, and the sheer number of shows starting to take advantage of digital imagery means a growing number of positions that need to be filled.

Working on a series as a digital artist can be intense. It is definitely not for everyone. It's a fast-paced production with insane weekly deadlines. The payoff is that you get to see the work that you just created the same week you worked on it—and sometimes even on the same day of finishing the job.

[Figure 15.4] These frames from the children's series *Waybuloo* show stylized digital character models composited with live action backgrounds.

© The Foundation TV Productions Limited/Decode/Blue Entertainment 2011

Commercials

The average American watches over two million TV commercials by the age of 65. These commercials are sometimes fully animated, have digital characters or products, or use hidden effects that you aren't aware of. Studios of all sizes work on commercials, from large houses like ILM, Rhythm & Hues, and Digital Domain, to small shops like my own studio, Applehead Factory.

Some of the most talented artists I know prefer to work on commercials rather than series work or even feature films. Why? Commercials usually take between 4–8 weeks to produce, which means that an artist can potentially put 6–12 completely unique productions under his or her belt each year. For example, **Figure 15.5** shows two distinctly different commercials created by the same team at Branit|FX (www.branitfx.com). Another reason could easily be that the small crew sizes allow artists to work across departments, giving them a more generalist experience versus being tied to just one area of production.

[Figure 15.5] These two commercials from Branit|FX provided digital modelers with both hard surface and organic modeling work.

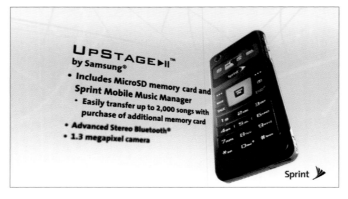

Games

Since the first commercial video game development began in the 1970s, gaming has grown more than any other market and is making money like never before. The video game industry is even starting to overshadow feature films. Many artists from the film and television markets have migrated to gaming for its job security and longer development cycles.

Although console and computer games still dominate this market, game apps for mobile devices and slot machine production have opened up new career options for digital artists to explore.

Console and computer games

The spotlight is definitely on the console and computer game sector of the gaming market. I like to think of console (PlayStation, Wii, Xbox, and so forth) and computer games as interactive storytelling where the viewer is no longer a passive observer but is an active participant. The artists I know working in the games industry have a passion for playing games, which in turn helps drive their creativity to produce them.

The production pipeline of a game is very similar to that of film and television, and usually requires large teams of artists. Games used to take 6–18 months to produce, but most modern games now take 1–3 years or more. *Duke Nukem Forever* may hold the record with a mind-blowing 14-year development cycle.

Although this sector of the market is dominated by larger studios, an increasing number of small shops are producing games commercially with great success. Many of these studios pull from the hobbyist *modding* (creating new content for existing games) communities, which is a great place for new artists to gain experience.

Nearly all games take advantage of real-time 3D graphics. From characters to environments and from weapons to props, digital modelers are needed to create every asset. This is good news for any modeler interested in finding work in gaming. **Figure 15.6** shows a game mesh created by Baj Singh (http://bajsingh.wordpress.com), a digital modeler who has worked on games such as *Runscape* and *Stellar Dawn*.

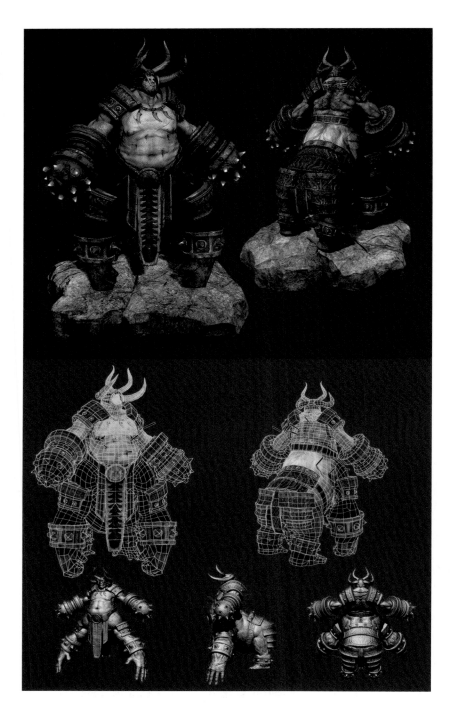

[Figure 15.6] This highly detailed game mesh created by Baj Singh is representative of the types of digital models being created for games.

Mobile apps

Mobile application development is the new gold rush of gaming. Hundreds of these apps are released every week, developed for small, low-power handhelds, such as iPhone, iPad, and Android devices. New developers are sprouting up like weeds in every city, so opportunities for artists could be just around the corner—literally.

Digital artists work with either *sprite sheets* (a single large image containing several frames of an animation) for pre-rendered graphics or low-poly count, real-time assets. Working with teams that are developing apps is a great way to hone your skills in gaming art production. It can also be a lucrative area to be involved in if you know what you are doing.

Dustin Adair—who worked on movies, TV, and video games, such as *Fringe*, *Battlestar Galactica*, *Terminator: Sarah Connor Chronicles*, *Transformers: War for Cybertron*, and *Halo 3*—developed an app called Poker with Bob (www. pokerwithbob.com) that became an instant hit, allowing him to focus on his own intellectual property full time. This is an example of how you never know where your career will take you.

Figure 15.7 shows a mobile app developed by Frima (www.frimastudio.com) for FunGoPlay's *Powerhouse Punter*, which runs on the iPad. The digital character models were used for both the online virtual world (www.fungoplay.com) and the mobile app.

[Figure 15.7]
I created the digital character models for Frima's *Powerhouse Punter* mobile app developed for FunGoPlay.

Video slot machines

I'm hoping you're still reading this section and didn't pass it over due to the title. This is gaming's best kept secret market. Video slot machines are not to be confused with the old-school gambling machines with three reels that spin when a lever is pulled. Rather, they are the more recent variant that is essentially like playing a computer game with interactive elements and advanced 3D graphics.

You won't see your name on the big screen at the end of a movie or read about your game in *GamePro* or *Game Informer* magazines, but you could find yourself working on slot machine versions of *Star Wars*, *Indiana Jones*, *Aliens*, and other big name properties. These machines display graphics and *cutscenes* (a sequence in a game that breaks up the gameplay to advance the story, introduce new elements, or keep the player interested) that can include scenes from your favorite movies, re-created digitally. So you might find yourself modeling Darth Vader one week and the Predator the next. One company flew Cassandra Peterson, the actress who plays Elvira, out to the studio to performance capture her for an Elvira video slot machine.

The people I know working in this market are paid well, get great benefits, and have some of the best job security this industry can offer. They also produce the same type of work as other entertainment markets except the end product is for a different platform. Marv Riley (www.marvriley.com), for example, has created digital models for video slot machines for several years and has worked on titles like *The Addams Family*, *Soul Train*, *Terminator*, *The Munsters*, and more. **Figure 15.8** shows a couple examples of the digital models he's created for games.

Visualization

Visualization is the art of using images, diagrams, or animations to communicate a message. 3D graphic software development has helped to advance visualization, increasing the number of visualization markets over the years, which continues to open up new opportunities for digital artists. 3D visualization has an endless array of applications in education, architecture, science, product, forensic, medical, military, archaeological, and many other areas. Two of the most popular visualization markets for digital artists are architectural and product.

[Figure 15.8] Artists working on video slots create everything from organic characters to hard surface vehicles, as shown here in some of Marv Riley's digital modeling work.

Architectural

Architectural visualization is used to show an image, animation, or real-time walkthrough of a proposed architectural design or renovation. Digital artists make it possible for architects to experiment with a building's visual aspects and design. The images and animations are used for presentations and greatly aid in real-estate sales. This can be a rewarding and secure career path for someone interested in hard-surface modeling. **Figure 15.9** shows a couple of examples of architectural visualization work by Sylvain Saintpère (http://5500k.carbonmade.com).

[Figure 15.9] These images created by Sylvain Saintpère are excellent examples of the work being created by digital artists in the architectural visualization market.

Product

Like architectural visualization, product visualization uses graphics applications to generate virtual products that allow you to experiment with shape, color, materials, and mechanisms. 3D product visualization allows you to create a physical mock-up of the 3D model using rapid prototyping (3D printing) as well as product simulations, giving it several advantages over 2D drawings.

Product visualization is ideal for market research, which is one of the benefits that my studio takes advantage of with product visualization. The ability to showcase a product before it is ever manufactured can allow for changes before manufacturing begins. We've done this for several years on products we've produced, such as the collectible vinyl figure Tofu the Vegan Zombie, as well as Drink Master Says SuperQuarters shown in **Figure 15.10**.

Product visualization is big business, and its use can be found in every facet of our daily lives. In fact, the United States Mint in Philadelphia uses sculpting software, such as Freeform and ZBrush, to visualize and produce coins.

[Figure 15.10] This 3D render of the Drink Master Says SuperQuarters product was used to showcase the product before it was manufactured.

Print Graphics

A revolution has occurred over the last 15 years in the print graphics market: Software traditionally seen as an animation tool is being used by designers and illustrators to create imagery for print and illustration.

Creative artists have adopted the power of these applications to help quickly generate everything from photorealistic to stylized images for product shots, industrial imagery, magazine covers, newspaper infographics, children's books, and any other media that traditional artists would normally produce illustrations for. **Figure 15.11** shows an illustration for M&M's that I worked on with Joe Zeff Design at Splashlight in New York. This image was used in magazines, billboards, and other forms of print.

[Figure 15.11] This 3D illustration for M&M's that I created digital models for was used in magazines, billboards, and other forms of print.

It's common for people to mistake photo-real 3D illustrations for photographs. Art directors have picked up on this and now choose to hire a digital artist to create a 3D model and render a product rather than have a photographer photograph it. Almost all car ads and product shots used in the media today are digital illustrations. The render can be just as convincing, more affordable, and much more flexible than a full-scale photo shoot.

Thousands of advertising agencies serve as potential clients for a professional digital artist, making this an ideal market for freelance digital artists.

Demo Reels

A demo reel is an important weapon in a digital artist's arsenal for promoting his or her experience in the 3D industry. It's equal in importance to a traditional artist's portfolio and is a requirement for entry into this field.

An artist's demo reel is like a prospector's gold pan; it's an artist's main tool when looking for a job. And when the right studio has been discovered and researched, an artist can use that demo reel to strike gold.

The art of putting together a demo reel has been discussed to death over the years, and endless resources are available online. With that said, I have pretty strong opinions about what should go into a successful demo reel, and I just can't resist including that information in this book.

To be part of the great CG gold rush, you must be sure to bring the right equipment. Having amazing examples of work to show is not enough to gain employment in the industry. You should be mindful of key attributes when developing a professional demo reel, and overlooking any element could be the single reason you are passed over by a studio. Trust me; you'll want to pay close attention to the following details concerning your demo reel.

Demo Reel Case and Sleeve

The case that houses your demo reel disc and the sleeve that decorates it are important. They give potential employers a first impression about you as an artist. How you handle your own work provides insight as to how you will handle the work they will task you with as an employee of the studio.

The case should be in pristine condition with no torn or scuffed plastic. This may seem obvious, but I've seen artists send out reels in cases that looked like their dog used it as a chew toy. I've also seen old Blockbuster rental cases used instead of purchasing a new, unused case. A standard DVD case is less than ten cents. There isn't an excuse in the world that could justify saving ten cents when something as valuable as your career is on the line.

Don't feel like you need anything other than a standard black case. Some artists invest in very expensive cases thinking that it will make their reel stand out. That's an unnecessary expense. I guarantee that a fancy case will play no role in whether you get an offer or not, so save your money for more important things. Keep it simple.

I can't stress enough how important your reel's sleeve is. It's your personal crowd barker, trying to "reel in" employers and get them to crack open the case to see your work.

When teaching students about the presentation of their demo reels, I used to use the comparison of walking the aisles of Blockbuster as an example, but that has become quite dated. So here's the new and improved way I explain the power of the sleeve. Think about when you're scanning through Netflix trying to decide which movie you're going to stream. Movie cover art is basically a little ad trying to sell you on the movie and screaming "pick me, pick me!" This is similar to reels at a studio. Usually, the HR department delivers stacks of reels to the various departments, and the department heads have to squeeze in time during their busy schedules to watch them. They try to speed up the process by selecting reels that look like they might be *the one* based on the sleeve. Once they've found a reel that could be a fit, they may stop looking and place a call to bring in that artist for an interview, or even to go ahead and offer that artist a position.

Your sleeve should be attractive and instantly sell a studio on the quality of your work and the breadth of your skill set. Have an image of your best work on the front. It should be something that will get viewers excited about what they are about to see. The worst thing you can do is handwrite your information on the case, no matter the level of your penmanship. Those reels usually end up getting thrown in the trash without a viewing.

Information that you'll want on the front of your sleeve includes

- Strong imagery, usually your best work

- Your name in an easy-to-read typeface (Adobe Garamond, Trade Gothic, and so on)

- A job title (Digital Modeler, 3D Generalist, and so on)

- Your phone number, email address, and web address

- Date, year, or at least season (example: Spring 2012)

Whose work this reel represents, as well as how to contact that person, should be clear. It goes without saying that without the proper contact information, the chance of getting a job is zero. Make the date clear so that prospective employers know they have your latest reel. You can just include the year, but if you're more specific, it could avoid confusion should you send an updated reel later that same year.

Here's what you want on the spine of your sleeve:

- Your name
- Title
- Date

I see quite a few reels with blank spines. If the studio shelves reels, a blank spine could easily be overlooked, even if someone is specifically looking for yours by name. Always make it easy for potential employers to know whose reel it is they are looking at, no matter what angle they are looking at the case.

Make sure the back of your sleeve contains the following:

- Strong imagery, usually your best work
- Your name in an easy-to-read typeface
- Title
- Your phone number, email address, and web address
- An optional shot breakdown

You basically want the same information on the back that you have on the front. Why? Quite simply, you don't know which side they will see first. You should use alternate imagery for the back to try to take advantage of the real estate and show more samples of your best work.

It's become increasingly popular to include a demo reel breakdown on the sleeve, giving viewers details about each shot that they can read as they watch the reel. It's not necessary, but it's incredibly useful to the studio. **Figure 15.12** shows an example of a demo reel sleeve with all the required elements for the front, spine, and back.

[Figure 15.12] This demo reel sleeve mockup makes it easy for the viewer to contact the artist and know what the artist's responsibilities were for each shot.

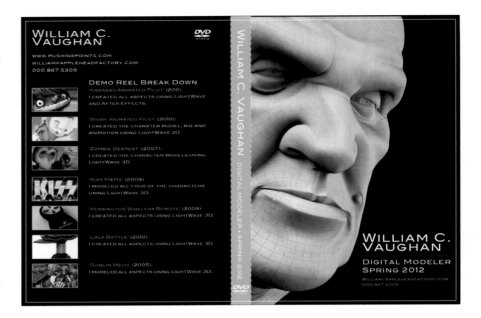

Before you're ready to print, you—or even better, a friend or two—need to proof your copy to ensure that there are no typos or other mistakes. It doesn't send a good message to the studio if you don't have enough interest in your own work to proof it. I once received a reel where the artist spelled his own name wrong; needless to say, he didn't get the gig.

When printing the sleeve design, make sure the print doesn't suffer from low ink, oversaturation, or any other quality issues. If you have to reprint it ten times to get it right, it's worth the extra effort.

Take your time trimming the sleeve as well. Make sure it's the correct size and that your cuts are straight and clean. Don't let sloppy craftsmanship destroy a first impression of the quality of your work.

The ultimate goal you are trying to achieve with the sleeve is to get viewers to watch your reel. Again, keep it simple and make the information as clear as possible. Your sleeve is like a one-frame trailer for a movie; it's got to sell the audience in a short amount of time.

Demo Reel Content

If employers are watching your reel, it means you have accomplished the goal of having a professional-looking case and sleeve, and viewers have enough interest in your work to put the reel in the player. Now you have to do the hard sell. This is where the rubber hits the road.

Basic requirements the industry expects to see on the reel include

- Beginning title card

- Content

- Demo reel breakdown

- Ending title card

Title cards

Title cards need to include your name and contact information—phone and email are the bare minimum. I like to include a job title under my name to make it as clear as possible what position I'm applying for. You can keep the design of the title cards to a simple black screen with white text, although I prefer to carry over the style of the front of the sleeve design for consistency, as shown in **Figure 15.13**.

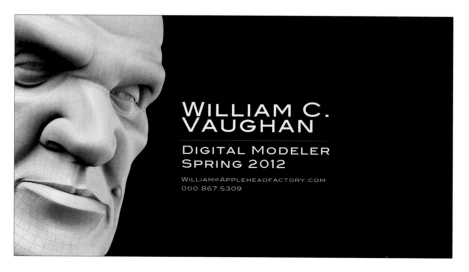

[Figure 15.13] Having a title card at the beginning and end of your reel allows the viewer to easily collect your name and contact information.

The title card at the beginning only needs to stay onscreen long enough to read all the information. If it stays on too long, it only delays the viewer from seeing your work.

The title card at the end should be identical to the intro card but last much longer. The show is over, and you want to give the viewer enough time to write down your info without having to pause the reel.

Main content

A demo reel should contain only *your best work*. Your content should match the quality of the studio you are applying to. If it doesn't, don't send it. This isn't a race. Don't rush to get a reel out that isn't up to the standard needed to get a job. Also, don't make viewing your demo reel an exercise in panning for gold; make sure your best work is visible right away.

Avoid using work created from tutorials. Tutorials are a great resource for enhancing your skills but make for weak demo reel material, because they don't offer any information about your skill set to the viewer other than the fact that you can follow steps.

When showcasing your digital models, displaying the mesh's wireframe to give viewers an idea of the efficiency of the model is important. They'll be looking at polygon count as well as polygon flow.

I also like to include a lower-third that is visible throughout the entire content section that has my name and contact info. This allows viewers to easily contact me while they are watching the reel. Make sure it is subtle and doesn't detract attention from the content by taking up too much of the screen real estate. Figure **15.14** shows an example of a subtle lower-third.

Demo Reel Breakdown (DRB)

Immediately following your content, you'll need to explain exactly what you did for each segment of your reel in a DRB. Leave no question in the mind of the viewer. It's also useful to the studio if you include the date of the production and the software used. I like to display a small thumbnail of the model or shot next to this information to make it easier for the viewer to recall what I'm describing in the DRB. Here are some DRB description examples:

- "Kanakas Animated Pilot" (2011): I created all aspects using LightWave 3D and After Effects.

- "Bigby Animated Pilot" (2010): I created the character model, rig, and animation using LightWave 3D.

- "Zombie Dearest" (2007): I created the characters using LightWave 3D.

Figure 15.15 shows an example of a DRB that would follow the main content of a demo reel.

[Figure 15.14] Adding your name and contact information throughout your reel allows viewers to easily contact you while they are watching the reel.

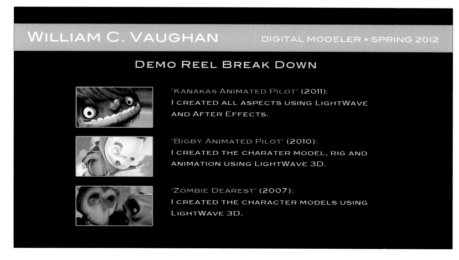

[Figure 15.15] DRBs leave no question in the mind of the viewer about what your involvement was for each shot shown.

Demo Reel Length

Demo reel length has been debated for years, and all artists have their own idea of how long a reel should be. Trying to lock down how long a reel should be is really the wrong way to approach creating a strong reel. If I say a reel should be between two and four minutes, most artists would try to fill their reel with enough content for a four-minute reel.

Remember that you only want to put your best work on your reel. Padding it with mediocre work just to add length will only diminish the overall quality of the reel and can leave a bad impression on viewers. They may think that the mediocre shots are true examples of the quality of your work and that you just got lucky on the better examples.

There is no limit to how short a reel should be. If you have an amazing ten-second clip on your reel with nothing else, it could be enough to land your dream job.

With that said, the average reel is between one and two minutes long. Make sure you spend enough time on each model or shot for the viewer to be able to fully take in what you are trying to show. Just be careful about spending too much time on each model or shot. You don't want the viewer to become bored looking at the same content and move on to another artist's reel.

Demo Reel Audio

Don't get too caught up in finding the perfect sound track to complement your images. Most studios could care less about music on a demo reel—in fact, they usually turn off the sound!

If you're going to add music to your reel, make sure it's appropriate. I'm a huge KRS-One fan, but I'd never use one of his songs on a reel, because not everyone agrees with the messages in his lyrics. However, movie sound tracks are very popular and seem to be a good fit for reels. Choose music that won't dominate the reel, and find audio that blends into the background and lets your work take center stage.

Demo Reel DVD Burning and Labeling

The final steps in the creation of your demo reel are to burn a DVD and print a DVD label. When burning your reel, make sure you use the auto play and looping options so that the viewer can watch your material again without having to reach for the remote. For similar reasons, avoid using any kind of menu system.

Most importantly, test each reel that you burn to ensure that it actually plays. I've received several reels over the years that simply didn't work. Why go through all the trouble to create a demo reel and not take the time to make sure it plays correctly?

Burn copies on an as-needed basis, because there is no all-purpose reel. Creating 100 copies at one time might seem efficient, but you won't have the freedom to customize each reel for the intended studio. You also run the risk of having several copies of an outdated reel, which is a waste of materials.

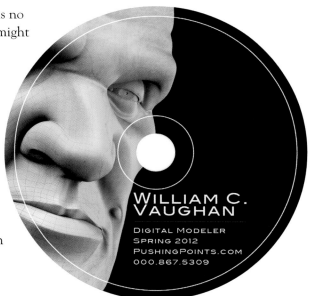

You want the label to be consistent with the sleeve so if they get separated it's easy for someone to pair the two back together. It's also important to include your name and contact information so that if all the studio has is the disc, they can still reach you. **Figure 15.16** shows a label design with the required information that matches the design on the example sleeve.

Your demo reel is your number one resource for getting a job. Take as much time to create the reel that is needed to land the job you are aiming for. Anything less is unacceptable.

[Figure 15.16] Having your name and contact information on your DVD label is helpful, especially when it gets separated from the case.

Personal Site

Right out of school, I landed my first job as a designer/illustrator for a large ad agency in Houston, Texas. Occasionally, the on-staff artists would be asked to create illustrations in a range of styles to present the clients with more options. However, when a client wanted a look that we couldn't deliver, we would reach for *The Directory of Illustration*, a veritable yellow pages for artists, featuring samples from hundreds of illustrators and their contact information. It was an invaluable tool for business, and an even better tool to help artists get business.

I bought a half-page ad in the directory for one year for $3,000 dollars. Although it was a lot of money to me, I knew it was worth the gamble. Later that year, I landed two clients who found me through my ad. The work those two clients generated easily covered the cost of placing the ad and helped me get my name in front of more people than I could possibly ever hope to meet.

But although source books are still a great way to get exposure to clients, one of the best tools for self-promotion, especially for digital artists, is the Internet. The source books are not as successful for a few reasons: many struggling artists can't afford the expense of buying an ad, the books have to compete with the Web, and the industry has evolved.

The traditional way to get work as a commercial artist was to put a physical portfolio of your work together and personally visit the agencies in your city. It required a great deal of time pounding the pavement and going door to door. It's always been the case that creating amazing work isn't enough to succeed; you have to get said work in front of as many people as possible.

The introduction of the Internet opened the door for artists to have their work instantly seen by people worldwide. Whether you're looking for a staff position or a freelance gig, having a personal site is no longer an option—it's a necessity. It is akin to mailing out millions of portfolios that never get thrown out. Your site can be filed away by potential clients or employers and called up in seconds.

A personal Web site can showcase your work, resume, personal information, links to other sites that showcase your work, and much more. Digital artists have compressed downloadable versions of their demo reels and movies on their site for easy offline viewing. Having a personal site is the most affordable and fastest way for you to get your work in front of employers.

Your site's link may go to thousands of people without your even knowing about it. For example, if one person discovers your Web site and sends a link to eight people who may be interested in your art, they can forward it to eight people, and so on. The distribution channel is endless. This type of pass-along is called viral marketing, and the Internet is the best place to take advantage of it.

Sending a one-link portfolio to potential clients or employers, for example, is much easier then compiling a collection of images and writing a long, detailed email every time you pitch a new client. In fact, put the link in your email signature and profile on online forums. If clients or employers see an image posted in a forum that they like, they can easily visit your site to see more samples or, if you're so inclined, your entire collection of work.

Any artist with a site has a huge advantage over an artist with just a portfolio or demo reel. Whether you're a student ready to break into the industry or a seasoned professional, having a Web site can help get your work in front of the right people. Today, a personal site is probably the strongest marketing tool you can have. Hardware and software companies figured this out years ago and invest a great deal of time and money in their sites.

I've helped place many graduates, and those who have personal sites make it very easy for me to shoot off links to contacts, letting them know that these artists will be graduating soon and will be available for hire. I can get immediate feedback. It's unlike anything that was available when I graduated.

If you have trouble building a site and don't know someone who can help, try using some of the template tools that ship with Adobe Photoshop, or you can take advantage of template Web sites like WordPress (www.wordpress.com), Blogger (www.blogger.com), or other free online resources. These options are very inexpensive and are a cinch to set up. Both my personal and company sites were created with WordPress, as shown in **Figure 15.17**.

[Figure 15.17] My personal site (left) and the Applehead Factory site (right) were both created using WordPress.

Unless you are promoting your Web creation skills, a simple site that showcases your work without any bells and whistles will suffice. It doesn't have to be flashy. You want viewers to notice your art, not your Flash programming.

These sites are great examples of personal sites:

- **Glen Southern:** www.southerngfx.co.uk

- **Ryan Etter:** www.ryanetterillustration.com

- **Chris ORiley:** www.chris3d.com

- **Jason Lee:** www.jasonallenlee.com

- **Kory Heinzen:** http://retroactivities.blogspot.com

The overused phrases *keep it simple* and *less is more* hold true for personal sites. Here are a few basic guidelines that I've found useful when setting up an online portfolio:

- The most important rule to remember when creating a personal online site is to make sure your contact information is easy to locate. If someone finds your site and loves your work but can't get in touch with you, what's the point?

- Have an easy to remember and easy to spell Web address. Using your name is a great idea unless your name can be spelled in different ways, and then some potential visitors to your site might misspell your address.

- Remember that your site is your "professional" portfolio. Don't be afraid to make it a visually fun site that shows off your personality, but keep professionalism in mind.

- Show only your best work. Follow the same basic rules you would when creating a printed portfolio or demo reel.

- Compress your content for easy downloads. If a site takes too long to download, you will lose visitors. Most people have a short attention span (just like my dog Jack). If they have to wait too long to see your work, they will simply move on. Use JPEG, GIF, or PNG file formats, and if you host your demo reel online, keep the file size small, but don't compress your work too much because it will degrade the quality.

- Always keep your site updated with your latest work and contact information. If you update your site when you finish new work, you'll never become overwhelmed with a backlog of projects to upload.

- Be sure to check the spelling on your site. Take the time to run a spell checking program on all the text that will be added to your site.

- Use small images that initially load in and link to larger versions. This allows your page to load quickly, and visitors can decide what they want to see in more detail without having to wait.

- Don't have music on your site unless you offer visitors a quick and easy way to turn it off. Music can drive people away faster than slow downloads.

- Visit your Web site daily to make sure that it is still live. Your hosting server could be down, and you wouldn't know it.

When it comes to self-promotion, a Web site can be your greatest promotional tool. Over the years, I've received freelance work and job offers, and established many long-lasting, professional relationships through my various personal sites. I'm certain job hunting would have been much more difficult without them.

Remember to start simple and be sure to get the word out that you have an online presence. Adding your URL to your email signature is an easy way to let people know about your site.

The Seven Deadly Job Search Sins

Over the years, I've given guidance to hundreds of students and colleagues in search of jobs as digital artists, and I've seen many mistakes that could easily have been avoided. I'll discuss some of these common blunders here and offer suggestions on how to avoid them when you're searching for work—whether it is your first CG position or the next rung up on your career ladder.

Each of the seven items I discuss in this section are key to landing a gig in this field and are the most common areas where I have seen artists go wrong. You may have personal goals and restrictions that may not allow you to be as flexible in each area described, and that's OK. The goal is to be open to each as much as possible for the maximum number of job opportunities.

Sin #1: Homesickness

I've seen some amazingly talented artists go jobless by limiting themselves to one city when looking for work. Especially early on in your career, you want to be as open as possible to relocating for work.

Anyone who knows me will tell you that I'm very vocal about how much I love Texas and how proud I am to be a Texan. But I left Texas back in 2000 to work for a game company up north. A great opportunity came up that fit with my career goals and I took it, although it meant leaving the motherland.

Your current location will determine the likelihood that you'll have to move in order to get work. Someone living in Los Angeles, California, is probably less likely to have to relocate compared to someone living in Santa Fe, New

Mexico. Unless of course you happened to live in California when DNA Productions was hiring artists to work on *Jimmy Neutron* in Texas.

Remember that you don't have to move to a given city for the rest of your life. It might just be a temporary relocation, or you might find that you really enjoy living there. A friend of mine from Texas moved up north and was surprised to find that he liked it better. Shame on him.

Being open to relocation greatly increases the pool of jobs that you can apply for and could speed up the job search process. Remember that it's all about location, location, location.

Sin #2: Greed

We all want to make as much money as possible, but we need to enter into each job search with a realistic idea of what is possible for our current experience level. I've seen a recent graduate turn down an amazing first job because he heard that the starting salary was $1,000 a week but was only offered $850. Even if this offer was more than he had ever made before, he was "insulted" and turned down the position.

On the other hand, I've seen graduates go to work for companies for free as interns, just to get a foot in the door, and weeks later be offered staff positions working on feature films. Have patience, work hard, and prove to the studio that you're worth more. Don't be in such a rush to make your millions, and you'll get there much faster.

Something I've heard more times than I'd like to admit is, "I can't afford to work for that little pay!" Meanwhile, the artist goes several months, sometimes more, without a job in the field. Ask yourself whether you can afford to not be working at all. Every position you accept builds your resume and your demo reel for the next position. With realistic budgeting, you might be surprised at how far your money will take you. Sometimes sacrifices are necessary when trying to attain your goals. Peanut butter and bread can go a long way (for those with peanut allergies, it's Ramen noodles).

Being realistic about the wages you can expect will help get you into a job quicker than holding out for the massive salary that may not come your way early on in your career. Wages and experience are directly linked.

Sin #3: Inflexibility

When I first saw what Will Vinton Studios was doing with computer animation, I knew I had to dive head first into 3D. My main passion has always been character work, but there was little or no work like that in Houston at the time, so I spent a few years creating animation for the oil and gas industry.

It wasn't exactly what I wanted to do, but I was excited that I was being paid to grow my 3D skills, and it quickly led to the character work I was after. Too often I see artists pass up great opportunities while they sit and wait for the ultimate job to come their way. Take, for example, the guy who has turned down more offers than you can imagine, holding out for a character modeling job, only to end up unemployed for almost three years. No one is suggesting that you give up your dream of working in a particular area of production. Simply work toward that goal while doing some kind of work in the industry.

One thing I have learned over the years is that you're more likely to get work if you're already working. But why is that? It could be that when you're working, you have a larger social network, or maybe it's that your confidence is better when you're working. When you're working, you are constantly expanding your network of contacts in the industry and staying on the minds of those contacts. When employers have work that needs to be done or a position opens up, you will be on their minds, while the guy sitting at home waiting for a great job to open up may get passed over. Whatever the reason, it's good to always have employment, even when you're looking for work. Your first and/or second gig might not be the exact position you're looking for, but don't let that keep you from kicking off your career.

I can also tell you that if you have generalist skills, you'll find that you have more options. Be a skilled digital modeler, but be able to handle all aspects of production. I've seen some of the best hard surface modelers take work as technical directors to get in the door and found that they moved over to the modeling department once they had worked for the company for a while.

One last example is a good friend of mine who had always wanted to work in the game industry but was having trouble getting his start. He landed a job at an architectural visualization firm, and his lighting skills improved tenfold.

After a year of being happily employed and increasing his skill set, he landed a job in the game industry, making much more than he had originally been asking for. Again, wages and experience are directly linked.

Being flexible with the type of work you take on early in your career can be a faster route to landing the type of work you have always dreamed of doing.

Sin #4: Putting All Your Eggs in One Basket

When looking for work, don't limit the number of places that you apply to. The majority of recent graduates send out a handful of reels and sit back to wait for one of those places to contact them. If you apply my previous rules to your job search, you will find that there are an unbelievable number of places that you can apply to.

This doesn't mean that you should send out hundreds of reels randomly. Make sure that you are a fit for the type of work the studios would be looking for, but if you do your homework, you will find that a lot of options are available. When I graduated years ago, I sent out 75 portfolios and was offered seven job opportunities. If I had sent out seven portfolios I might not have had a single offer. Target the companies that are currently looking to fill open positions, but also send your reel to companies not currently advertising.

For artists new to the industry, make sure the work on your reel matches the work coming from the studios you are applying to. I see a lot of recent grads limiting their reels to Pixar, ILM, Digital Domain, Weta Digital, and other top studios, and they can't figure out why they haven't found work. It's great to have goals of working at these studios, but look at the path that most of the artists who work at those places have taken. You might find that you can start working at a smaller studio doing amazing work, getting your skill set up to speed, and be working towards your end goal of a job at Pixar or DreamWorks. You might also discover along the way that you are quite happy at the smaller studio.

Artists who do their homework and send out their reels to a wide audience will find that more opportunities will arise.

Sin #5: Sloppiness

This sin is the big one! It's sad to say, but I've seen a lot of jobs slip through artists' hands due to poor presentation. Even if you have the best material on your demo reel, if the case is sloppy, viewers may never watch it. The number one pet peeve of mine (and many companies) is handwritten labels, which for some reason still show up. If you've read any information about demo reels, you'll find this one on the list of *don't's*—yet it still happens. Cover letters are another area where artists seem to struggle. Do your homework and create a cover letter that is professional and aimed at the target studio. I hear complaints from studios all the time that "Studio A" has received a cover letter that is addressed to "Studio B." This kind of mistake speaks to a lack of attention to detail—not a good quality in an employee.

Presentation also includes the personal interview. If you visit the studio, your personal appearance is a factor. Don't overdress for the studio and the industry, but find something that is business casual and not wrinkled. And although I shouldn't need to say it, bathe before you go to the interview. No one wants to work with the "stinky guy," although I think we all have at some point in our careers.

Be prepared for the interview, whether it is over the phone or at the studio. Research the studio before the interview so that you have good questions to ask, and listen carefully to the questions being thrown your way. Listen to the information being conveyed by the interviewer so that you don't ask a question that has already been answered. Your work is not enough to land you the job in most cases. The majority of studios are also looking for whether or not you will gel with the other artists on the team.

Artists who present themselves and their work professionally are more likely to seal the deal when looking for a job.

Sin #6: Playing Hard to Get

Lack of follow-through is probably the most unforgivable job search sin. Follow-through can consist of staying on top of all the studios you've applied to as well as studios that show an interest in you. Keep records of all the studios to which you have applied and their responses. If a studio asks you to should get back in touch in a few months, that is an open invitation to keep in contact with that studio. If you haven't heard back from the studio, a single call (no stalking!) a couple weeks after you send your reel is a good way to make sure that the studio received the reel and to see whether the studio has any questions or would like to see more examples of your work.

If a studio shows interest in you, stay on top of anything the studio throws at you. I've seen artists lose the opportunity to work at a studio simply because they didn't follow through on the next stage of discussions.

If a studio sends you a "test," you should jump on it. That means the studio is excited about you but wants to make sure you can handle the work they need you to do. I've seen more artists drop the ball during this stage than any other, simply by not taking the test seriously or by not taking the test at all.

Drop everything you're doing to follow up with a studio that is interested in you. You may have to go through several interviews and send additional work or references. Whatever the studio is asking for, make sure you tackle it right away. Think of it as a tennis match. You want to get the ball back in the studio's court as fast as possible. Remember not to drop the ball at this stage of the game.

Artists who keep records of all communication and follow through with the studios where they have applied are more prepared when job opportunities arise.

Sin #7: Sloth

Energy and persistence conquer all things. Lack of persistence is a seductive job search sin. After you've sent out a batch of your reels, the last thing you should do is sit and wait. Continue to research the job market to find new studios and be ready to submit your reel as new jobs hit the boards. Sometimes being quick to respond to a job post is the key to landing the job.

You should also continue to work on new projects to build up your skills. It's very common for studios that have had your reel for a while to contact you and ask to see what you've been working on. Having nothing new is a giant red flag to studios.

Constantly working on new projects also lets you refine your reel over time. Remember that if the fish aren't biting, it may be time to change your bait. If the company you want to work for just landed the *Battlestar Galactica* series, it may be time for you to add a Cylon to your reel. Don't wait for a job posting —be proactive, update your reel often, and stay knee deep in production while you're looking for work. Enter contests and share your work in online galleries and magazines. Artists who realize that searching for work is a full-time job usually find work quickly.

Get a Job!

The more you can work at not falling victim to the seven deadly job search sins, the more likely it is that you will find work. I've yet to see an artist who really wants to work, and works hard at finding a job, not land a gig in this industry. In the end, the ticket to finding work is to be flexible, put everything you have into searching, and be persistent. You can be a success story and make a living doing what you truly want to do.

Staying Current

Like a shark, your career should be in perpetual motion. If you don't stay current in this industry, your career will sink. Every digital artist should keep on top of several areas in order to have longevity in this industry. This section discusses these areas.

Skill Set

Your skill set is the easiest area in which to stay current if you are working at or for a studio. Every project you work on will help you hone your skills to become a better artist. If you're not currently employed in the industry, you should still be working on personal projects to keep your skills sharp.

Unfortunately, digital modeling isn't the same as riding a bike. Even the best modelers can lose valuable skills if they aren't exercised on a regular basis. Improving your skills is only the first part of keeping your skill set current. You also want to add new skills and techniques to your bag of tricks that will allow you to take on bigger and more challenging work.

So many sources are available today in the forms of books, magazines, DVDs, online resource sites for digital artists, and more that can aid you in evolving as an artist. Take advantage of these resources and soak up as much information as you possibly can to increase your knowledge in as many areas as possible.

A good way to test whether you are advancing as an artist is to go back and review a model you were most proud of six months to a year ago and make a list of aspects you would do differently to improve on it. If you can't come up with anything, you may be stagnating as an artist.

As a digital artist, you can only produce to the level of your skill set, so you want to keep improving to raise the bar on your work.

Software

As mentioned earlier in the book, like an artist's skill set, software is constantly evolving, and new software is released every year. It would be impossible to master all the applications that are associated with this industry, but it is more than possible to be aware of the majority of them.

As an artist working in this industry, you will constantly be tasked with projects that require you to solve new problems. Knowing the available software gives you more options to pull from and could save you a massive amount of time when devising a plan of attack on your current project.

The software you currently use will eventually be updated as well. You want to keep informed on these updates as they come out; otherwise, more and more new components will be added over time, and you will find your knowledge of the software to be as outdated as the old version you're using.

Being an early adopter of new software can also lead to advancing in your career. You can quickly become one of the most knowledgeable artists in that software, which can lead to interesting opportunities. I got my big break in the game industry this way.

Over ten years ago, the Croteam released the first *Serious Sam* game, and I immediately fell in love with it. Having never worked in the game industry, I started teaching myself level design using the Level editor that came with the game. As I learned the *Serious Sam* Level editor, I posted my findings to share with the online community, and within three weeks a large game studio contacted me with an offer using the Serious engine as a level designer on *Carnivores Cityscape*. This was how I got my start working in the game industry where I later became a producer.

Software will always play a role in a digital modeler's career, so remaining current with your applications should be one of your top priorities.

Networking: Online Communities

Networking refers to meeting and associating with people, and making connections with them to strengthen your network, both personally and professionally. You've heard, "It's not what you know, it's who you know." But in the world of CG, it's not who you know but who knows you.

I would never have sculpted Pokemon and Littlest Pet Shop toys, given 3D training to Dick Van Dyke, or written this book if it weren't for the people who know me. Those people recommended me to someone that was not part of my network at the time.

Your network needs to evolve and expand more than anything else discussed here. The people you know and the people who know you are important when looking for a job or advancing in your career.

You can expand your network by attending industry events and conferences, and participating in social networking sites like Facebook (www.facebook. com), LinkedIn (www.linkedin.com), Google Groups (groups.google.com), and any other avenue that involves meeting, conversing, and talking business with people.

When my career in 3D was beginning, I set out to meet others who shared a passion for art and animation like me, and wanted to make a career of their craft. What I found was a flourishing art community online. Many CG forums consist of talented artists and animators who share ideas, offer feedback and critique, and help others with tools and techniques to work around creative design and animation challenges. Not only are these portals excellent information resources, but they are a way to get your art in front of literally thousands of people. The only investment you have to make is your time, but with a little perseverance, the commitment can really pay off.

Several years ago, I became active in a handful of online forums, many of which I am still involved with today, as a way to get my art in front of other artists and animators for their feedback. I began by posting sample sketches, works in progress, and final renders. At the time, my goal was simply to meet other artists who shared my passion for the medium and maybe exchange a few modeling and animation tips. It never occurred to me that I was actually showcasing my work to potential clients.

Since my initial introduction to online communities, I have posted more than 400 3D characters in online forums, many of which were spotted by companies and studios looking for contract artists and animators. Those online communities were conduits for contract jobs. If my work had not been highly visible on these online forums, I'm certain the job opportunities would never have come my way and the contractors would have never seen my work. But the job opportunities go beyond project work. I've been asked to speak at events and judge award shows, and have even been offered full-time positions based solely on my work posted in online forums.

Finding the right online community

Before jumping online, check your 3D software toolkit and see if the software developers, such as Autodesk, Luxology, or Newtek, have online support forums. Other companies, such as Adobe, have product-specific forums that are a good place to meet others and share information.

Great communities to investigate include

- **CG Society:** www.cgsociety.org

- **3DTotal:** www.3dtotal.com

- **Foundation 3D:** www.foundation3d.com

- **Polycount:** www.polycount.com

Once you find online forums that seem right for you, get active within the communities by showing your work, critiquing the work of others, and helping answer questions that you may have experience with. Use them to share the latest news you may have heard, software you may have discovered, or techniques you created.

Being a good online citizen

Here are some basic guidelines you should follow when participating in an online community:

- Always remember that you are representing yourself as a professional CG artist.

- Show respect to the other members in the community.

- Give constructive critiques and be ready to hear both positive and negative feedback about your work.

- Fill in your profile with your real name and offer a way for others to contact you. Someone may be interested in hiring you and will need a way to reach you.

- Dedicate time each week to spend with one or more online communities. Stay updated with what is being shared in the community and be a regular presence.

By being proactive and helpful in online forums, not only will you be giving back to the community, but it could lead to a contract project or even a full-time job. Remember that everyone—from students and hobbyists to studio artists and owners—are members of forums. You never know when someone will notice you.

I'm a big fan of online networking. These communities have opened up many doors for me, both personally and professionally. Online community forums are some of the best promotional tools for CG artists. If you're trying to get established in your career and community, it's a no-brainer!

Networking may not come easy to you, but it is an important skill to hone. As with most things, the more networking you do, the easier it gets.

Staying on Top of Industry Trends and News

As animation and visual effects continue to change and expand, it is important to remain updated on information regarding this industry.

One of the easiest ways to stay up to date on industry trends is to visit several of the CG-related news sites daily and absorb as much information as you can. Think of it this way: Someone who has invested a large sum of money in the stock market wouldn't go a day without checking what's happening in the market, so why do any different with your investment in your career?

Some industry details to look for include

- Studios and the projects they are working on

- Artists' names and their titles

- Event announcements

- Software news

- New technologies being developed

- Anything else that directly (or indirectly) plays a role in your career

As mentioned earlier, some sites that I visit daily are 3DTotal (www.3dtotal.com), CG Society (www.cgsociety.org), CG Arena (www.cgarena.com), and software-specific sites. It's never been easier to stay on top of industry news, and the best part is that it's free. Subscriptions to trade magazines like *3D World*, *Cinefx*, *3D Artist*, and *Computer Graphics World* are another way to discover what's happening in this industry, and they're tax deductible, which can help justify the expense.

Remember to take advantage of your network. A good portion of the industry news that I find out about comes to me by email from artists within my network. It's important to keep in touch with these contacts and keep the relationships active, so be sure to pass along news that you discover as well.

Reel and Resume

Keeping your reel updated is extremely important when looking for a job, but it's also something to think about doing even when you're happily employed. You never know when you'll need an updated reel, and it's always easier to update as you finish new work along the way than to try and do it all at once after too much time has passed.

Sometimes it can be too late to get finished frames or content from a production you worked on if you postpone asking the studio for them. In those unfortunate cases, you're limited to low-resolution footage from compressed files or simply not having any version to use.

I worked on a project a couple of years ago for an online interactive Web site, and by the time I went to get screen shots of the site for my online gallery, the project had already run its course and was removed. I then had to jump through some exhausting hurdles to get them from the client.

If you have trouble remembering dates and other important information that is useful on your resume, you should frequently update it as well. It's also a good idea to request letters of recommendation on a regular basis to keep on file for future use. I've regretted not doing this in the past on projects that I'm extremely proud of. I've also missed getting one in time to use for an interview.

Keeping your reel and resume current can help you to avoid running into similar situations and will allow you to gain the upper hand when you find you need updated versions quickly.

Health

Our health is one of the most important and also the most overlooked areas in this industry. As digital artists, we spend the majority of our time in the studio on a computer. If we're not working on a paying gig, we're either improving our skill set by practicing or keeping up to date with the latest game or movie. That doesn't leave much time to stay on top of the one thing that allows us to do all of this—our health.

Make sure that you work some form of exercise into your daily schedule. Take frequent breaks throughout a modeling session to get up and stretch, or even to take a walk. Not only will this help you to avoid back problems later in life, but it will also allow you to come back with a fresh perspective to what you're working on. I love to take my chocolate lab, Jack, for long walks at least twice a day, and find that I do some of my best problem solving during those trips.

Regrettably, it's taken me years to realize the importance of attending to this part of my life. A healthy body leads to a healthy mind, which then leads to being able to think clearer when problem solving.

If you're like me, you have a bucket list of things you'd like to do in your career, and keeping up with your health allows you more time to accomplish them.

Advancing in Your Career

Staying current is key to advancing in your career, but there are other measures you can take to climb the ladder. An easy one for those passionate about their job is to take on more responsibilities and do more than is expected of you. If a director or supervisor is looking for someone to take on a special assignment or if another department is falling behind schedule, offer assistance. The trick is to be aware of what's happening on the project and offer help before being asked to do it. Be careful not to step on the toes of your colleagues because no one appreciates someone butting in with, "I can do that," all the time.

On the other hand, if you are unsure about a task or are having problems, don't hide it from your team or supervisor; be honest and up front before the issue gets worse. A great way to handle this situation is to deliver every problem with a possible solution. Hiding a problem is a quick way to bring the production to a screeching halt and may be the quickest way to end your time at that studio.

If the studio you're working at offers on-the-job training or there are courses you can take to learn important skills needed for a higher position, sign up. Learn as much as you can about the studio and its production pipeline, and try to find ways to enhance the process and reduce expenses for the company.

An obvious way to advance your career in a studio is to simply ask to be moved into a higher position. Be prepared to give solid reasons to justify why the company should promote you and make sure your superiors view you as an indispensible resource.

If you find that you have gone as far as you can go in a studio, know when to move on. It's very common for an artist to outgrow a studio. If you are honestly doing everything you can to advance in a studio and there doesn't seem to be any forward progress in your career after a few years, a new studio may be just the thing you need.

Even if you're satisfied with your job, there is never a time you should feel that your job hunting days are over. It's a good idea to keep current with what is happening in the job market because you never know what the future holds.

In closing I'd like to add one more valuable suggestion that may be the most important: A lot of people have this idea that the 3D industry is extremely large; they couldn't be more wrong. The markets we work in are quite small, and only a few degrees of separation lie between all of the artists that make up our industry. Word travels fast throughout this network, so make sure any words spoken in regards to you and your work are positive. I've seen a lot of artists unnecessarily burn bridges and think their actions wouldn't follow them, only to find that within 24 hours the news had spread like wildfire. Your reputation can be your most powerful asset when trying to advance in your career, so take good care of it. You only have one!

Always remember that you are in control of your career and that you have to treat yourself like a valuable commodity. You need to market this commodity, improve it, and most importantly, sell it.

Final Thoughts

It was bound to happen. The cat's out of the bag! You've reached the end of the book and discovered that there is no real secret to producing professional digital models. You now know that creating efficient, production-ready models is easy. When you apply good observation, do a little preplanning, and foster solid problem-solving skills, the process of making a production-ready model can be a walk in the park.

In this final chapter, I leave you with a few closing thoughts and suggestions before setting you loose on the world of digital modeling.

One of the most important suggestions I'd like to pass on to you is to never stop learning. Remember that experience comes from the repetition of modeling and constantly challenging yourself. As a digital modeler, you will face new challenges with every new project; many will require new and innovative solutions that you must discover on your own. Remember what I always say: "I know everything I need to know to do the things I've already done."

As you've seen throughout the chapters in this book, there is more to digital modeling than learning the specific tools that make up 3D software, and there is more than one way to go about modeling.

I hope this book has left an impression on the way you will approach future modeling assignments. As a digital modeler, you play an important role that carries a great deal of responsibility, not only to yourself, but most importantly, to the entire production team.

Don't forget what the working professionals shared in Chapter 2. Each had invaluable information about how they viewed a modeler's role and how a modeler's work affects them. When you complete a model, always think back to what those artists said and ask yourself if they would call your model "production ready." At this point it might be a good time to revisit Chapter 2 and see how much more prepared you are now that you have a better understanding of professional modeling practices.

Remember to apply the concepts you have learned throughout this book to all of your modeling projects, whether they are for personal or professional use. Always be mindful of your models' poly-count and topology, giving great care and thought to every piece of geometry you create. Don't forget to be organized, pay attention to detail, and gain full control over the mesh. Taking pride in ownership will allow you to be a successful artist in this field and will set you apart from the average modeler.

The most important advice I can leave you with is to *have fun*. Digital modeling is an amazingly cool job. Be an artist, explore, and create. Remember that the more models you create and the more modeling methods you add into the mix, the more proficient you will be as a professional modeler.

I'd like to thank you for investing the time you have in reading this book, and I encourage you to return to it from time to time, not only as a refresher, but to check on your progress and to see how far you advance as a digital modeler over time. I also encourage you to contact me through my Web site www.pushingpoints.com, share your thoughts on this book, and keep me posted on your modeling work. I'd love to hear from you!

It's now time for me to give Jack the long outing I've been promising him ever since I started writing this book. As you can see in **Figure 16.1**, he's been waiting patiently.

[Figure 16.1] My best friend Jack is extremely happy that the book has come to an end and he gets to hit the road!

Index